PRACTICAL
ENGLISH
HANDBOOK

HOUGHTON MIFFLIN COMPANY · BOSTON

DALLAS   GENEVA, ILL.   PALO ALTO   PRINCETON, N.J.

PRACTICAL ENGLISH HANDBOOK

Eighth Edition

Floyd C. Watkins

EMORY UNIVERSITY

William B. Dillingham

EMORY UNIVERSITY

Authors of works quoted in the text are identified with the quotations.

Grateful acknowledgment is made to the following publishers and authors for permission to reprint from their works.

American Heritage Dictionary. Definition of *double* reprinted by permission from the *American Heritage Dictionary, Second College Edition.* © 1982, 1985 by Houghton Mifflin Company.

Sissela Bok. Excerpt from Sissela Bok, *Secrets: On the Ethics of Concealment*, reprinted by permission of Pantheon Books, a Division of Random House, Inc. Copyright © 1983.

Walter Pritchard Eaton. Material from "Up Attic" from *The Virginia Quarterly Review*, 21 (Spring 1945). Reprinted by permission.

Gerard J. Gormley. Extract from a letter reprinted by permission of Mr. Gormley.

Mary Oliver. "The Black Walnut Tree" from *Twelve Moons* by Mary Oliver. Copyright © 1978. First appeared in *The Ohio Review*. By permission of Little, Brown and Company and Molly Malone Cook Literary Agency, Inc.

Richard Wilbur. "A Game of Catch." Reprinted by permission; © 1953, 1981 *The New Yorker Magazine*.

Cover: *Ocean Park Series No. 40*. 1971. Richard Diebenkorn, private collection.

Library of Congress Catalog Card Number 88-81366

Student's Edition ISBN: 0-395-43243-x

Instructor's Edition ISBN: 0-395-49262-9

ABCDEFGHIJ-M-9543210-898

CONTENTS

SENTENCE ERRORS   29

PREFACE

Those familiar with *Practical English Handbook* will notice that this Eighth Edition includes many new ideas about writing, some of our own, some from recent theories of composition. Nothing, however, has been added that has not been tested in the crucible of practicality, and nothing has been changed simply for the sake of change. Among the new features are

- techniques for discovering good subjects for short papers and the research paper
- strategies for getting started with the process of writing
- a brief section on writing about film, with model paper
- new models for the essay, the literary paper, and the research paper
- the short story "A Game of Catch" by Richard Wilbur and the poem "The Black Walnut Tree" by Mary Oliver in the section on writing about literature
- a section on writing with a word processor
- expanded commentary on using the library

In addition, the Eighth Edition contains expanded glossaries of usage and grammatical terms; revised exercises, with 30 percent new sample sentences; revised sections on the paragraph and logic; an improved system of grading symbols; and an expanded ancillary package.

Practical English Handbook, Eighth Edition, is accompanied by the following ancillaries:

- *Practical English Workbook,* Fourth Edition—A collection of exercises that follows the organization of *Practical English Handbook,* but can be used independently. Instruction is grouped at the beginning of each part so that exercises are freestanding on perforated pages. An Instructor's Manual contains answers to the exercises.

- Diagnostic Test Package—Three forms of a fourteen-page test provided on photocopying masters, free to adopters.

- Computerized Diagnostic Test Package—Interactive software using the same items as in the three printed diagnostic tests, available for IBM-PC and APPLE. Available at no cost to adopters.

- Reference Chart—A complimentary sheet based on the Contents and correction symbols in *Practical English Handbook* for use in grading papers.

- PEER: Practical English Exercises and Review—Computerized exercises for IBM-PC complement *Practical English Handbook* and give practice in the areas of grammar, sentence structure, punctuation, mechanics, and diction and style. Students locate errors in sample sentences, then enter corrections. Correct answers appear superimposed above the original sentence on the screen. The relevant formal precept from *Practical English Handbook* is cited, with carefully tailored instructional commentary applying the rule to the specific sentence in the exercise. PEER thus helps to reinforce students' understanding of important grammatical principles. PEER is available at no cost to adopters.

- WIP: Works-in-Progress—An easy-to-use basic word-processing program originally developed by Houghton Mifflin

Company College Division for the IBM-PC and APPLE. WIP is available at no cost to adopters.

- PC-Write—A commercial-quality word-processing program for the IBM-PC. Software and short manual with tutorial are available at no cost to adopters.
- GPA: Grade Performance Analyzer—An electronic grade management and evaluation program for IBM-PC and APPLE, available at no cost to adopters.

In our work on the Eighth Edition, we have received more assistance than we could possibly acknowledge in a list. Help has come from every corner of the country. In particular we thank our colleagues and the staff of the Department of English at Emory University. We offer our gratitude to the entire staff of the Reference Department, Woodruff Library, Emory University—especially Eric and Marie Nitschke and Betsy Patterson. Members of that exceptional staff have taught us much, and they continue to be our partners in the teaching of our students. For guidance and ideas, we express our deepest appreciation to the following reviewers:

Irma Ned Bailey, San Antonio College, Texas

Joan Bell, University of Nebraska at Omaha

Elizabeth T. Coffman, Faulkner State Junior College, Alabama

John W. Crawford, Henderson State University, Arkansas

Robert Dees, Orange Coast College, California

David Galef, Columbia University, New York

John Harty, The University of Florida

Joan Haug, Sacramento City College, California

T. Mark Ledbetter, Wesleyan College, Georgia

Martin Light, Purdue University, Indiana

Blair Morrissey, Muskegon Community College, Michigan

John V. Pastoor, Montcalm Community College, Michigan

William Peirce, Prince George's Community College, Maryland

Joseph S. Podrasky, University of Wisconsin—Marathon Center

Joel Rudinger, Firelands College, Bowling Green State University, Ohio

Richard J. Schrader, Boston College, Massachusetts

F.C.W.
W.B.D.

TO THE STUDENT

Using this Book

Your instructor may use *Practical English Handbook,* Eighth Edition, as a basis for class discussions and for various kinds of exercises in writing or may simply ask you to buy a copy of the book to use on your own. This book is designed to be equally useful in class and as a reference book. Thumb through it. Consider how it is organized. Use the reference numbers and the index. Learn where you can find the help you need on particular and general problems. As you write a paper, refer to the following sections for help:

Selecting a topic	Sections **44a** and **44b,** pp. 228–232
Organizing your paper	Sections **44c** and **44d,** pp. 232–237
Writing and rewriting	Sections **44e** through **44h,** pp. 237–247
Avoiding errors in sentences, mechanics, diction, and style	Sections **1** through **43,** pp. 30–225. See Contents or Index for location of specific information.

Writing and Revising Papers

Good writers develop a well-planned system of working. Generally, they think hard, search diligently for information, set certain times aside for writing, and shape and reshape their work.

Take your writing seriously. If you write only to satisfy a requirement, your papers probably will lack thoughtfulness and conviction. Earnestness of purpose and true interest show in all types of writing. Conversely, casualness and lack of interest are also easily apparent.

How people write changes with the times, sometimes rapidly and drastically. Manual typewriters and then electric ones probably did not change how words were put on paper in decades as much as microcomputers have in the past few years. Now many first-year students come to college with word processors and the ability to use them. (See pp. 254–255.) Also, changes in thinking about writing have undergone a revolution: in advancements in methods of selecting topics, in gathering information, in preparing notes and materials, and in putting papers together. See the discussions of prewriting, brainstorming, journal jotting, listing, clustering, freewriting, and writing rough drafts in the chapter on writing college papers (pp. 228–232 and 239–247).

Once you have written the first draft of a paper, either in longhand or on a word processor, study it as if you were seeing it for the first time. Good writers look at their writing as their readers will see it. Imagine that you are two people—the writer and a stranger who will read what you write. When you learn to find your own problems and correct them before another reader sees the paper, you will then be well on the way to realizing your full capabilities.

Before giving your paper to your instructor, give it a final check for minor errors. The value of a clean and correct manuscript is based partly on the impression it conveys. A final draft marred by careless errors bespeaks a sloppy writer (and, by implication, a fuzzy thinker). If you submit a paper that is riddled with the kinds of mistakes you can catch by proofreading, everything in your paper is rendered questionable.

Allow nothing short of an emergency to prevent you from completing and submitting your work on time. By establishing sensible priorities, using what time you do have wisely, and then meeting your responsibilities, you are learning how a mature writer works under pressure.

The process of revising and the act of learning do not come to an end when you submit your paper. Most teachers mark strengths and weaknesses on papers, and many write comments in the margins and at the end. Their purpose is to offer constructive advice about future writing. Learn to accept and use criticism. It can be a valuable tool in helping you improve your writing.

F.C.W.
W.B.D.

PRACTICAL
ENGLISH
HANDBOOK

GRAMMAR

Anyone who can use a language, who can put words together to communicate ideas, knows something about grammar without necessarily being aware of it. Grammar is the methodology of the way a language works. It is also the formal study of that system, its laws or rules. For example, a person who says "They are" is using grammar. A person who says that *they* is a plural pronoun and takes the plural verb *are* is using terms of grammar to explain the proper use of the language. The technical study of grammar can be pursued almost for its own sake, for the pleasure of a scholar, a grammarian. Much of this system is helpful in discussions about *how* to speak or to write.

This book introduces a minimum amount of the grammatical system—all that is needed—to develop effective writing and speaking.

The Parts of Speech

Knowing the part of speech of a word in its context may be the most basic aspect of grammar.

The eight parts of speech are **nouns, pronouns, verbs, adjectives, adverbs, conjunctions, prepositions,** and **interjections.** Each of these is explained and illustrated below.

NOTE: Much of the time, the function of a word within a sentence determines what part of speech that word is. For example, a word may be a **noun** in one sentence but an **adjective** in another.

noun
↓
She teaches in a *college.*

adjective
↓
She teaches several *college* courses.

Nouns

Nouns are words that name. They also have various forms that indicate **gender** (sex—masculine, feminine, neuter), **number** (singular, plural), and **case** (see **Glossary of Grammatical Terms**). There are several kinds of nouns.

(a) **Proper nouns** name particular people, places, or things (*Thomas Jefferson, Paris, Superdome*).

Meet me in *San Francisco* at *Fisherman's Wharf*.

(b) **Common nouns** name one or more of a class or a group (*reader, politician, swimmers*).

The *women* stared hard and listened intently.

(c) **Collective nouns** name a whole group though they are singular in form (*navy, team, pair*).

It has been said that an *army* moves on its stomach.

(d) **Abstract nouns** name concepts, beliefs, or qualities (*courage, honor, enthusiasm*).

Her *love* of *freedom* was as obvious as her *faithfulness*.

(e) **Concrete nouns** name tangible things perceived through the five senses (*rain, bookcase, heat*).

The *snow* fell in the *forest*.

Pronouns

Most **pronouns** stand for a noun or take the place of a noun. Some pronouns (such as *something, none, anyone*) have general or broad references, and they do not directly take the place of a particular noun.

Pronouns fall into categories that classify both how they stand for nouns and how they function in a sentence. (Some of the words listed below have other uses; that is, they sometimes function as a part of speech other than a pronoun.)

(a) **Demonstrative pronouns** point out (see **demonstrative adjectives,** p. 9). They can be singular *(this, that)* or plural *(these, those).*

demonstrative pronoun
↓
Many varieties of apples are grown here. *These* are winesaps.

(b) **Indefinite pronouns** do not point out a particular person or thing. They are usually singular, though sometimes plural. (See **8d.**) Some of the most common are *some, any, each, everyone, everybody, anyone, anybody, one,* and *neither.*

indefinite pronoun
↓
Everyone knows that happiness is relative.

(c) **Intensive pronouns** end in *-self* (singular) or *-selves* (plural). An intensive pronoun is used to emphasize a word that precedes it in the sentence.

intensive pronoun
↓
The clown *himself* refused to walk the tightrope.

intensive pronoun
↓
I *myself* will carry the message.

(d) **Reflexive pronouns** end in *-self* or *-selves* and indicate that the subject acts upon itself.

reflexive pronouns ———
↓
I hurt *myself*.

Members of an athletic team sometimes defeat *themselves*.

(e) **Interrogative pronouns** are used in asking questions: *who, whom, whose,* and *which. Who* and *whom* combine with *ever: whoever, whomever.*

interrogative pronoun
↓
Who was chosen?

(f) **Personal pronouns** usually refer to a person, sometimes to a thing. (See **9h.**) They have many forms, which depend on their grammatical function.

	SINGULAR	PLURAL
First person	I, me, mine	we, us, ours
Second person	you, yours	you, yours
Third person	he, she, it, his, hers, its	they, them, theirs

(g) **Relative pronouns** are used to introduce dependent adjective or noun clauses: *who, whoever, whom, whomever, that, what, which, whose.* (See **9i** and **7j.**)

relative pronoun
↓
The director decided *who* was to act the role of the hero.

They may function as connectives as well as stand for a noun.

relative pronoun—connective
↓
The director had not read the play *that* was chosen.

■ Exercise 1

Identify and distinguish between the nouns and pronouns in the following sentences.

         N   P   P   P   N

1. The director himself told those who wanted to join the choir
that they were welcome to audition to show him that they
could not only sing on pitch but also sight-read with confidence.

2. Someone has said that a person who works hard and plays
little will be dull.

3. Yosemite National Park is far west of the Mississippi River.

4. The two speakers said that a person who completes
college is educated, but they should have said that one who
completes college has been exposed to knowledge.

5. No one was surprised when the wind blew branches from
the dead maple tree onto the roof of the metal tool shed,
denting it badly.

Verbs

Verbs can assert an action or express a condition. (See **3.**)

action
↓

Twenty-seven mallards *flew* south.

condition
↓

The twenty-seven birds *were* mallards.

A main verb may have helpers, called **auxiliary verbs,** such as *are, have, will be, do,* and *did.*

auxiliary verb   *main verb*
    ↘   ↙

Twenty-seven mallards *did fly* south.

auxiliary verbs *main verb*
 ↙ ↘   ↓

Leif Erickson *may have preceded* Columbus to America.

Linking verbs express condition rather than action: *appear, become, feel, look, seem, smell, sound,* and *taste.* The most common linking verbs, however, are the many forms of the verb *to be* (*is, are, was, were,* etc.). See p. 445.

linking verb
↓

The woman with the plastic fruit on her hat *is* an actress.

linking verb
↓

In the presence of so many toys the child *appeared* joyful.

Verbs are either **transitive** or **intransitive** (see pp. 47, 449). For **verb tenses,** see **4.** For **verbals,** see pp. 22–24, 449.

■ **Exercise 2**

Identify the verbs in each of the following sentences.

1. The arrival of jets flying in formation <u>will signal</u> the end of the air show.

2. The flight attendant <u>walked</u> among the passengers and <u>looked</u> for the lost purse.

3. The symphony <u>was performed</u> by a renowned orchestra, but the audience <u>was</u> not enthusiastic.

4. Spectators at the hockey game <u>were</u> ecstatic when the rookie <u>scored</u> a goal.

5. An appointment with a famous person <u>can be</u> an anxious experience.

Adjectives

Adjectives modify a noun or a pronoun. They limit, qualify, or make more specific the meaning of another word. Generally, they describe. Most adjectives appear before the word they modify.

> *adjective*
> ↓
> *Sour* apples are often used in cooking.

Predicate adjectives follow linking verbs and modify the noun or pronoun that is the subject of the sentence.

subject   predicate adjective

A nap in the afternoon is *restful.*

The three **articles** *(a, an, the)* are classified as adjectives.

Some **possessive adjectives** have forms that are the same as some **possessive pronouns:** *her, his, your, its, our, their. (Your, our,* and *their* have endings with *-s* in the pronoun form.)

Demonstrative adjectives, which have exactly the same forms as demonstrative pronouns, are used before the nouns they modify.

this dog or *that dog; these dogs* or *those dogs*

Indefinite adjectives have the same form as indefinite pronouns: for example, *some, any, each, every.*
(See **10.**)

Adverbs

Adverbs (like adjectives) describe, qualify, or limit other elements in the sentence. They modify verbs (and verbals), adjectives, and other adverbs.

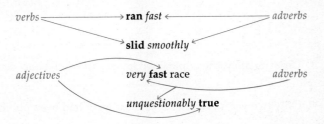

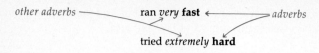

other adverbs ⟶ ran *very* **fast** ⟵ *adverbs*

tried *extremely* **hard**

Sometimes adverbs modify an entire clause:

Frankly, *she did not speak the truth.*

Many adverbs end in *-ly (effectively, curiously),* but not all words that end in *-ly* are adverbs *(lovely, friendly).*

Adverbs tell how *(slowly, well);* how much *(extremely, somewhat);* how often *(frequently, always);* when *(late, afterward);* where *(there, here).* These are the main functions of adverbs, but not the only ones. Adverbs must be identified by their use in the sentence; that is, they cannot all be memorized. (For a discussion of the degrees of adverbs, see **10.**)

■ **Exercise 3**

Identify the adverbs and adjectives in the following sentences. Tell what each one modifies. (A, an, and the are adjectives.)

     adv.   adv.   adj./adj.   adj.
1. Slowly and quietly the large automobile glided to a stop.

   adj. adj.   adj.   adv.
2. The huge sign was a warning: "Drive carefully and live

   adj. adj.
   a long time."

   adv.   adj. adj.   adj.   adv. adv.   adj.
3. Unfortunately, the white linen tablecloth is still badly stained.

   adv.   adj.   adj. adj. adj.
4. Only two years after her first short work had been published

adj. adj.   adj.   adj. adj.

in the college literary magazine, the young writer became

compound adj.   adj. adj.

book-review editor of the local newspaper.

    adj.   adj.   adv.   adj.

5. Many young couples are carefully restoring the beauties of

adj.   adv.   adv.

old homes that have been almost entirely ignored for

adj.

many years.

Conjunctions

Conjunctions connect words, phrases, or clauses. They are classified as **coordinating, subordinating,** or **correlative.**

    Coordinating conjunctions connect elements that are—grammatically speaking—of equal rank. Those most frequently used are *and, but, or, nor, for,* and *yet.*

coordinating conjunction

The orchestra played selections from *Brahms, Beethoven,* **and** *Wagner.*

coordinating conjunction

The angry candidate left the podium, **and** *he did not return.*

    Subordinating conjunctions introduce a subordinate or dependent element of a sentence. Examples are *although, because, if, since, though, unless, when, where, while.*

subordinating conjunction
↓
Although *many painters sell their work,* few become wealthy.

Some words (such as *before, after*) may function as conjunctions and also as other parts of speech.
Correlative conjunctions are always used in pairs. Examples are *both . . . and, either . . . or, not only . . . but also, neither . . . nor.* (See **18.**)

correlative conjunctions

Not only a well-balanced diet *but also* adequate sleep is needed for good health.

■ Exercise 4

Identify all conjunctions in the following sentences, and tell whether each is coordinating or subordinating or correlative.

1. subordinating
   <u>Although</u> the players protested, the coach scheduled two extra practices <u>and</u> (coordinating) warned that latecomers <u>not only</u> (correlative) would run extra laps <u>but also</u> (correlative) would sit on the bench during the first period of the next game.

2. subordinating
   <u>When</u> the sun comes up, the world takes on an entirely new appearance, <u>and</u> (coordinating) hope seems to bloom again.

3. The ceilings of the old room were high, <u>but</u> (coordinating) the windows were narrow, <u>and</u> (coordinating) the wind blew hard <u>and</u> (coordinating) whistled through the cracks around the door.

4. After the electricity came on again, the manager discovered
that neither the meats nor the vegetables were spoiled
or even discolored.

subordinating — After

correlative — neither   *correlative* — nor

coordinating — or

5. The mayor recommends an increase not only in property
taxes but also in wage taxes unless the budget deficit de-
creases dramatically.

correlative — not only

correlative — but also   *subordinating* — unless

Prepositions

Prepositions connect a noun or a pronoun (the **object of the
preposition**) to another word in the sentence.

Most prepositions are short single words: *above, across, after,
against, along, among, at, before, behind, below, beneath, beside, between, by, from, in, into, of, on, over, through, up, upon, with, without.*

Groups of words can also serve as prepositions: *along with,
according to, in spite of.*

A preposition introduces and is part of a group of words, a
phrase, that includes an object. The phrase is used as a unit in the
sentence, a single part of speech—usually an adjective or an adverb.

above the clouds	*across* the tracks	*after* the game
by the creek	*through* the hallways	*under* the floor

(See **37f** for a discussion of the idiomatic use of prepositions.)

■ Exercise 5

Identify prepositions, objects of prepositions, and prepositional phrases in the following sentences.

1. Piles of leaves on the curb were collected by the street-cleaning trucks.

2. According to the rules of the game, the contestant at the front of the line must turn quickly and race toward the rear.

3. There on the table was the book the hostess had borrowed from her friend.

4. Never in the history of the province had so devastating an event occurred.

5. After a brisk walk around the block, everyone was ready for dessert.

Interjections

Interjections are words that exclaim; they express surprise or strong emotion. They may stand alone or serve as part of a sentence.

Ouch!
Well, that was a shame.

Because of their nature, interjections are most often used in the spontaneity of speech, not writing, which is generally more planned than exclamatory.

■ **Exercise 6**

Name the part of speech of each word underlined and numbered in the following sentences.

```
      1        2      3   4    5      6       7      8    9
    Well, questions do not always have answers, but that does
```

not mean we should stop asking.

```
      10          11     12         13         14
    Movie   stars and well-known athletes hobnobbed with
       15         16      17               18         19
    government and business leaders at the fund-raiser, which
       20
    was held last night.
```

1. interjection	5. adverb
2. noun	6. verb
3. verb	7. noun
4. adverb	8. conjunction
9. pronoun	15. adjective
10. adjective	16. adjective
11. conjunction	17. noun
12. adjective	18. noun
13. noun	19. pronoun
14. preposition	20. verb

The Parts of Sentences

A sentence, a basic unit of language, has a complete meaning of its own. The essential parts of a sentence are a **subject** and a **predicate.**

A **subject** does something, has something done to it, or is identified or described.

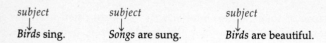

subject
↓
Birds sing.

subject
↓
Songs are sung.

subject
↓
Birds are beautiful.

A **predicate** expresses what the subject does, what is done to it, or how it is identified or described.

predicate
↓
Birds *sing*.

predicate
⌐‾‾‾¬
Songs *are sung*.

predicate
⌐‾‾‾‾‾¬
Birds *are beautiful*.

Simple subjects, complete subjects, compound subjects

The essential element of a subject is called the **simple subject.** Usually it consists of a single word.

simple subject
↓
The large *balloon* burst.

The subject can be understood rather than actually stated. A director of a chorus might say, "Sing" meaning, "You sing." But here one spoken word would be a complete sentence.

understood subject   predicate
↘   ↙
[You] Sing.

All the words that form a group and function together as the subject of a sentence are called the **complete subject.**

complete subject
⌐‾‾‾‾‾‾¬
The large balloon burst.

When any similar units of a sentence—subjects, verbs, adjectives —are linked together and function together, they are said to be **compound**.

compound subject

The large *balloons* and the small *bubbles* burst.

Of course pronouns as well as nouns may make up compound subjects.

compound pronoun subject

She and *I* sang.

■ **Exercise 7**

Identify the subjects and the complete subjects. Tell whether each sentence has a single subject or a compound subject.

C 1. The old furniture and dishes stored in the attic are worthless.

S 2. In the middle of the campus stood a tall, beautiful tower.

S 3. Swimming against the current, the otter returned to her young.

C 4. The George Washington Bridge and the Golden Gate Bridge are both well known.

C 5. The piano teacher and her youngest pupil played a duet at the recital.

Simple predicates, complete predicates, compound predicates

The single verb (or the main verb and its auxiliary verbs) is the **simple predicate.**

simple predicate
↓
Balloons *soar.*

simple predicate
Balloons *are soaring.*

The simple predicate, its modifiers, and any complements form a group that is called the **complete predicate.**

complete predicate
Balloons *soared over the pasture.*

When two verbs in the predicate express actions or conditions of a subject, they are a **compound predicate**—just as two nouns may be a **compound subject.**

compound predicate
Balloons *soar and burst.*

compound, complete predicate
Balloons *soared over the pasture and then burst.*

(For errors in predication, see **15b.**)

■ **Exercise 8**

Identify the verbs (including auxiliaries) and the complete predicates. Tell whether each sentence has a single predicate or a compound predicate.

c 1. The scientist left the laboratory and walked to the library.

s 2. All day long the caravan moved through long valleys and over steep hills.

s 3. Build beautiful and lasting buildings.

c 4. Playgoers arrived at the theater early and waited eagerly for the box office to open.

c 5. Children at the picnic played softball, swam in the pool, and rowed on the lake.

Complements

Complements, usually a part of the predicate, complete the meaning of the sentence. They are nouns, pronouns, or adjectives. They function as predicate adjectives or predicate nominatives (both sometimes called **subjective complements**) and direct or indirect objects.

Predicate adjectives

A **predicate adjective** follows a linking verb and modifies the subject, not the verb.

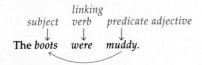

Predicate nominatives

A predicate nominative follows a linking verb and renames the subject. (Compare **predicate adjectives** above and **appositives,** p. 440.)

```
              predicate
              nominative
                 ↓
Bears are omnivores.
```

Direct objects

A **direct object** receives the action indicated by a transitive verb. It is always in the objective case. See **9.**

```
   verb  direct object
    ↓        ↓
Bears eat honey.
```

Indirect objects

An **indirect object** receives the action of the verb indirectly. The subject (through the verb) acts on the direct object, which in turn has an effect on the indirect object. Indirect objects tell to whom or for whom something is done.

```
              indirect  direct
      verb    object    object
       ↓        ↓         ↓
Rangers fed the bears honey.
```

The sentence can be rearranged to read

```
                                    indirect
      verb   object  understood     object
       ↓       ↓          ↓           ↓
Rangers fed honey     [to]      the bears.
```

When the preposition (*to*, as above, or *for*) is understood, the word is an indirect object. When the preposition is expressed, the word is an object of a preposition:

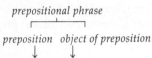

prepositional phrase

preposition   object of preposition

Rangers fed honey *to* the *bears.*

(Grammatically, the sentence above has no indirect object.)

Objective complements accompany direct objects. They can modify the object or be synonymous with it.

The editor considered the manuscript *publishable.*

The corporation named a former clerk its *president.*

■ **Exercise 9**

Underline and identify the predicate adjectives, predicate nominatives, direct objects, and indirect objects in the following sentences.

1. Those who possess <u>talents</u> (DO) should develop and use <u>them</u> (DO) wisely.

2. The gardener already had many <u>cactuses</u> (DO), but a neighbor was <u>happy</u> (PA) to give him some more.

3. Good peaches are <u>sweet</u> (PA) and <u>juicy</u> (PA).

4. Give <u>each</u> (IO) of the men and the women a <u>book</u> (DO) and a <u>candle</u> (DO).

5. Whoever comes to the party will be a welcome <u>guest</u> (PN).

Phrases

A **phrase** is a cluster of words that does not have both a subject and a predicate. Some important kinds of phrases are **verb phrases, prepositional phrases,** and **verbal phrases.**

Verb phrases

The main verb and its auxiliary verbs are called a **verb phrase:** *were sitting, shall be going, are broken, may be considered. Were, shall be, are, may be,* and verbs like them are often auxiliary verbs (sometimes called "helping" verbs).

verb phrase

The bear *had been eating* the honey.

Prepositional phrases

Prepositional phrases function as adjectives or adverbs.

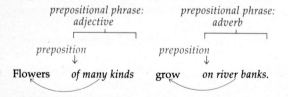

Flowers *of many kinds* grow *on river banks.*

Verbals and verbal phrases

A **verbal** is a grammatical form derived from a verb. No verbal is a complete verb. It may have an object and modifiers. (Adverbs modify verbals as they modify verbs.) A verbal and the words associated with it compose a **verbal phrase.**

There are three kinds of verbals: **gerunds, participles,** and **infinitives.** A gerund is always a noun; a participle is an adjective; an infinitive may be either a noun, an adjective, or an adverb, depending on its use in the sentence.

GERUNDS AND GERUND PHRASES
Gerunds always end in *-ing* and function as nouns.

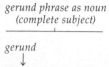

gerund phrase as noun
  (complete subject)

gerund
  ↓
Playing the xylophone requires skill.

PARTICIPLES AND PARTICIPIAL PHRASES
Participles usually end in *-ing* or *-ed* (there are many irregular forms also) and always function as adjectives.

participial phrase as adjective
    (modifies he)

participle
↓
Jumping aside, he dodged the ball.

INFINITIVES AND INFINITIVE PHRASES
Infinitives begin with *to,* which is sometimes understood rather than actually stated. They can be used as nouns, adjectives, or adverbs.

USED AS NOUN

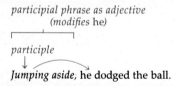

infinitive phrase
used as subject

infinitive

To rescue the swimmer was easy.

USED AS ADJECTIVE

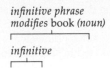

infinitive phrase
modifies book *(noun)*

infinitive

Charlotte's Web is a good book *to read to a child.*

USED AS ADVERB

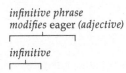

infinitive phrase
modifies eager *(adjective)*

infinitive

The novelist was eager *to read a story.*

■ **Exercise 10**

Identify phrases in the following sentences and tell what kind each is —infinitive, gerund, participial, prepositional, or verb.

1. Patting your head and rubbing your stomach at the same time is not as easy as you may be thinking it is.
   - gerund / gerund / prepositional / verb

2. Candidates for local office will be attending the parent-teacher association meeting to make themselves known and to express their views.
   - prepositional / verb / infinitive / infinitive

3. Working through the night, they completed the musical score to be included in the play.
   - participial / prepositional / infinitive / prepositional

gerund   prepositional
4. Taking the census in modern times is not as simple as it was

two thousand years ago.

participle   verb
5. Insisting that his vegetables had been grown organically, the

    infinitive   prepositional
gardener refused to sell them at a lower price.

Clauses

A **clause** is a group of words containing a subject and a predicate. There are two kinds of clauses: **independent** and **dependent** (or **subordinate**).

Independent clauses

An **independent clause** can stand alone; grammatically, it is like a complete sentence. Two or more independent clauses in one sentence can be joined by coordinating conjunctions, conjunctive adverbs, semicolons, and other grammatical devices or punctuation marks.

> Some birds soar, but others constantly beat their wings during flight.
> Some birds soar; others constantly beat their wings during flight.

Dependent clauses or subordinate clauses

Like verbals, **dependent clauses** function as three different parts of speech in a sentence: nouns, adjectives, and adverbs. Unlike independent clauses, dependent clauses do not express a complete thought in themselves.

DEPENDENT CLAUSE NOT IN COMPLETE SENTENCE
> *When the auction began.*

USED AS NOUN (usually subject or object)
> *That the little child could read rapidly* was well known.
>> *(noun clause used as subject)*

> The other students knew *that the little child could read rapidly.*
>> *(noun clause used as direct object)*

USED AS ADJECTIVE

> Everyone *who completed the race* won a shirt.
> *(modifying pronoun subject)*

USED AS ADVERB

> *When spring comes* many flowers bloom.
> *(modifying verb)*

The Kinds of Sentences

A **simple sentence** has only one independent clause (but no dependent clause). A simple sentence is not necessarily a short sentence; it may contain several phrases.

> Birds sing.
> After a long silence, *the bird began to warble a sustained and beautiful song.*

A **compound sentence** has two or more independent clauses (but no dependent clause).

independent clause   *independent clause*

Birds sing, and bees hum.

A **complex sentence** has both an independent clause and one or more dependent clauses.

┌─────────*dependent clauses*─────────┐ ┌─*independent*─

When spring comes and [when] new leaves grow, migratory birds
─clause─┐

return north.

A **compound-complex** sentence has at least two independent clauses and at least one dependent clause. A dependent clause can be part of an independent clause.

dependent adverb   *independent*
┌─── *clause* ───┐ ┌── *clause* ──┐ ┌─ *independent clause*

When heavy rains come, the streams rise, and farmers know
dependent noun clause
used as object

┌──────────────┴──────────────┐
└──────────────────────────────┘

that there will be floods.

■ **Exercise 11**

Underline each clause. Tell whether it is dependent or independent. Explain the use of each dependent clause in the sentence. Tell whether each sentence is simple, compound, complex, or compound-complex.

  complex   **independent**
1. People in some towns are awakened in the morning when a
                    dependent-adverb
   factory whistle blows to signal the change in a shift of

   workers.

2. Moving down the hills and around the curves, <u>the procession of cars was not able to proceed faster than twenty miles an hour</u>.

simple   *independent*

3. Officials hope <u>that the new primate center at the zoo will attract scholars as well as busloads of schoolchildren</u>.

complex   *entire sentence independent*   *dependent-noun*

4. <u>On the Friday after Thanksgiving, in spite of heavy rain, we took the train downtown to join the throngs of shoppers and sightseers piling into the beautifully decorated department stores</u>.

simple   *entire sentence independent*

5. <u>The visitor politely asked to be allowed to speak</u>, <u>and the moderator agreed</u>.

compound   *independent*   *independent*

SENTENCE
ERRORS

1 Sentence Fragments *frag*

Write complete sentences.

Fragments are parts of sentences written and punctuated as complete sentences. They take the form of dependent clauses, phrases, or other word groups without independent meaning and structure and often without subject, verb, or subject-verb.

Notice how the fragments below are revised and made into complete sentences.

FRAGMENT (phrase)
    Fear of heights, one of the most common phobias.

COMPLETE SENTENCE (verb added)
    Fear of heights is one of the most common phobias.

FRAGMENT (dependent clause)
    Although several large rivers have been cleaned up.

COMPLETE SENTENCE (dependent conjunction *although* omitted)
    Several large rivers have been cleaned up.

FRAGMENT (noun and phrase—no main verb)
    The green fields humming with sounds of insects.

COMPLETE SENTENCE (modifier *humming* changed to verb *hummed*)
    The green fields hummed with sounds of insects.

Fragments are often permissible in dialogue when the meaning is clear.

    "See the geese."
    "Where?"
    "Flying north."

Fragments are occasionally used for special effects or emphasis.

> The long journey down the river was especially pleasant. A time of rest and tranquillity.

■ Exercise 1

Make the following fragments complete sentences. Delete one word; add one word or a verb phrase; change one word; attach a fragment to a sentence; or rewrite.

1. The various colors and designs of academic regalia revealing~~ing~~ ^ed^

   the wearers' schools, degrees, and fields of learning.

2. ~~That~~ ^T^the bald eagle flies high over the mountaintops looking

   for prey.

3. An empty attic and an uncluttered basement suggest~~ive of~~ a

   life without a meaningful past.

4. The young artist who won first prize in the autumn exhibit of

   watercolors.

5. That is, ~~if~~ it ^may^ becomes possible to travel at a rate exceeding the

   speed of light.

6. ^Have you lost t^The ability to solve simple arithmetic problems mentally/

   ~~Have you lost it~~ because you use your pocket calculator so

   often?

7. Lakes provide a wide range of recreation ~~.~~ ⌃ , including w~~W~~ading, swim-

   ming, fishing, and boating.

8. Meadows of deep green grass, hills with trees soaring almost

   into the white clouds, one superhighway, and a small dirt

   road ⌃ make up ~~—~~a landscape of contradictions.

9. The post office is closed ~~.~~ ⌃ b~~B~~ecause July 4 is a national holiday.

10. Although the range of her voice was limited ⌃ , s~~S~~he had perfect

    pitch.

2 Comma Splices and Fused Sentences   *cs/fus*

Join two independent clauses clearly and appropriately, or write two separate sentences.

A **comma splice** or **comma fault** occurs when a comma is used between two independent clauses (and when there is **no** coordinating conjunction).

SPLICE OR FAULT

Human nature is seldom as simple as it appears, hasty judgments are therefore often wrong.

A **fused sentence** or **run-on sentence** occurs when the independent clauses have neither punctuation nor coordinating conjunctions between them.

FUSED OR RUN-ON

> Human nature is seldom as simple as it appears hasty judgments are therefore often wrong.

Comma splices and fused sentences fail to indicate the break between independent clauses. Revise in one of the following ways:

1. Use a *period* and write two sentences.

   Human nature is seldom as simple as it appears. Hasty judgments are therefore often wrong.

2. Use a *semicolon.* (See also **22**.)

   Human nature is seldom as simple as it appears; hasty judgments are therefore often wrong.

Before *conjunctive adverbs* (see **20f** and **22a**), use a *semicolon* to join *independent clauses.*

   The rare book had a torn flyleaf; *therefore* it was advertised at a reduced price.

3. Use a *comma* and a *coordinating conjunction (and, but, or, nor, for, yet, so).* (See also **20a**.)

   Human nature is seldom as simple as it appears, *so* hasty judgments are often wrong.

4. Use a *subordinating conjunction* (see pp. 11–12, 448) and a *dependent clause.*

   Because *human nature is seldom as simple as it appears,* hasty judgments are often wrong.

■ **Exercise 2**

Identify comma splices and fused sentences with CS or FS. Correct them. Write C by sentences that are already correct.

CS 1. Television sometimes offers worthwhile programs as well as
                                                        and *or* . It *or* ;
      trivia, it should not be condemned entirely.

C 2. After twelve years of silence, the composer finished two

      symphonies within six months.
                                                        ;
FS 3. Conflicts almost always exist within a family nevertheless it

      is still the most enduring of social units.
                              ;   ;
FS 4. The bread stuck in the toaster the smoke detector went off

      the smell of burned toast permeated the apartment.

CS 5. Signs warning about riptides and the undertow were posted
                              so
      on the beach, no one ventured into the water.

■ **Exercise 3**

Identify each of the following as correct (C), *a comma splice* (CS), *a fused sentence* (FS), *or a fragment* (F).

CS 1. Vitamins are necessary for health, however, excessive
      amounts of some of them are dangerous.

C 2. Vitamins are necessary for health; however, excessive
      amounts of some of them are dangerous.

FS 3. Vitamins are necessary for health however, excessive amounts of some of them are dangerous.

F 4. Vitamins are necessary for health. Excessive amounts of some of them, however, dangerous.

C 5. Vitamins are necessary for health, but excessive amounts of some of them are dangerous.

■ Exercise 4

Identify fragments (F), comma splices (CS), or fused sentences (FS) and correct them. Write C by correct sentences.

CS 1. Buying and assembling an unpainted table may save you money,/however, you will need tools, space, and time to put

    ;

it together.

FS 2. Bus and subway fares are going up next month fewer people

    Because b

will be using public transportation.

C 3. Fresh seafood is plentiful even in inland cities. It can be flown in from the coasts without being frozen.

FS 4. Styles of clothing are not always planned for comfort belts

    ; *or* . B

and seams may be designed to look good rather than to fit natural contours of the body.

F 5. Predictions were that videotapes of films would seriously

harm the motion picture industry./Another instance of how

— or , a

difficult it is to see into the future.

C 6. New York's Washington Square has changed considerably

since it was a haven for writers in the 1890s.

F 7. Snow ~~continuing~~ to fall, increasing the likelihood that classes

continued

would be canceled.

FS 8. All over the city new buildings are springing up the skyline is

; or . T

rapidly changing.

C 9. For many, swimming is more pleasant than jogging, espe-

cially when the weather is hot.

CS 10. An adventurer will sometimes participate in a pastime de-

spite its great danger/sky diving, for example, is perilous.

; or . S

■ **Exercise 5**

Follow the instructions for Exercise 4.

F 1. The class project was to design and make sweaters for the

homeless,/Instead of doing research and writing a report.

i

CS 2. After all, the student argued, any imbecile can punctuate, *; or . S or , so*
studying the mechanics of composition is a complete waste
of time.

CS 3. Most generous people are naive, *; or . T* they simply do not realize
when they are being imposed upon.

FS 4. Some families agreed that for two weeks they would keep
their television sets turned off, *; or . T* the children were doubtful
about the experiment.

CS 5. Science and art are not incompatible, *; or . S* some learned scientists
are also philosophers or poets.

F 6. The art of pleasing is very necessary, *, b (comma optional)* but difficult to acquire.

FS 7. Finding someone to repair or clean mechanical watches is
difficult *; or . M* most of the watches sold now are electronic.

C 8. Writing on a blackboard frequently creates a scraping sound
that causes an unpleasant sensation.

FS 9. Some hobbies are for rich people, *. O or ;* only the wealthy can collect
diamonds.

F 10. Fossils and oil are often found in cold regions where ice and

                    This is e

snow never entirely melt. Evidence that the climate and the

earth change drastically over long periods of time.

or rewrite: Finding fossils and oil in cold regions where ice and
snow never entirely melt proves that the climate and the earth
change drastically over long periods of time.

3   Verb Forms   *vf*

Use the correct form of the verb.

All verbs have three principal parts: the present infinitive, the
past tense, and the past participle. Verbs are regular or irregular.

Regular verbs form the past tense and the past participle by
adding *-d* or *-ed* or sometimes *-t*. If only the infinitive form is
given in a dictionary, the verb is regular.

INFINITIVE	PAST TENSE	PAST PARTICIPLE
close	closed	closed
dwell	dwelled, dwelt	dwelled, dwelt
help	helped	helped
open	opened	opened
talk	talked	talked

Irregular verbs usually form the past tense and the past participle by changing an internal vowel. For irregular verbs a dictionary gives the three principal parts and also the present participle. For the verb *see*, the dictionary lists *see, saw, seen,* and *seeing*.
For *think*, it shows *think, thought* (for past and past participle), and
thinking (the present participle). The present and past participial
forms always have auxiliary (helping) verbs (see p. 7).

    Know the following irregular verbs so well that you automat-
ically use them correctly.

INFINITIVE	PAST TENSE	PAST PARTICIPLE
awake	awoke, awaked	awoke, awaked
be	was	been
begin	began	begun
bid (to offer as a price or to make a bid in playing cards)	bid	bid
bid (to command, order)	bade, bid	bidden, bid
blow	blew	blown
bring	brought	brought
build	built	built
burst	burst	burst
choose	chose	chosen
come	came	come
deal	dealt	dealt
dig	dug	dug
dive	dived, dove	dived
do	did	done
drag	dragged	dragged
draw	drew	drawn
drink	drank	drunk
drive	drove	driven
drown	drowned	drowned
fly	flew	flown
freeze	froze	frozen
give	gave	given
go	went	gone
grow	grew	grown
know	knew	known
lead	led	led
lend	lent	lent
lose	lost	lost
ring	rang	rung
run	ran	run
see	saw	seen
sing	sang	sung
sink	sank, sunk	sunk
slay	slew	slain
sting	stung	stung
swim	swam	swum
swing	swung	swung

INFINITIVE	PAST TENSE	PAST PARTICIPLE
take	took	taken
teach	taught	taught
think	thought	thought
throw	threw	thrown
wear	wore	worn
write	wrote	written

Some verb forms are especially troublesome. *Lie* is confused with *lay; sit,* with *set;* and *rise,* with *raise.*

Lie, sit, and *rise* are intransitive (do not take objects) and have the vowel *i* in the infinitive form and the present tense.

Lay, set, and *raise* are transitive (take objects) and have *a, e,* or *ai* as vowels.

TRANSITIVE	lay (to place)	laid	laid
INTRANSITIVE	lie (to recline)	lay	lain
TRANSITIVE	set (to place)	set	set
INTRANSITIVE	sit (to be seated)	sat	sat

In special meanings the verb *set* is intransitive (a hen *sets;* the sun *sets;* and so forth).

TRANSITIVE	raise (to lift)	raised	raised
INTRANSITIVE	rise (to get up)	rose	risen

■ Exercise 6

Underline the incorrect verb and write the correct form above it. Write **C** *by correct sentences.*

1. The lake had froze over, and the ice gleamed on the surface.
    frozen

2. The bricklayer begun work late yesterday because he seen an
    began   *had seen*

    automobile accident and stopped to offer his help.

3. Before the government began restocking national forests
    with wild game, hunters taken few vacations for hunting be-
                              took
    cause they use to see few deer and wild turkeys.
                    used

4. Before the cement could sit, someone written a name on it.
                          set   *wrote/had written*

5. The builder lead the owner of the property to the back of the
              led
    lot and showed him where someone had drug old cars onto
                                        dragged

    his land and left them there as eyesores.

6. The passenger give a tip to the cab driver, who frowned and
                gave
    sunk in his seat.
    sank

7. One person bidded fifteen dollars, and then another setting
                bid   *sitting*
    in the front row bidded twenty.
                    bid

C 8. The artist laid the brush on the stand just after he had

    painted the portrait, and it has been lying there ever since.

9. The carpenter promised to sit the bucket on the tile, but it has
                            set
    been setting on the carpet for a week.
        sitting

                              hung
10. The balloon that <u>hanged</u> over the doorway suddenly
    burst
    <u>busted</u>.

 Tense and
Sequence of Tenses   *t / shift*

Use appropriate forms of verbs and verbals to express time
sequences. Avoid confusing shifts in tense.

   The present tense expresses an action or condition occurring
in present time; the past, an action or condition that occurred in
past time but is now completed; the future, an action or condition
expected to occur in future time.

4a Tense forms

For each kind of time—present, past, and future—verbs have a
different form: simple, progressive, and perfect.[1]

SIMPLE	REGULAR	IRREGULAR
Present	I walk	I go
Past	I walked	I went
Future	I shall (will) walk	I shall (will) go

---

[1] There are in addition the emphatic forms with the auxiliary *do* or *did* (I *do go*
there regularly).

PROGRESSIVE	REGULAR	IRREGULAR
Present	I am walking	I am going
Past	I was walking	I was going
Future	I shall (will) be walking	I shall (will) be going

PERFECT	REGULAR	IRREGULAR
Present	I have walked	I have gone
Past	I had walked	I had gone
Future	I shall (will) have walked	I shall (will) have gone

4b Consistency (see 15)

Relationships between verbs should be consistent:

TWO PAST ACTIONS
> The sailor *stood* on the shore and *threw* shells at the seagulls. (not *throws*)
>
> He *turned* away when he *saw* me watching him.

TWO PRESENT ACTIONS
> As the school year *draws* to a close, the students *are* swept into a whirl of activities.

4c Special uses of the present tense

In general, the **present tense** or the **present progressive** expresses present time, but there are exceptions:

PRESENT—TO EXPRESS FUTURE ACTION
> The plane *leaves* for New York tomorrow. (present tense—future action)

> The plane *is leaving* in ten minutes. (present progressive tense—future action)

PRESENT—TO MAKE STATEMENTS ABOUT THE CONTENT OF LITERATURE AND OTHER WORKS OF ART (HISTORICAL PRESENT). (See **15** and **47e**.)
> In Henry James's *The Turn of the Screw,* a governess *believes* that the ghosts *are* real.

PRESENT—TO EXPRESS TIMELESS TRUTHS
> In 1851, Foucault proved that the earth *rotates* on its axis.

BUT
> Ancient Greeks *believed* that the earth *was* motionless.

Past tense is used for anything once believed but now disproved.

4d Perfect tenses

The three perfect tenses indicate one time or action completed before another.

PRESENT PERFECT WITH PRESENT
> I *have bought* my ticket, and I **am waiting** for the bus.

The controlling time word may not be a verb.

> I *have bought* my ticket **already.**

PAST PERFECT WITH PAST
> I *had bought* my ticket, and I **was waiting** for the bus.
> I *had bought* my ticket before the bus **came.**

FUTURE PERFECT WITH FUTURE

I *shall have eaten* by the time we **go.** (The controlling word, *go,* is present tense in form but future in meaning.)

I *shall have eaten* by **one o'clock.**

The future perfect is rare. Usually the simple future tense is used with an adverb phrase or clause.

RARE

I shall have eaten before you go.

MORE COMMON

I shall eat before you go.

4e Verbals and sequence

An infinitive (see pp. 23–24) generally takes the present tense when it expresses action that occurs at the same time as that of the controlling verb.

NOT

I wanted *to have gone.*

BUT

I wanted *to go.*

NOT

I had expected *to have met* my friends at the game.

BUT

I had expected *to meet* my friends at the game.

NOT
    I would have preferred *to have waited* until they came.

BUT
    I would have preferred *to wait* until they came.

The perfect participle expresses an action that precedes another
action.

    Having finished the manuscript, the aged author stored it away in
    her safe.

■ **Exercise 7**

*Underline the incorrect verb or verbal and write the correction above
it. Write C by correct sentences.*

1. In looking back, public officials almost always say they
                                to remain
   would have preferred to have remained private citizens.

                                    began *or* opens and begins
2. The actor opened the Bible and begins reading the Song of

   Solomon.

3. Having agreed to sing a solo at the Christmas concert, the so-
                began
   prano begins to hunt for a suitable piece of music.

4. The periodic table showed that the symbol for the element
                is
   mercury was Hg, not Me.

5. Joseph Conrad was well into his thirties before he began / ~~having begun~~

    to write his novels.

6. In Gérôme's painting "The Cadet," the young man has / ~~had~~ a

    slight sneer on his face.

C 7. The fall semester begins in August this year.

8. Having written his paper, the author placed his pen on the
   table and contemplated / ~~contemplates~~ what he had / ~~has~~ said.

9. The heroine is / ~~was~~ young throughout the novel.

10. The horses rushed out of the starting gate and headed / ~~head~~ for the

    first turn.

5   Voice   *vo*

Use the active voice for conciseness and emphasis.

A transitive verb is either active or passive. (An intransitive verb
does not have voice.) When the subject acts, the verb is active. In
most sentences the actor is more important than the receiver.

PASSIVE	The entire book was read by only half the class.
USE THE ACTIVE	Only half the class read the entire book.

PASSIVE   Satisfactory solutions for economic prob-
                          lems are being sought by the governor.

USE THE ACTIVE   The governor is seeking satisfactory solu-
                          tions for economic problems.

In the sentences above, the active voice creates a more vigorous
style.

When the subject is acted upon, the verb is passive. A passive verb is useful when the performer of an action is unknown or
unimportant.

The book about motorcycles *was misplaced* among books about cos-
metics.

The passive voice can also be effective when the emphasis is on
the receiver, the verb, or even a modifier.

The police *were* totally *misled.*

■ Exercise 8

*Rewrite the following sentences. Change the voice from passive to ac-
tive.*

  The leaders of the tribe destroyed t   used
1. The cameras that ~~were used by~~ the anthropologists to take

    pictures of the ancient village ~~were destroyed by the leaders~~

    ~~of the tribe.~~

2. ~~The trucks were finally loaded by~~ **W**
   workers who used fork-

   finally loaded the trucks.
   lifts./

3. ~~Some ancient objects of art were discovered by~~ **T**
   the amateur

   discovered some ancient objects of art.
   archaeologist./

4. The ~~road~~ **reporter** had ~~been~~ traveled **the road** many times, ~~by the reporter,~~ but

   she
   ~~the old house~~ had never before ~~been~~ noticed ~~by her~~. **the old house.**

5. The ~~cherry pie~~ **party-goers** will ~~be~~ devoured ~~by~~ the ~~party-goers~~ **cherry pie** although

   most of them
   ~~chocolate cake is~~ preferred ~~by most of them~~. **chocolate cake.**

■ **Exercise 9**

Change the voice of the verb when it is ineffective. Rewrite the sentence if necessary. Write E by sentences in which the verb is effective.

1. **Mowing the grass and pruning the hedges**
   ~~The appearance of the yard was~~ dramatically improved

   the appearance of the yard.
   ~~by mowing the grass and pruning the hedges~~.

E 2. Some young people are learning the almost lost art of black-

       smithing and shoeing horses.

E 3. The horse lost the race because the shoe was improperly

       nailed to its hoof.

       Elderly people can have a   **they maintain**
     4. A good time ~~can be had by elderly people~~ if relatively good

       health ~~is maintained by them~~.

       The gardener did not properly care for t
     5. The rare plants ~~were not properly cared for by the gardener.~~

6   Subjunctive Mood   *mo*

Use the subjunctive mood to express wishes, orders, and
conditions contrary to fact. (See **Mood,** p. 446.)

WISHES
     I wish I *were* a little child.

ORDERS
     The instructions are that ten sentences *be* revised.

CONDITIONS CONTRARY TO FACT
     If I *were* a little child, I would have no responsibilities.
     If I *were* you, I would not go.

Had the weather *been* good, we would have gone to the top of the mountain.

In modern English the subjunctive survives mainly as a custom in some expressions.

SUBJUNCTIVE
The new manager requested that ten apartments *be* remodeled.

SUBJUNCTIVE NOT USED
The new manager decided to have ten apartments remodeled.

■ **Exercise 10**

Change the mood of the verbs to subjunctive when appropriate in the following sentences. Put a C by those sentences that already use the correct subjunctive.

 1. If happiness ~~was~~ **were** measured by money and wealth, more people would be happy.

 2. The lock is broken. The owner of the building said that if it ~~was~~ **were** not, he would not press charges against the intruder.

C 3. The buyer of the Roman coin would demand that his money be refunded if the expert were to determine that it is a fake.

C 4. This coin would be worth more money if it were not smooth.

 5. The dealer required that the catalog ~~was~~ **be** reprinted.

7 Subject and Verb: Agreement   *agr*

Use singular verbs with singular subjects, plural verbs with plural subjects.

The *-s* or *-es* ending of the present tense of a verb in the third person (*she talks, he wishes*) indicates the singular. (The *-s* or *-es* ending for most *nouns* indicates the plural.)

SINGULAR	PLURAL
The dog barks.	The dogs bark.
The ax cuts.	The axes cut.

7a A compound subject (see p. 17) with *and* takes a plural verb.

Work and play **are** not equally rewarding.

Golf and polo **are** usually outdoor sports.

EXCEPTION: Compound subjects connected by *and* but expressing a singular idea take a singular verb.

The rise and fall of waves **draws** a sailor back to the sea.

When the children are in bed, *the tumult and shouting* **dies.**

7b After a compound subject with *or, nor, either . . . or, neither . . . nor, not . . . but,* the verb agrees in number and person with the nearer part of the subject. (See **8b**.)

NUMBER

Neither the *photographs* nor the *camera* **was** damaged by the fire.

Either *fans* or an *air conditioner* **is** necessary.

Either an *air conditioner* or *fans* **are** necessary.

PERSON

Neither *you* nor your *successor* **is** affected by the new regulation.

7c Intervening phrases or clauses do not affect the number of a verb.

Connectives like *as well as* and *along with* are not coordinating conjunctions but prepositions that take objects; they do not form compound subjects. Other such words and phrases include *in addition to, together with, with, plus,* and *including.*

SINGULAR SUBJECT, INTERVENING PHRASE, SINGULAR VERB

The *pilot* as well as all his passengers *was* rescued.

Written with a coordinating conjunction, the sentence takes a plural verb.

The *pilot* **and** his *passengers were* rescued.

NOTE: Do not be confused by inversion.

From these angry speeches *arises* [not *arise*] conflict.

7d A collective noun takes a singular verb when referring to a group as a unit, a plural verb when the members of
a group are thought of individually.

A collective noun names a class or group: *family, flock, jury, con-
gregation.* When the group is regarded as a unit, use the singular.

The *audience* at a concert sometimes **determines** the length of a performance.

When the group is regarded as separate individuals, use the
plural.

The *audience* at a concert **vary** in their reactions to the music.

7e Most nouns plural in form but singular in meaning
take a singular verb.

News and *economics* (and other words like *genetics, linguistics,*
etc.) are considered singular.

The *news* of the defeat **is** disappointing.

Economics **is** often thought of as a science.

Trousers and *scissors* are treated as plural except when used after *pair*.

> The *trousers* **are** unpressed and frayed.

> An old *pair* of jeans **is** sometimes stylish.

> The *scissors* **are** dull.

> That *pair* of scissors **is** dull.

Other nouns that cause problems are *measles, politics,* and *athletics.* When in doubt, consult a dictionary.

7f Indefinite pronouns *(each, either, neither, one, no one, everyone, someone, anyone, nobody, everybody, somebody, anybody)* usually take singular verbs.

> *Neither* of his papers **was** acceptable.

> *Everybody* **has** trouble choosing a subject for a paper.

> *Each student* **has** chosen a subject.

7g Some words such as *none, some, part, all, half* (and other fractions) take a singular or a plural verb, depending on the noun or pronoun that follows.

> *singular*

> *Some* of the *sugar* **was** spilled on the floor.

> *plural*

> *Some* of the *apples* **were** spilled on the floor.

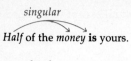

singular

Half of the *money* **is** yours.

plural

Half of the *students* **are** looking out the window.

When *none* can be regarded as either singular or plural, a singular or plural verb can be used.

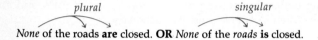

plural   *singular*

None of the roads **are** closed. **OR** *None* of the *roads* **is** closed.

The number is usually singular.

singular

The number of people in the audience **was** never determined.

A number when used to mean *some* is always plural.

plural

A number of the guests **were** whispering.

7h   In sentences beginning with *there* or *here* followed by verb and subject, the verb is singular or plural, depending on the subject.

There and *here* (never subjects of a sentence) are sometimes **expletives** used when the subject follows the verb. (See Section **38**.)

There **was** a long *interval* between the two discoveries.

There **were** thirteen *blackbirds* perched on the fence.

Here **is** a *thing* to remember.

Here **are** two *things* to remember.

The singular *is* may introduce a compound subject when the first noun is singular after an expletive.

There is *a swing and a footbridge* in the garden.

In sentences beginning with *It,* the verb is always singular.

It **was** many years ago.

7i A verb agrees with its subject, not with a predicate nominative.

NO

His horse and *his dog* **are** his main source of pleasure.

NO

His main *source* of pleasure **is** his horse and his dog.

7j After a relative pronoun *(who, which, that)* the verb has the same person and number as the antecedent.

antecedent ⟶ *relative pronoun* ⟶ *verb of relative pronoun*

Those→*who*→came **were** invited.

We→*who*→ **are** about to die salute you.

The *costumes*→*which*→ **were** worn in the ballet were dazzling.

He was the *candidate* →*who* →**was** able to carry out his pledges.

He was one of the *candidates* →*who* →**were** able to carry out their pledges.

BUT

He was *the* only *one* of the candidates *who* **was** able to carry out his pledges.

7k A title or a word used as a word is singular and requires a singular verb even if it contains plural words and plural ideas.

The Canterbury Tales **is** a masterpiece of comedy.

''Prunes and Prisms'' **was** a syndicated newspaper column on grammar and usage.

Hiccups is a word that imitates the sound it represents.

7L Expressions of time, money, measurement, and so forth take a singular verb when the amount is considered a unit.

Two tons **is** a heavy load for a small truck.

Forty-eight hours **is** a long time to go without sleep.

■ **Exercise 11**

Correct any verb that does not agree with its subject. Write C by correct sentences.

1. The sound of hammers mingle ∧ with the screech of seagulls

   and the crash of waves on the beach.

   (insertion above "mingle": s)

2. In O'Neill's *Long Day's Journey into Night,* Mary's smiles and
   laughter ~~is~~ **are** increasingly forced, her resentment is more obvi-

   ous, and her journey into night is more plainly marked.

3. *The Aspern Papers* deal ∧ with the subject of the right of pri-

   vacy.

   (insertion above "deal": s)

C 4. A large number of students are now moving away from

   housing provided by universities and colleges.

5. Two years ~~were~~ **was** a long time to wait for a raise.

6. Either *cacti* or *cactuses* ~~are~~ **is** acceptable for the plural form of

   cactus.

7. Molasses ~~were~~ **was** used in a great number of early New England

   recipes.

8. This tribal custom is enforced by strict taboos, the violation of

   which bring ∧ ostracism.

   (insertion above "bring": s)

9. Childish sentences or dull writing ~~are~~ **is** not improved by a

   sprinkling of dashes.

10. Neither the senator's son nor the senator's daughter wants a
career in politics, which ~~have~~ **has** always fascinated their father.

■ Exercise 12

Follow the instructions for Exercise 11.

1. Two weeks away on a glorious vacation ~~are~~ **is** the dream of many Americans.

2. All year long, the worker who is shackled to his job ~~look~~ **looks** forward to the time when he can lounge upon the shore of a mountain lake or the white sands by the sea.

3. It is highly improbable that either the white sands or the mountain lake ~~are~~ **is** the answer for this tense city-dweller.

4. Anybody who ~~live~~ **lives** a life of quiet desperation for months or even years can hardly expect to forget anxieties at once.

5. Nevertheless, realizing a need to slow down, the American vacationer, along with his entire family, ~~take~~ **takes** a trip.

6. Plan after plan ~~have~~ **has** been made; nothing can go wrong.

7. The trouble is that the family ~~have~~ **has (optional)** made so many plans that neither parents nor children ~~has~~ **have** time for side trips.

8. Father is determined to relax; he somehow fails to see that relaxation and two weeks of feverish activity <s>is</s> **are** not compatible.

9. This man's situation, like that of thousands of others, <s>are</s> **is** the
result of his desire on the one hand to slow down and on the
other to forget himself, to escape the thoughts that <s>haunts</s> **haunt**
him for fifty weeks of the year.

c 10. Physical relaxation and at the same time escape from frustra-
tions is impossible for him.

c 11. He returns to his job more weary or more worried or both
than when he left.

12. The roots of this man's problem <s>goes</s> **go** very deep, and he must
search deep within himself for the solution.

c 13. He must learn to stop frequently and to take account of himself and his values.

14. He must identify himself with values that <s>has</s> **have** proved
lasting.

15. He should also ask his wife and children whether any of
them <s>have</s> **has** ideas about how to make a vacation more enjoy-
able.

⑧ Pronouns: Agreement, Reference, and Usage *agr / ref*

Use singular pronouns to refer to singular antecedents, plural pronouns to refer to plural antecedents. Make a pronoun refer to a definite antecedent.

The *writer* finished **his** story.

The *writers* finished **their** stories.

8a In general, use a plural pronoun to refer to a compound antecedent linked with *and*.

The *owner* and the *captain* refused to leave **their** distressed ship.

If two nouns designate the same person, the pronoun is singular.

The *owner and captain* refused to leave **his** distressed ship.

8b After a compound antecedent linked with *or, nor, either . . . or, neither . . . nor, not only . . . but also,* a pronoun agrees with the nearer part of the antecedent. (See **7b.**)

Neither the chess *pieces* nor the *board* had been placed in **its** proper position.

Neither the *board* nor the chess *pieces* had been placed in **their** proper positions.

A sentence like this written with *and* is less artificial and stilted.

The chess *pieces* **and** the *board* had not been placed in **their** proper positions.

8c A singular pronoun follows a collective noun antecedent when the members of the group are considered as a unit; a plural pronoun, when they are thought of individually. (See **7d**.)

A UNIT
The student *committee* presented **its** report.

INDIVIDUALS
The *committee*, some of **them** defiant, filed into the room and took **their** seats.

8d Such singular antecedents as *each, either, neither, one, no one, everyone, someone, anyone, nobody, everybody, somebody, anybody* usually call for singular pronouns.

Not *one* of the linemen felt that **he** had played well.

Be consistent in number within the same sentence.

INCONSISTENT   *singular*   *plural*

Everyone takes **their** seats.

CONSISTENT

Everyone who is a mother sometimes wonders how **she** will survive the day.

Traditionally the pronouns *he* and *his* were used to refer to both men and women when the antecedent was unknown or representative of both sexes: "Each person has to face **his** own destiny." *He* was considered generic, that is, a common gender. Today this usage is changing because many feel that it ignores the presence and importance of women: there are as many "she's" as "he's" in the world, and one pronoun should not be selected to represent both.

Writers should become sensitive to this issue and strive to avoid offense without at the same time indulging in ridiculous alternatives. Here are three suggestions:

1. Make the sentence plural.

   All *persons* have to face *their* own destinies.

2. Use *he or she* (or *his or her*).

   Each person has to face *his or her* own destiny.

NOTE: Be sparing in the use of *he or she, his or her.* Monotony results if these double pronouns are used more than once or twice in a paragraph.

3. Use *the* or avoid the singular pronoun altogether.

   > Each person must face *the* future.
   > Each person must face destiny.

8e   *Which* refers to animals and things. *Who* and *whom* refer to persons and sometimes to animals or things called by name. *That* refers to animals or things and sometimes to persons.

The *boy* **who** was fishing is my son.

The *dog,* **which** sat beside him, looked happy.

Secretariat, **who** won the Kentucky Derby, will be remembered as one of the most beautiful horses of all time.

Sometimes *that* and *who* are interchangeable.

A mechanic *that (who)* does good work stays busy.

A person *that (who)* giggles is often revealing embarrassment.

NOTE: *Whose* (the possessive form of *who*) may be less awkward than *of which,* even in referring to animals and things.

The *car* **whose** right front tire blew out came to a stop.

8f   Pronouns should not refer vaguely to an entire sentence or to a clause or to unidentified people.

Some people worry about wakefulness but actually need little sleep. *This* is one reason they have so much trouble sleeping.

This could refer to the worry, to the need for little sleep, or to psychological problems or other traits that have not even been mentioned.

CLEAR

Some people have trouble sleeping because they lie awake and worry about their inability to sleep.

They, them, it, and *you* are sometimes used as vague references to people and conditions that need more precise identification.

VAGUE

> *They* always get *you* in the end.

The problem here is that the pronouns *they* and *you* and the sentence are so vague that the writer could mean almost anything pessimistic. The sentence could refer to teachers, deans, government officials, or even all of life.

NOTE: At times writers let *this, which,* or *it* refer to the whole idea of an earlier clause or phrase when no misunderstanding is likely.

> The grumbler heard that his boss had called him incompetent. *This* made him resign.

8g Make a pronoun refer clearly to one antecedent, not uncertainly to two.

UNCERTAIN

> The agent visited her client before she went to the party.

CLEAR

> Before the client went to the party, the agent visited her.

8h Use pronouns ending in *-self* or *-selves* only in sentences that contain antecedents for the pronoun.

CORRECT INTENSIVE PRONOUN

> The cook *himself* washed the dishes.

FAULTY

> The antique dealer sold the chair to my roommate and *myself.*

CORRECT

The antique dealer sold the chair to my roommate and *me.*

■ Exercise 13

Revise sentences that contain errors in agreement of pronouns.

1. The captain of the freighter let each member of the crew decide whether ~~they~~ he wished to remain with the ship.

2. On behalf of my wife and ~~myself~~ me, I welcomed the visitors.

3. The cat ~~who~~ that was judged best of show belongs to a woman

   who lives in Atlanta.

4. The wire fence did not stop either the owner's dog or the

   neighbor's cat from ~~their~~ its efforts to get into the enclosure.

5. The drifter, along with his many irresponsible relatives,

   never paid back a cent ~~they~~ he borrowed.

6. In the early days in the West, almost every man could ride
   ~~their~~ his horse well.

7. The League of Nations failed because ~~they~~ it never received

   full support from the member countries.

                                                                you
8. Was the prize awarded to your assistant or to ~~yourself~~?

                                                          her
9. Neither of the two women ever accepted ~~their~~ prize from the

    advertising agency.

                                                    she
10. None of the bridesmaids believed ~~they~~ would ever again
      her
    wear ~~their~~ gown after the wedding was over.

■ **Exercise 14**

Revise sentences that contain vague or faulty references of pronouns.

                                                            employers
1. The typical industrial worker is now well paid, but ~~they~~ have

    not been able to do much about the boredom.
    The government   s
2. ~~They~~ tell you that you must pay taxes, but most of the time
                                                it   s
    you do not know what ~~they~~ use your money for.
      T
3. ~~In~~ the recipe on the back of the box ~~it~~ says that three eggs are

    needed.
    Mints
4. ~~They~~ use much less silver in modern coins; so the metal in

    the coins is worth less.

5. The collision slammed the car into the side of the house and
                                  the car (or the house).
    damaged ~~it~~.

■ **Exercise 15**

Revise sentences that contain errors in reference of pronouns. Write C by correct sentences.

1. The passerby ~~which~~ **who** saved the two children did not know how to swim.

2. ~~The soles of his~~ **His** shoes ~~were~~ worn **with** ∧ **soles** made him self-conscious.

3. Lawyers generally charge their clients ∧ a standard fee ~~unless they are unusually poor~~ **who are not unusually poor**.

4. One difference between dry, new boots and boots that have been worn and carefully oiled is that ~~they~~ **unoiled ones** will not keep your feet dry if you are crossing a swamp.

5. The ~~instructions were~~ brief and clear ~~which was~~ **instructions were** helpful.

6. On the night of July 14, the patriots stormed the doors of the jail/, and ~~they were~~ immediately smashed ∧ **them** open.

7. The lecturer may have ignored the heckler because ~~he~~ **the heckler (or the lecturer)** was obviously unwell.

8. The poet is widely read, but it is very difficult indeed to make a living ~~at it~~ **by writing poetry.**

c 9. The osprey feeds on fish, which it captures by diving into the

water.

10. Even after the suit was altered, it did not fit, ~~which~~ was a
    _{. That}

great disappointment.

9 Case *c*

Use correct case forms.

Case expresses the relationship of pronouns *(me, I)* and nouns to other words in the sentence by the use of different forms. Nouns are changed in form only for the possessive case *(child, child's;* see p. 441).

Following is a chart of the cases of pronouns:

	PERSONAL PRONOUNS		
SINGULAR	SUBJECTIVE	POSSESSIVE	OBJECTIVE
First person	I	my, mine	me
Second person	you	your, yours	you
Third person	he, she, it	his, her, hers, its	his, her, it

PLURAL	SUBJECTIVE	POSSESSIVE	OBJECTIVE
First person	we	our, ours	us
Second person	you	your, yours	you
Third person	they	their, theirs	them

	RELATIVE OR INTERROGATIVE PRONOUNS		
NUMBER	SUBJECTIVE	POSSESSIVE	OBJECTIVE
Singular	who	whose	whom
Plural	who	whose	whom

To determine case, find how a word is used in its own clause—for example, whether it is a subject or a subjective complement or an object.

9a Use the subjective case for subjects and for subjective complements that follow linking verbs.

SUBJECT

This month my *sister* and *I* have not been inside the library. (never *me*)

It looked as if my *friend* and *I* were going to be blamed. (never *me*)

SUBJECTIVE COMPLEMENT

The guilty ones were *you* and *I*.

In speech, *it's me, it's us, it's him,* and *it's her* are sometimes used. These forms are not appropriate for formal writing.

9b Use the objective case for a direct object, an indirect object, or the object of a preposition.

Errors occur especially with compound objects.

FAULTY

    The manager gave the jobs *to* **you and I.**

    The manager had to choose *between* **he and I.**

CORRECT

    The manager gave the jobs *to* **you and me.**

    The manager had to choose *between* **him and me.**

Be careful about the case of pronouns in constructions like the following:

FAULTY

    A few *of* **we campers** learned to cook.

CORRECT

    A few *of* **us campers** learned to cook.

When in doubt, test by dropping the noun:

    A few *of* **us** learned to cook.

CORRECT (when pronoun is subject)

    We campers learned to cook.

9c   Use the objective case for subjects and objects of infinitives.

subject of infinitive

The editor considered **her** *to be* the best reporter on the staff.

9d Give an appositive and the word it refers to the same case.

The case of a pronoun appositive depends on the case of the word it refers to.

SUBJECTIVE
Two *delegates* — Esther Giner and **I** — were appointed by the president.

OBJECTIVE
The president appointed two *delegates* — Esther Giner and **me.**

9e The case of a pronoun after *than* or *as* in an elliptical (incomplete) clause should be the same as if the clause were completely expressed.

subject of understood verb

No one else in the play was as versatile as **she** *(was)*.

object of understood subject and verb

The director admired no one else as much as *(he did)* **her.**

9f Use the apostrophe or an *of* phrase to indicate the possessive case. (See **33.**)

The club's motto was written in Latin.
The motto *of the club* was written in Latin.

9g   Use the possessive case for pronouns and nouns preceding a gerund.

> **My** *driving* does not delight my father. (*My* here may be called a pronoun or an adjective.)
>
> The **lumberman's** *chopping* could be heard for a mile.

A noun before a gerund (see pp. 22–23) may be objective when a **phrase** intervenes:

> The *baby* **in the next apartment** *crying* kept us awake.

when the noun is **plural:**

> There is no rule against **men** *working* overtime.

when the noun is **abstract:**

> I object to **emotion** *overruling* judgment.

when the noun denotes an **inanimate object:**

> The policeman did not like the **car** *being* parked in the street.

When a verbal is a participle and not a gerund, a noun or pronoun preceding it is in the objective case. The verbal functions as an adjective.

> No one saw **anyone** *running* from the scene.

9h   The possessive forms of personal pronouns have **no** apostrophe; the possessive forms of indefinite pronouns **do have** an apostrophe.

PERSONAL PRONOUNS
> *yours   its   hers   his   ours   theirs*

INDEFINITE PRONOUNS
> *everyone's   other's   one's   anybody else's*

9i   The case of an interrogative or a relative pronoun is determined by its use in its own clause.

Interrogative pronouns (used in questions) and relative pronouns are *who (whoever), whose, whom (whomever), what, which. Who* is used for the subjective case; *whom,* for the objective case.

In formal writing always use *whom* for objects.

> The hostess did not tell her family **whom** she had invited to dinner.

In speech, *who* is usually the form used at the beginning of a sentence, especially an interrogative sentence.

> **Who** was the foreman talking to?

The case of pronouns is clear in brief sentences.

> **Who** *defeated* the challenger?

But when words intervene between the pronoun and the main verb, determining the case can be difficult.

> **Who** do the reports say *defeated* the challenger?

Mentally cancel the intervening words:

> **Who** *defeated* the challenger?

Do not confuse the function of the relative pronoun in its clause with the function of the clause as a whole. Pick out the relative clause and draw a box around it. Then the use of the pronoun in the dependent clause is more easily determined.

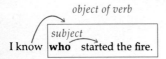

Try to avoid writing sentences with elaborate clauses that make the choice between *who* and *whom* difficult.

■ Exercise 16

Underline the correct word in each of the following sentences.

1. There was in those days in Paris a singer (<u>who</u>, whom) the secret police knew was a double agent.

2. On the platform stood the man (<u>who</u>, whom) they all believed had practiced witchcraft.

3. On the platform stood the man (who, <u>whom</u>) they all accused of practicing witchcraft.

4. The speaker defended his right to talk critically of (whoever, <u>whomever</u>) he pleased.

5. (Whoever, Whomever) is elected will have to deal with the

   problem.

6. (Who, Whom) do you think you are fooling?

7. On skid row is a little mission that gives (whoever, whom-

   ever) comes a hot meal, a dry place to sleep, and a word of

   encouragement.

8. Will the delegate from the Virgin Islands please indicate

   (who, whom) she wants to support?

9. Does anyone know (who, whom) this copy of *Animal Farm* is

   being reserved for?

10. Truth is there for (whoever, whomever) will seek it.

■ **Exercise 17**

Cross out the incorrect forms of pronouns and nouns, and write in the correct forms.

1. The director said that the stunt man and ~~myself~~ ^I^ were the

   ones most afraid of the white water on the trip downriver.

2. After much discussion between the Navajo and ~~she~~ ^her^, they

   agreed that the first chance to buy the turquoise bracelet was
   ~~her's~~ ^hers^ rather than the man's.

3. No one was able to make more intricate designs than ~~him~~ *he*.

4. Just between you and ~~I~~ *me*, whom is it that the judges are favoring?

5. Evan and ~~him~~ *he* appeared just before sunset in that old car, waving and shouting at Eileen and me.

6. The physician said that he had not objected to the employee *'s* returning to work.

7. Deep thinkers have motives and secrets that ~~us~~ *we* ordinary people can never fathom.

8. ~~Who's~~ *Whose* theory was it that matter can be neither created nor destroyed?

9. No one enjoyed Peking duck more than ~~her~~ *she*.

10. I apologized because I wanted no ill feelings between ~~she~~ *her* and ~~I~~ *me*.

10 Adjectives and Adverbs *adj / adv*

Use adjectives to modify nouns and pronouns, adverbs to modify verbs, adjectives, and other adverbs.

Most adverbs end in *-ly*. Only a few adjectives (such as *lovely, holy, manly, friendly*) have this ending. Some adverbs have two forms, one with *-ly* and one without: *slow* and *slowly, loud* and *loudly*. Most adverbs are formed by adding *-ly* to adjectives: *warm, warmly; pretty, prettily*.

Choosing correct adjectives and adverbs in some sentences is simple.

> They stood *close.*
> The barber gave him a *close* shave.
> Study the text *closely.*

Adjectives do not modify verbs, adverbs, or other adjectives. Distinguish between *sure* and *surely, easy* and *easily, good* and *well, real* and *really, some* and *somewhat*.

NOT
> Balloonists *soar* over long distances **easy.**

BUT
> Balloonists *soar* over long distances **easily.**

10a Use the comparative to refer to two things, the superlative to more than two.

> *Both* cars are fast, but the small car is (the) **faster.**
> All *three* cars are fast, but the small car is (the) **fastest.**

10b Add *-er* and *-est* to form the comparative and superlative degrees of most short modifiers. Use *more* and *most* (or *less* and *least*) before long modifiers.

	COMPARATIVE	SUPERLATIVE
ADJECTIVES		
	-er/-est	
dear	dearer	dearest
pretty	prettier	prettiest
	more/most	
pitiful	more pitiful	most pitiful
grasping	more grasping	most grasping
ADVERBS		
	-er/-est	
slow	slower	slowest
	more/most	
rapidly	more rapidly	most rapidly

Some adjectives and adverbs have irregular forms: *good, better, best; well, better, best; little, less, least; bad, worse, worst.* Consult a dictionary.

Some adjectives and adverbs are absolute; that is, they cannot be compared *(dead, perfect, unique).* A thing cannot be more or less dead, or perfect, or unique (one of a kind). Acceptable forms are *more nearly perfect* or *almost dead.*

10c Use a predicate adjective, not an adverb, after a linking verb (see p. 7) such as *be, seem, become, look, appear, feel, sound, smell, taste.*

ADJECTIVE

  He feels **bad.** (He is ill or depressed. An adjective modifies a pronoun.)

ADVERB

> He *reads* **badly.** (*Reads* is not a linking verb. An adverb modifies a verb.)

ADJECTIVE

> The *tea* tasted **sweet.** (*Sweet* describes the tea.)

ADVERB

> She *tasted* the tea **daintily.** (*Daintily* tells how she tasted.)

10d Use an adjective, not an adverb, to follow a verb and its object when the modifier refers to the object, not to the verb.

Verbs like *keep, build, hold, dig, make, think* are followed by a direct object and a modifier. After verbs of this kind, choose the adjective or the adverb form carefully.

ADJECTIVES—MODIFY OBJECTS

> Keep your *clothes* **neat.**
>
> Make the *line* **straight.**

ADVERBS — MODIFY VERBS

> *Keep* your clothes arranged **neatly** in the closet.
>
> *Draw* the line **carefully.**

■ **Exercise 18**

Underline unacceptable forms of adjectives and adverbs, and write the correct form. If a sentence is correct, write **C**.

1. The new miniskirts look ~~similarly~~ (similar) to the ones our aunts are wearing in that photo taken ~~near~~ (nearly) twenty-five years ago.

2. The jackhammer made so much noise that we could ~~scarce~~ (scarcely) hear the speaker, though his shirt ~~sure~~ (surely) was loud.

3. The old clockmaker looked ~~sadly~~ (sad) when he spoke of the way the years whirl by.

4. It ~~sure~~ (surely) cannot be denied that Tennyson was one of the ~~popularlest~~ (most popular) poets of his time.

5. Hungry birds strip a holly bush of its berries ~~rapid~~ (rapidly) and swoop away seeking ~~frantic~~ (frantically) for other food.

6. The computer, a ~~real~~ (really) complicated mechanical mind, is ~~the~~ (a) ~~most unique~~ (unique) instrument of modern civilization.

C 7. The athlete played awkwardly and badly but was the better of the two choices.

8. The stockholders were ~~mighty~~ (extremely) unhappy but not ~~real~~ (really) sur-

prised when the corporation lost money for another year.

9. In times of tribulation, a leader must think logical.
   (logically)

10. The manager never knew which of the two sales programs
    was likely to be the most successful.
    (more)

SENTENCE STRUCTURE

11 Choppy Sentences and Excessive Coordination *chop / coord*

Do not string together brief independent clauses or short sentences. (See **19.**)

Wordiness and monotony result from choppy sentences or from brief independent clauses connected by coordinating conjunctions *(and, but, or, nor, for, yet, so)*. Excessive coordination does not show precise relationships between thoughts. Skillful writers vary their sentences by using phrases that connect ideas.

STRINGY

>   Sugarloaf Mountain is four thousand feet high, and it is surrounded by fields and forests, and the air currents are favorable for hang gliding, and many gliding enthusiasts go there in the summer.

CHOPPY

>   Sugarloaf Mountain is four thousand feet high. It is surrounded by fields and forests. The air currents are favorable for hang gliding. Many gliding enthusiasts go there in the summer.

Consider the last clause or sentence the central idea. Subordinating the other elements creates a more effective sentence.

IMPROVED

>   Surrounded by fields and blessed with air currents favorable for hang gliding, four-thousand-foot-high Sugarloaf Mountain attracts many gliding enthusiasts in the summer.

■ **Exercise 1**

Improve the following sentences by subordinating some of the ideas. Combine choppy sentences into longer sentences.

1. Fort Smith ~~is in~~' Arkansas/' ~~It is~~ across the state line from

   Oklahoma/' ~~It~~ was founded as a military supply post in 1817.

   It was a supply point for people heading west ^to California^ in 1849 to look

   for gold. ~~They were going to California.~~

2. ^The dentist billed t^ ^who^ The patient ^forgot~~^~~ to cancel his dental appointment ^,~~and so~~^ .

   ~~the dentist billed him anyway, and then~~ ^Although^ the patient ~~was~~

   ~~angry and~~ paid the bill ^, he was angry^ and changed dentists.

3. Some vacationers leave home in search of quiet/ ^and^ ~~so they~~ find

   a place without a telephone or television, but other people

   ^who^ want complete isolation/ ~~but they discover that it is diffi-~~ ^usually cannot^

   ~~cult to~~ find a park that is not crowded with trailers and tents.

4. The instructor gave the new student an assignment/ ~~and he~~ —

   ~~had~~ to write just one sentence/ ~~but~~ ^;^ he ^because^ could not think of an

   interesting subject, ~~and so~~ he did not do the required work.

5. Famous books are not always written by admirable people.

                  or

Some authors are arrogant/ ~~Some are~~ even immoral.

     graceful   **, also called a devilfish,** **.**

6. The ˄ manta ray ˄ has a wide, flat body/ ~~and it is also called a~~

~~devilfish, and it is graceful.~~

  While s   **and t**   **, p**   **waiting for the bus**

7. ˄Snow fell/ ˄The wind howled/ ˄˄People ˄stood on the corner/

~~They were~~ shivering. ~~They were waiting for the bus.~~

  Sacred   **pagodas, which**

8. ~~Pagodas are~~ temples or ~~sacred buildings, and they~~ are found

in several Eastern countries, ~~and they~~ often have many

stories and upward-curving roofs.

  Although   **sharks**

9. ~~Sharks are~~ ferocious/ ~~And they~~ attack many bathers each

year, ~~but~~ they seldom kill, so their reputation as killers is in

part undeserved.

               ,   **who**

10. Benjamin Franklin ˄~~was~~ an American/ ~~He~~ was at home

wherever he went. ~~He~~ gained wide popularity in France.

and   became
~~He was~~ also well known in England.
        ∧

12 Subordination   *sub*

Use subordinate clauses to achieve proper emphasis and effective, varied construction.

Putting the less important idea of a sentence in a subordinate clause emphasizes the more important thought in the independent clause. Piling one subordinate clause on top of another awkwardly stretches out sentences and obscures meaning.

12a Express main ideas in independent clauses, less important ideas in subordinate clauses.

An optimistic sociologist wishing to stress progress despite crime would write:

> Although the crime rate is high, society has progressed in some ways.

A pessimistic sociologist might wish the opposite emphasis:

> Although society has progressed in some ways, the crime rate is high.

Putting the main idea in a subordinate clause **(upside-down subordination)** places the stress on the minor instead of the major thought.

> Although the patient recovered fully, the burn had at first been thought fatal.

12b Avoid excessive overlapping of subordinate clauses.

Monotony and even confusion can result from a series of clauses in which each depends on the previous one.

OVERLAPPING

> Pianos are instruments
>
> that contain metal strings
>
> that make sounds when struck by felt-covered hammers
>
> that are operated by keys.

IMPROVED

> Pianos are instruments containing metal strings that make sounds when struck by felt-covered hammers operated by keys.

■ Exercise 2

The following is an exercise in thinking about relationships. The sentences used are designed to point out differences in meaning that result from subordination. Read the pairs of sentences carefully, and answer the questions.

1. A. Although the lecturer had a speech defect, she was a good teacher.
   B. Although the lecturer was a good teacher, she had a speech defect.

   Which sentence stresses the lecturer's handicap? B
   Which stresses her accomplishment? A

2. A. Although short skirts are in fashion again, she will not wear them.
   B. Although she will not wear short skirts, they are in fashion again.

   Which sentence stresses her attitude toward clothing? A

3. A. Although a lifetime is short, much can be accomplished.
   B. Although much can be accomplished, a lifetime is short.

   Which of these sentences expresses more determination? A

4. A. When in doubt, some drivers apply the brakes.
   B. When some drivers apply the brakes, they are in doubt.

   With which drivers would you prefer to ride? A

5. A. While taking a bath, Archimedes formulated an important principle in physics.
   B. While formulating an important principle in physics, Archimedes took a bath.

   Which sentence indicates accidental discovery? A
   In which sentence does Archimedes take a bath for relaxation? B

■ **Exercise 3**

Rewrite the following sentences to avoid overlapping subordination.

1. The platypus is an egg-laying mammal ~~that is~~ found ~~in~~ Aus-
tralia, which ~~is the continent that~~ is also home to the koala.
(on the continent of)

2. Each musician ~~who plays~~ in the orchestra ~~that performs~~ in
the club ~~that is~~ on the side of the lake has at least fifteen years
of professional experience.
(performing)

3. Lobster Newburg is ~~a dish that consists of~~ cooked lobster
meat ~~which is~~ heated in a chafing dish ~~that contains~~ a special
cream sauce.
(with)

4. The dresses ~~that are~~ modeled in fashion shows ~~that take
place~~ in expensive surroundings sell for prices that are
usually well beyond the means of some of the viewers who
attend.

5. ~~The elevator stuck that had~~ The board member ~~who~~ could
have cast a vote that would have changed the future of the
corporation.
(T) *(stuck on the elevator)*

13 Completeness *compl*

Make your sentences complete in structure and thought.

Every element of a sentence should be expressed or implied clearly to prevent inconsistency and misunderstanding.

13a Do not omit a verb or a preposition that is necessary to the structure of the sentence.

OMITTED PREPOSITION
> The baby was both frightened and attracted **to** the new kitten.

IMPROVED
> The baby was both frightened **by** and attracted **to** the new kitten.

BETTER
> The baby was both frightened **by** the new kitten and attracted **to** it.

OMITTED VERB
> The cabinet *drawers* **were** open and the glass *door* shattered. (The door **were** shattered?)

VERB STATED
> The cabinet *drawers* **were** open, and the glass *door* **was** shattered.

When the same form is called for in both elements, it need not be repeated:

> To err is human; to forgive, divine.

13b Omission of *that* sometimes obscures meaning.

INCOMPLETE

The labor leader reported a strike was not likely.

COMPLETE

The labor leader reported **that** a strike was not likely.

14 Comparisons *comp*

Make comparisons logical and clear.

Compare only similar terms.

The *laughter* of a loon is more frightening than an **owl.**

This sentence compares a sound and a bird. A consistent sentence would compare sound and sound or bird and bird.

The *laughter* of a loon is more frightening than the **hoot** of an owl.

A *loon* is more frightening than an **owl.**

The word *other* is often needed in a comparison.

ILLOGICAL

The Sahara is larger than any desert in the world.

RIGHT

The Sahara is larger than any *other* desert in the world.

Avoid awkward and incomplete comparisons.

AWKWARD AND INCOMPLETE

The new cars appear to be *as small* if not *smaller than* last year's models. (*As small* requires *as*, not *than*.)

BETTER

The new cars appear to be as small as last year's models if not smaller. (Note that *than last year's model* is understood.)

AWKWARD AND INCOMPLETE

Canoeing in white water is one of the most dangerous if not the most dangerous water sport. (After *one of the most dangerous,* the plural *sports* is required.)

BETTER

Canoeing in white water is one of the most dangerous water sports if not the most dangerous one.

OR

Canoeing in white water is one of the most dangerous water sports.

AMBIGUOUS

After many years my teacher remembered me better than my roommate. (Better than he remembered my roommate, or better than my roommate remembered me?)

CLEAR

After many years my teacher remembered me better than my roommate did.

OR

After many years my teacher remembered me better than he did my roommate.

■ **Exercise 4**

Correct any errors in completeness and comparisons. Write C by correct sentences.

1. At one time poodles were more popular as house pets than
   any breed of dog.
   (caret with "other" inserted before "breed")

2. The dress rehearsal went as well if not better. ~~than ex-pected.~~
   (above: "as expected" inserted after "well", "(preferred)")
   or **The dress rehearsal went as well as if not better than expected.**

3. Storms on the open ocean are usually more severe than small
   seas.
   (caret with "those on" inserted before "small")

4. Sunny days usually create more cheer than rain.
   (caret inserting "y days." after "rain")

5. The baboons ate more ~~of the~~ bananas than the ants.
   (caret with "did." inserted after "ants")

6. Statistics reveal that our nation's population is and will continue to ~~grow older.~~ do so.
   (above: "growing older" inserted after "is")

7. The veterinarian read an article contending that horses like
   dogs better than cats.
   *(caret with "they do *or* cats do." inserted after "than")*

8. For good health, plain water is as good <s>if not better than</s> most
   ^{as}

   other liquids, if not better.

9. The lighthouse stood as a symbol and guide to safety.
   ^{of}   ^{as a}

C 10. Some laws are so broad that they allow almost unlimited in-

   terpretations.

■ **Exercise 5**

Follow the instructions for Exercise 4.

1. The river was shallower than any in the area.
   ^{other}

2. The squirrels climbing up the rainspout were less tame than
   ^{those}

   in the park.

3. The editors say that the headlines have been written and the

   type set.
   ^{has been}

4. The attorney saw the witness's composure was lost.
   ^{that}

5. Shoppers standing in the checkout line are sometimes both
                          about *or* about the tabloids on the display racks and
   curious ᨈand disapproving of the tabloids on the display racks.
   disapproving of them.

15 Consistency   *cons*

Write sentences that maintain consistency in form and
meaning.

15a Avoid confusing shifts in grammatical forms.

Tenses and verbs

PRESENT AND PAST
SHIFT

> The architect *planned* the new stadium, and the contractor *builds* it.
> (Use *planned . . . built* or *plans . . . builds.*)

CONDITIONAL FORMS *(SHOULD, WOULD, COULD)*
SHIFT

> Exhaustion after a vacation *could* be avoided if a family *can* plan bet-
> ter. (Use *could . . . would* or *can . . . can.*)

Person

> In department stores, *good salespersons* **(3rd person)** first ask
> whether a customer needs help or has questions. Then *they* **(3rd per-
> son)** do not hover around. If *you* **(2nd person)** do, *you* **(2nd person)**
> run the risk of making the customer uncomfortable or even angry.

> (The third sentence should read, "If they do, they run. . . . ")

Number

A *witness* may see an accident one way when it happens, and then *they* remember it an entirely different way when *they* testify. (Use *witness* and a singular pronoun or *witnesses* and *they . . . they*.)

Mood

SHIFT

First the job-seeker *mails* an application; then *go* for an interview.

CONSISTENT

First the job-seeker *mails* an application; then he *goes* for an interview.

First *mail* an application; then *go* for an interview.

Voice

SHIFT

The chef *cooks* **(active)** the shrimp casserole for thirty minutes, and then it *is allowed* **(passive)** to cool. (Use *cooks* and *allows*.) See **5.**

Connectors

RELATIVE PRONOUN

She went to the chest of drawers *that* leaned perilously forward and *which* always resisted every attempt to open it. (Use *that . . . that*).

CONJUNCTIONS

The guests came *since* the food was good and *because* the music was soothing. (Use *since . . . since* or *because . . . because*.)

Direct and Indirect Discourse

MIXED

The swimmer says that the sea is calm and why would anyone fear it?

CONSISTENT

The swimmer says, "The sea is calm. Why would anyone fear it?"
The swimmer says that the sea is calm and asks why anyone would fear it.

■ Exercise 6

Correct the shifts in grammar in the following sentences.

                you *or* one buys a refrigerator, one should
1. Before ~~one~~ buys a refrigerator, you should find out how ex-

   pensive it will be to operate.

2. A boy who writes an appealing letter to his girlfriend will

                          he sees   he
   seem to have personality, but the next time ~~you see~~ her ~~you~~

                          he is   he writes.
   should be as interesting in person as ~~you are~~ when ~~you write.~~
                                 or was when he wrote.

3. The failures in the experiments will be avoided this time if

              will
   the assistants ~~would~~ follow the instructions precisely.

4. The retreating actor backed out of the door, jumped on a

           rode
   horse, and ~~rides~~ off into the sunset.

             Start   use
5. ~~It is wise to start~~ a fire with a wood like pine, and then ‸ a

   heavier wood like oak.~~is used.~~

                         because

6. Use pine first to start a fire ~~since~~ it ignites easily and because

     it will then make the oak burn.

                that
7. The corn ~~which~~ is in the basket and that needs to be husked

     was picked only two hours ago.

8. Dedicated joggers want to run every day, but occasionally

                   is
     the weather ~~would be~~ too bad to get outside.

9. For days the engaged couple plans a picnic, but then he de-

                          s (*or* use all past tense)
     cides to go bowling; so she gets angry and call~~ed~~ off the wed-

     ding.

10. The losing candidate demanded a recount, and the judge

      ordered *or* demands a recount, and the judge orders
     ~~orders~~ the ballots to be secured.

15b   Make subjects and predicates fit together. Avoid
faulty predication.

Test the consistency of a sentence by mentally placing the subject
and predicate side by side. If they do not fit together **(faulty
predication)**, rewrite for consistency.

FAULTY PREDICATION

   Tragedy, according to Aristotle, *is when* a person of high estate falls.
   (*Tragedy . . . is when* makes no sense.)

LOGICAL

Tragedy, according to Aristotle, *occurs when* a person of high estate falls.

FAULTY

After *eating* a large meal is a bad *time* to go swimming.

CONSISTENT

The *period* immediately after eating a large meal is a bad *time* to go swimming.

FAULTY

The *use* of a mediator *was hired* so that a compromise could be achieved.

CONSISTENT

A *mediator was hired* so that a compromise could be achieved.

■ **Exercise 7**

Correct faulty predication in the following sentences.

occurs

1. A first serious test of a marriage is when the couple's jobs

   force them to live apart.

the reason

2. Daily exercise is why that woman looks so fit.

3. By means of a fast ferry it could shorten the time it takes to

   cross the English Channel.

           P   only when

4. ~~The only time~~ people should be tardy ~~is if~~ they cannot possi-

   bly avoid being late.

                    C   regarded

5. ~~The question of~~ ¢ensorship is ~~the answer~~ often ~~given to~~
   as the solution to the problem of language in
   ~~the objectionable language of~~ many modern novels.

16   Position of Modifiers   *dg / mod*

Attach modifiers clearly to the right word or element in the sentence.

A misplaced modifier can cause confusion or misunderstanding. Usually a modifying adjective precedes its noun whereas an adverb may precede or follow the word it modifies. Prepositional phrases usually follow closely, but may precede; adjective clauses follow closely; and adverbial phrases and clauses may be placed in many positions. (See pp. 22–24, 25–26.)

16a   Avoid dangling modifiers.

A verbal phrase at the beginning of a sentence should modify the subject.

DANGLING PARTICIPLE

    Growing rapidly, new *shoes* are needed frequently by toddlers.

CLEAR

Growing rapidly, *toddlers* frequently need new shoes.

DANGLING GERUND

After **searching** around the attic, a *Halloween mask* was discovered.
(The passive voice in the main clause causes the modifier to attach
wrongly to the subject.)

CLEAR

After **searching** around the attic, *I* discovered a Halloween mask.

DANGLING INFINITIVE

To enter the house, the *lock* on the back door was picked. (*To enter
the house* refers to no word in this sentence.)

CLEAR

To enter the house, *he* picked the lock on the back door.

DANGLING PREPOSITIONAL PHRASE

During childhood, *my mother* was a consul in Italy. (In whose childhood?)

CLEAR

During **my** childhood, *my mother* was a consul in Italy.

DANGLING ELLIPTICAL CLAUSE

While still sleepy and tired, the *counselor* lectured me on breaking
rules.

CLEAR

While I was still sleepy and tired, the counselor lectured me on
breaking rules.

Loosely attaching a verbal phrase to the end of a sentence is unemphatic:

UNEMPHATIC
> Every member of the infield moved closer to the plate, preparing for a double play.

Revise by using simple coordination:

BETTER
> Every member of the infield moved closer to the plate and prepared for a double play.

Some verbal phrases that are **sentence modifiers** do not need to refer to a single word:

> *Strictly speaking,* does this sentence contain a dangling construction? *To tell the truth,* it does not.

16b   Avoid misplaced modifiers.

Placement of a modifier in a sentence affects meaning.

> He enlisted after he married *again.*
> He enlisted *again* after he married.

Almost anything that comes between an adjective clause and the word it modifies can cause confusion.

MISLEADING
> Even on a meager sheriff's salary, a family may have some comforts.

CLEAR
> Even on a sheriff's meager salary, a family may have some comforts.

16c A modifier placed between two words so that it can modify either word is said to squint.

SQUINTING

The secretary who was typing *slowly* rose from her chair.

CLEAR

The secretary who was *slowly typing* rose from her chair.

OR

The secretary who was typing *rose slowly* from her chair.

■ **Exercise 8**

Correct the faulty modifiers in the following sentences.

1. ~~To pass a difficult course,~~ ᶜcramming all night before the final

   examination seems to be the only choice for those who do

   not study consistently ∧**and who wish to pass a difficult course.**

2. ~~Looking~~ ᵀthrough a magnifying glass, the flaw in the diamond

   appeared as a dark spot.

3. Listeners ∧**who have strange beliefs** often call in to radio talk shows. ~~that have strange beliefs.~~

4. The teacher gave ∧**each child** a birthday present ~~to each child~~ wrapped in

   silvery paper.

5. ∧**Check the answer t** (*or* You must check the answer . . .)
   To be absolutely certain. ~~the answer must be checked.~~

6. The restaurant offers ᶦⁿᵉˣᵖᵉⁿˢᶦᵛᵉ meals for children. ~~that are inexpensive.~~

inexpensive

6. The restaurant offers ∧ meals for children. ~~that are inexpensive.~~

7. Serve one of the melons for dessert at lunch; keep one of

them ~~for the picnic~~ in the refrigerator. **for the picnic.**

8. ~~The carpenter inspected the board before sawing for nails.~~
   Before sawing, the carpenter inspected the board for nails.

9. ~~Slowly and relentlessly~~ ᵀ the lecturer said that witches ∧ attempt **slowly and relentlessly**

   to gain control over the minds of others.

10. The woman who was ∧ writing ~~hastily~~ rose ∧ from the desk and
    hastily *or* **hastily**

    left the room.

■ Exercise 9

Follow the instructions for Exercise 8.

1. Early explorers crossing the vast desert could ~~only~~ travel ∧ at
   only

   night.

2. ~~Without shoes,~~ ᵀ the rough stones cut the feet of the ∧ hikers.
   barefoot

3. Although hindered by the weather, ∧ the bridge. ~~was still built~~
   the workers still built

   ~~by the workers.~~

4. ~~To taste delicious,~~ ᵀ the chef should prepare a dressing pre-

   cisely suitable to ∧ the raw spinach salad. **taste delicious.**
   make

5. Divers entered the decompression chambers,~~and~~ thereby pre-
venting~~ing~~ the bends.

17 Separation of Elements   *sep*

Do not needlessly separate closely related elements.

Separation of subject and verb, parts of a verb phrase, or verb
and object can result in awkwardness or confusion.

AWKWARD

At last the trapper had after many weeks of isolation and hard
trudging through the snow returned to civilization.

IMPROVED

At last the trapper had returned to civilization after many weeks of
isolation and trudging through the snow.

PUZZLING

She is the man who owns the service station's wife.

CLEAR

She is the wife of the man who owns the service station.

Do not divide a sentence with a quotation long enough to cause
excessive separation.

AVOID

Stephen Clarkson's opinion that "politicians always create their
own reality; during campaigns they create their own unreality" is
pessimistic.

Split infinitives occur when a modifier comes between *to* and the verb form, as in *to loudly cheer*. Some writers avoid them without exception; others accept them occasionally. To avoid objections, do not use this kind of split construction.

18 Parallelism *paral*

Use parallel grammatical forms to express parallel thoughts.

Elements in a sentence are *parallel* when one construction matches another construction: a phrase and a phrase, a clause and a clause, a verb and a verb, a noun and a noun, a verbal and a verbal, and so forth.

(1) Parallelism in constructions with coordinating conjunctions (*and, but, for,* etc.):

NOT PARALLEL
                  adjective   *verb*
    Sailing ships were *stately* **and** *made* little noise.

PARALLEL
                  adjectives
    Sailing ships were *stately* **and** *quiet.*

NOT PARALLEL
                           nouns   *pronoun*
    Young Lincoln read widely for *understanding, knowledge,* **and** *he* just liked books.

PARALLEL
                                nouns
    Young Lincoln read widely for *understanding, knowledge,* **and** *pleasure.*

NOTE: Repeat an article *(the, a, an)*, a preposition *(by, in, on,* etc.), the sign of the infinitive *(to)*, or other key words in order to preserve parallelism and clarity:

UNCLEAR

The artist was *a* painter and sculptor of marble.

CLEAR

The artist was *a* painter and *a* sculptor of marble.

UNCLEAR

They passed the evening *by* eating and observing the crowds.

CLEAR

They passed the evening *by* eating and *by* observing the crowds.

(2) Parallelism in constructions with correlatives *(not only . . . but also, either . . . or,* etc.):

NOT PARALLEL

infinitive   *preposition*

Petroleum is used **not only** *to make* fuels **but also** *in* plastics.

NOT PARALLEL

verb   *preposition*

Not only *is* petroleum used in fuels **but also** *in* plastics.

PARALLEL

prepositions

Petroleum is used **not only** *in* fuels **but also** *in* plastics.

NOT PARALLEL

adverb   *pronoun*

The speeches were **either** *too* long, **or** *they* were not long enough.

NOT PARALLEL

          article   *adverb*

          ↓   ↓

     Either *the* speeches were too long **or** *too* short.

PARALLEL   *adverbs*

                                ╱   ╲

     The speeches were **either** *too* long **or** *too* short.

PARALLEL

     Either the speeches were too long, **or** they were too short.

(3) Parallelism with *and who* and with *and which:*

Avoid *and who, and which,* or *and that* unless they are preceded by a matching *who, which,* or *that.*

NOT PARALLEL

     The position calls for a person with an open mind *and who* is cool-headed.

PARALLEL

     The position calls for a person *who* is open-minded and *who* is cool-headed.

PARALLEL

     The position calls for a person with an open mind and a cool head.

NOT PARALLEL

     A new dam was built to control floods *and which* would furnish recreation.

PARALLEL

     A new dam was built to control floods and furnish recreation.

PARALLEL

A new dam was built *that* would control floods *and that* would furnish recreation.

■ **Exercise 10**

Revise sentences with faulty parallelism. Write C by correct sentences.

1. The chrysanthemums ~~bloomed~~ not only ^bloomed^ this year but also will bloom for several years to come.

2. The ~~performance was~~ ^performance^ long, boring, ~~and~~ made everyone in the audience restless.

3. Adjusting to a large college is difficult for a person who has always attended a small school and ~~being~~ ^who has been^ used to individual attention.

C 4. Roaming through the great north woods, camping by a lake, and getting away from crowds are good ways to forget the cares of civilization.

5. A good listener must have a genuine interest in people, a strong curiosity, and ^enough^ discipline ~~oneself~~ to keep the mind from wandering.

6. A young musician must practice long hours, give up pleasures, and ~~one has to~~ be able to take criticism.

7. A good trial lawyer must be shrewd, alert, and ~~a bold~~
   bold.
   ~~speaker.~~

8. The delegation found it impossible ~~either~~ to see the governor
   either ∧
   or any other official.

9. The archeologists decided to abandon the site after spending
   ing
   three months digging, sifting, and ~~able to~~ find∧nothing of significance.

10. The jaguar is swift, quiet, and ~~moves with~~ grace/
    ful.

19 Variety   *var*

Vary sentences in structure and order.

An unbroken series of short sentences may become monotonous
and fail to indicate such relationships as cause, condition, conces-
sion, time sequence, and purpose. (See **11.**)

The following description of a chimpanzee coming upon a
waterfall in a tropical forest is monotonous because of a lack of
variety in sentence structure.

The animal seemed lost in contemplation. He moved slowly closer and began to rock. He began to give a round of characteristic "pant-hoot" calls. He became more excited. He finally began running back and forth, jumping. He called louder and drummed on trees with his fists. He ran back again. The behavior was most reminiscent of that observed by Jane Goodall in groups of chimpanzees. It was at the start of a rainstorm. It has been called the "rain dance." But this one animal was alone. It was not surprised as the animals are by sudden rain. He had not deliberately sought the waterfall. He certainly knew where it was. He also knew when he had come to it.

Study the variety of the sentences in the passage as it was originally written by Melvin Konner:

The animal seemed lost in contemplation. He moved slowly closer and began to rock, while beginning to give a round of characteristic "pant-hoot" calls. He became more excited, and finally began running back and forth, jumping, calling louder, drumming on trees with his fists, running back again. The behavior was most reminiscent of that observed and described by Jane Goodall in groups of chimpanzees at the start of a rainstorm—the "rain dance," as it has been called. But this was one animal alone, and not surprised as the animals are by sudden rain; even if he had not deliberately sought the waterfall, he certainly knew where it was and when he had come to it.

MELVIN KONNER,
The Tangled Wing

Structure

Do not overuse one kind of sentence structure. Write simple, compound, and complex patterns. Vary your sentences among loose, periodic, and balanced forms.

A **loose sentence,** the most common kind, makes its main point early and then adds refinements.

LOOSE

Boys are wild animals, rich in the treasures of sense, but the New

England boy had a wider range of emotions than boys of more equable climates.

HENRY ADAMS

Uncle Tom's Cabin is a very bad novel, having, in its self-righteous, virtuous sentimentality, much in common with *Little Women*.

JAMES BALDWIN

A **periodic sentence** withholds an element of the main thought until the end to create suspense and emphasis.

PERIODIC

Under a government which imprisons any unjustly, the true place for a just man is also a prison.

HENRY DAVID THOREAU

PERIODIC

There is one thing above all others that the scientist has a duty to teach to the public and to governments: it is the duty of heresy.

J. BRONOWSKI

A **balanced sentence** has parallel parts that are similar in structure, length, and thoughts. Indeed, *balance* is simply a word for a kind of parallelism. (See **18.**) The following sentence has perfect symmetry:

Marriage has many pains, but celibacy has no pleasures.

SAMUEL JOHNSON

A sentence can also be balanced if only parts of it are symmetrical. The balance here consists of nouns in one group that are parallel to adjectives in the other.

> Thus the Puritan was made up of two different men, the one all self-abasement, penitence, gratitude, passion; the other proud, calm, inflexible, sagacious.
>
> THOMAS BABINGTON MACAULAY

Thus
the Puritan
was made up
of two different men,

the one ----- the other
all self-abasement,---proud,
penitence,------calm,
gratitude,-----inflexible,
passion;----- sagacious.

Order

If several consecutive sentences follow the order of subject-verb-complement, they can be monotonous. Invert the order occasionally; do not always tack dependent clauses and long phrases on at the end. Study the following variations:

NORMAL ORDER

   subject   *verb*   *object*   *modifiers* ⟶
      ↓   ↓   ↓
   She attributed these *defects* in her son's character to the general weaknesses of mankind.

SENTENCE BEGINNING WITH DIRECT OBJECT

   These *defects* in her son's character she attributed to the general weaknesses of mankind.

SENTENCE BEGINNING WITH PREPOSITIONAL PHRASE
> *To the general weaknesses of mankind* she attributed the defects in her son's character.

SENTENCE BEGINNING WITH ADVERB
> *Quickly* the swordfish broke the surface of the water.

INVERTED SENTENCE BEGINNING WITH CLAUSE USED AS OBJECT
> *That the engineer tried to stop the train,* none would deny.

SENTENCE BEGINNING WITH PARTICIPIAL PHRASE
> *Flying low over the water,* the plane searched for the reef.

■ **Exercise 11**

Rewrite the following sentences and make them periodic. If you consider a sentence already periodic, put a P next to it.

1. One machine/ ~~the typewriter~~/ revolutionized business practices and had a profound influence on the style of many authors/ : the typewriter.

2. ~~A sense of humor is one quality~~ ɴ no great leader can be without/ one quality: a sense of humor.

3. ~~Selfishness, some philosophers maintain, is~~ ᴛ the reason behind every action of any person/ , some philosophers maintain, is selfishness.

4. ~~Security men stood guard~~ ᴡ while the display windows broken during the earthquake were replaced/ , security men stood guard.

         W

5. ~~He studied~~ when all other possible methods of passing the

                      , he studied.

course proved unworkable/

■ **Exercise 12**

Rewrite the following sentences to give them balanced constructions.
Put a B by a sentence that is already balanced.

1. What the critic says is that parents should preview the film

                                         what

and decide whether to let their children see it, but he means

 is

that the film is so awful that everyone should ignore it.

2. A successful advertisement surprises and pleases, but ~~not~~

an unsuccessful advertisement bores and irritates.

~~all advertisements are successful because some are merely~~

~~boring and irritating.~~

B 3. Realists know their limitations; romantics know only what

they want.

4. Whereas being an only child is a condition you cannot alter,

having

~~to have~~ no friends is a circumstance you can do something

about.

5. A trained ear hears many separate instruments in an orches-

tra, but the ∧melody. ~~is usually all that is heard by the untutored.~~

^{untutored ear hears only the}

▪ Exercise 13

Rewrite the following passage so that it is more varied in sentence structure.

Cynicism, despair, and frantic slapstick now run through the pages of many composition texts. And the same is often true of tests. Grammar examples and test sentences do not exist inert,/ ~~They are not~~ detached from life/ ~~and they are not~~ in some neutral vacuum. Most of them, even when disfigured by deliberate mistakes, still reflect and reinforce attitudes/ ~~They~~ make claims about our world. Students surely cannot help responding, and we often hand them melodrama and morbidity. One of my colleagues has even ~~made a suggestion. She says~~ this message of despair is a welcome means of social control. Keep students' anxieties high and they will be more docile.

^{and}

^{ed that}

Adapted from Ellen Strenski,
"Grammar Sample Sentences and the Power of Suggestion"

PUNCTUATION

20 Commas   ,

Use commas to reflect structure and to clarify the sense of the sentence.

Commas are chiefly used (1) to separate equal elements, such as independent clauses and items in a series, and (2) to set off modifiers or parenthetical words, phrases, and clauses.

Elements that are set off within a sentence take a comma both *before* and *after*.

NOT

> This novel, a best seller has no real literary merit.

BUT

> This novel, a best seller, has no real literary merit.

20a Use a comma to separate independent clauses joined by a coordinating conjunction. (See p. 442.)

> *Nice* is a word with many meanings, and some of them are opposite to others.
>
> Sherlock Holmes had to be prepared, for Watson was full of questions.

NOTE: The comma is sometimes omitted between the clauses when they are so brief that there is no danger of misreading.

> The weather was clear and the pilot landed.

20b Use commas between words, phrases, or clauses in a series.

> The closet contained worn clothes, old shoes, and dusty hats.

The final comma before *and* in a series is sometimes omitted.

> The closet contained worn clothes, old shoes and dusty hats.

But the comma must be used when *and* is omitted.

> The closet contained worn clothes, old shoes, dusty hats.

And it must be used to avoid misreading.

> An old chest in the corner was filled with nails, hammers, a hacksaw and blades, and a brace and bit.

Series of phrases or of dependent or independent clauses are also separated by commas.

PHRASES
> We hunted for the letter in the album, in the old trunks, and even under the rug.

DEPENDENT CLAUSES
> Finally we concluded that the letter had been burned, that someone had taken it, or that it had never been written.

INDEPENDENT CLAUSES
> We left the attic, Father locked the door, and Mother suggested that we never unlock it again.

In a series of independent clauses, the comma is not omitted before the final element.

- **Exercise 1**

Insert commas where necessary in the following sentences.

1. Some prominent women authors took masculine pen names
   in the nineteenth century, for they felt that the public would
   not read novels written by women.

2. A good speaker should prepare well for a talk, enunciate
   clearly to be understood, and practice the art of effective tim-
   ing.

3. The house with the long driveway is not as old as some
   others on the block, but none of the historians can determine
   when it was built.

4. The sales manager and the trainee and sometimes a secretary
   visited branch offices in Pittsburgh, in Dallas, and in San
   Diego.
   ,(optional)

5. Professors sometimes hesitate to write full and honest letters
   of recommendation, for students are now allowed to read
   them unless waivers are signed.

6. The sensitive child knew that the earth was round, but she
   thought that she was on the inside of it.

7. The commissioner stated that taxes are already high, that personal incomes are low, and that rapid transit is expensive.

8. For breakfast the menu offered only bacon and eggs, toast and jelly, and hot coffee.

9. Careless driving includes speeding, stopping suddenly, turning from the wrong lane, going through red lights, and failing to yield the right of way.

10. Driving was easy, for the highway was completed, and traffic was light.

20c Use a comma between coordinate adjectives not joined by *and*. Do not use a comma between cumulative adjectives.

Coordinate adjectives modify the noun independently.

COORDINATE

We entered a forest of tall, slender, straight pines.

Ferocious, alert, loyal dogs were essential to safety in the Middle Ages.

Cumulative adjectives modify the whole cluster of subsequent adjectives and the noun.

CUMULATIVE

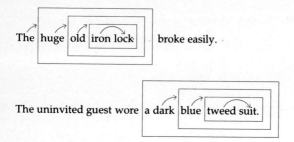

Two tests are helpful.

Test One

And is natural only between coordinate adjectives.

>   tall *and* slender *and* straight pines
>   ferocious *and* alert *and* loyal dogs

BUT NOT
>   dark *and* blue *and* tweed suit
>   huge *and* old *and* iron lock

Test Two

Coordinate adjectives are easily reversible.

>   straight, slender, and tall pines
>   loyal, alert, ferocious dogs

BUT NOT
>   tweed blue dark suit
>   iron old huge lock

The distinction is not always clear-cut, however, and the sense of the cluster must be the deciding factor.

She was wearing a full-skirted, low-cut velvet gown.

(a velvet gown that was full skirted and low cut, not a gown that was full skirted and low cut and velvet)

■ **Exercise 2**

Punctuate the following. When in doubt, apply the tests described above. Write C *by those that require no comma.*

1. a graceful, agile cat

C 2. large glass front doors

3. creamy, soft vanilla ice cream

4. light, fresh scent

5. a long, shrill, eerie cry

C 6. a wrinkled brown paper bag

7. a hot, sultry, depressing day

C 8. expensive new electric typewriter

9. a woebegone, ghostly look

C 10. beautiful Persian rugs

20d Use a comma after a long introductory phrase or clause.

LONG PHRASE

> With the severe part of the trek behind him, the traveler felt more confident.

LONG CLAUSE

> When the severe part of the trek was behind him, the traveler felt more confident.

When the introductory element is short and there is no danger of misreading, the comma is often omitted.

SHORT PHRASE

> After the ordeal the traveler felt more confident.

SHORT CLAUSE

> When the ordeal was over the traveler felt more confident.

Use of the comma in the above sentences may depend on personal taste. Commas after the introductory elements would be acceptable.

Introductory verbal phrases are usually set off by commas.

PARTICIPLE

> Living for centuries, redwoods often reach great heights.

INFINITIVE

> To verify a hypothesis, a scientist performs an experiment.

GERUND

> After surviving the ordeal, the traveler felt relieved.

A phrase or a clause set off by a comma at the beginning of a sentence may not require a comma if it is moved to the end of the sentence.

BEGINNING

Because of pity for creatures that must live in cages, some people do not go to the zoo.

END

Some people do not go to the zoo because of pity for creatures that must live in cages.

20e Use commas to set off nonrestrictive appositives, phrases, and clauses.

A **nonrestrictive modifier** or **appositive** adds information but does not point out or identify. When the modifier is omitted, the sentence loses some meaning but does not change radically.

In the following sentences the italicized elements add information that is not essential to the meaning of the sentence.

NONRESTRICTIVE

The painter's latest work, *a landscape,* has achieved wide acclaim.

Salt, *which is plentiful in this country,* is still inexpensive.

Abstract words, *which do not convey images,* are necessary in language.

NOTE: *That* should never introduce a nonrestrictive clause.

A **restrictive modifier** or **appositive** points out or identifies its noun or pronoun. When the modifier is removed, the sentence radically changes in meaning.

RESTRICTIVE

The Russian ruler *Nicholas* was married to Alexandra.

Huge signs *that are displayed along interstate highways* spoil the beauty of the countryside.

Words *that convey images* are important in poetry.

In all these sentences, the italicized expressions identify the words they modify; to remove the modifiers would be to change the meaning.

Some modifiers can be either restrictive or nonrestrictive; use or omission of the commas changes the sense.

The coin that gleamed in the sunlight was a Spanish doubloon. (There were several coins.)

The coin, which gleamed in the sunlight, was a Spanish doubloon. (There was only one coin.)

■ Exercise 3

The following pairs of sentences illustrate differences in meaning that result from use or omission of commas with modifiers. Answer the questions about each pair of sentences.

1. A. In Allison Long's novel, *Only Once,* the heroine is a physician.
   B. In Allison Long's novel *Only Once,* the heroine is a physician.

   In which sentence has Allison Long written only one novel? **A**

2. A. The tapes that we enjoyed last summer are worn out.
   B. The tapes, which we enjoyed last summer, are worn out.

   Which sentence suggests that all the tapes are worn out? **B**

3. A. The plant, which has an elaborately designed pot, is not as pretty as the container.
   B. The plant that has an elaborately designed pot is not as pretty as the container.

   Which sentence makes a false generalization? B

4. A. The moviegoers who did not understand Japanese welcomed the English subtitles.
   B. The moviegoers, who did not understand Japanese, welcomed the English subtitles.

   Which sentence suggests that some moviegoers did not depend on English subtitles? A

5. A. Anthropologists, who respect native ways, are welcome among most tribes.
   B. Anthropologists who respect native ways are welcome among most tribes.

   Which sentence reflects confidence in anthropologists? A

■ **Exercise 4**

Insert commas for nonrestrictive modifiers; circle all unnecessary commas. Write C by correct sentences.

1. The American composer, George Gershwin, wrote *Rhapsody in Blue*, which was performed last night, on the composer's birthday.

2. Barbers, who are bald, often authoritatively discuss baldness with their customers, who are worried about losing their hair.

C   3. The wealthy who keep their expensive jewelry in bank vaults sometimes hire people to wear their pearls for them so that the gems will not lose their luster.

C   4. Americans who have grown up on the prairies may feel shut in when they move to forest regions or to cities with buildings that have more than ten stories.

C   5. Adam's son Abel was a shepherd.

6. Abel, Adam's son, was a shepherd.

7. An American flag, that had flown over the Capitol in Washington, was presented to the students by their congressman, who needed favorable publicity in his home district.

8. Cars, that no one would buy off the lot, were sold for scrap.

9. The most beautiful photograph, a shadowy shot of a white bird against a dark sky, was made on a small island that is about a mile off the eastern coast.

10. The musical entitled, My Fair Lady, is based on Shaw's play, Pygmalion.

20f Use commas to set off sentence modifiers, conjunctive adverbs, and sentence elements out of normal word order.

Modifiers like *on the other hand, for example, in fact, in the first place, I believe, in his opinion, unfortunately,* and *certainly* are set off by commas.

> Only a few poets, unfortunately, make a living by writing.
>
> Thomas Hardy's poems, I believe, ask profound questions.

Commas are frequently used with conjunctive adverbs such as *accordingly, anyhow, besides, consequently, furthermore, hence, however, indeed, instead, likewise, meanwhile, moreover, nevertheless, otherwise, still, then, therefore, thus.*

BEFORE CLAUSE

optional

> The auditor checked the figures again; therefore, the mistake was discovered.

WITHIN CLAUSE

optional

> The auditor checked the figures again; the mistake, therefore, was discovered.

Commas **always** separate the conjunctive adverb *however* from the rest of the sentence.

> The auditor found the error in the figures; however, the books still did not balance.
>
> The auditor found the error in the figures; the books, however, still did not balance.

Commas are not used when *however* is an adverb meaning "no matter how."

> However fast the hare ran, he could not catch the tortoise.

Use commas if necessary for clearness or emphasis when part of a sentence is out of normal order.

Confident and informed, the young woman invested her own money.

OR

The young woman, confident and informed, invested her own money.

BUT

The confident and informed young woman invested her own money.

20g Use commas with degrees and titles and with elements in dates, places, and addresses.

DEGREES AND TITLES

Arthur Weiss, M.A., came to the picnic.

Louis Ferranti, Jr., chief of police, made the arrest.

DATES

Sunday, May 31, is her birthday.

August 1982 was very warm. (Commas around 1982 are also acceptable.)

July 20, 1969, was the date when a human being first stepped on the moon. (Use commas *before* and *after*.)

He was born 31 December 1970. (Use no commas.)

The year 1980 was a time of change. (Restrictive; use no commas.)

PLACES

Cairo, Illinois, is my home town. (Use commas *before* and *after*.)

ADDRESSES
Write the editor of *The Atlantic*, 8 Arlington Street, Boston, Massa-chusetts 02116. (Use no comma before the zip code.)

20h Use commas for contrast or emphasis and with short interrogative elements.

The pilot used an auxiliary landing field, not the city airport.
The field was safe enough, wasn't it?

20i Use commas with mild interjections and with words like *yes* and *no*.

Well, no one thought it was possible.
No, it proved to be simple.

20j Use commas with words in direct address and after the salutation of a personal letter.

Driver, stop the bus.
Dear John,
    It has been some time since I've written. . . .

20k Use commas with expressions like *he said, she remarked,* and *she replied* when used with quoted matter.

"I am planning to enroll in Latin," she said, "at the beginning of next term."
He replied, "It's all Greek to me."

20L   Set off an absolute phrase with commas.

An **absolute phrase** consists of a noun followed by a modifier. It modifies the sentence as a whole, not any single element in it.

┌—— *absolute phrase* ——┐
Our day's journey over , we made camp for the night.

┌—— *absolute phrase* ——┐
The portrait having dried , the artist hung it on the wall.

20m   Use commas to prevent misreading or to mark an omission.

After washing and grooming **,** the pup looked like a different dog.
When violently angry **,** elephants trumpet.
Beyond **,** the open fields sloped gently to the sea.

verb omitted
↓
To err *is* human; to forgive **,** divine. (Note that *is*, the verb omitted, is the same as the one stated.)

■ **Exercise 5**

Add necessary commas. If a sentence is correct as it stands, write C *by it.*

1. Inside **,** the convention hall resembled a huge, overcrowded barn.

2. A few hours before he was scheduled to leave **,** the mercenary

visited his father, who pleaded with him to change his mind and then finally said quietly, "Good luck."

3. Seeing a nightingale, the American ornithologist recognized its resemblance to other members of the thrush family.

4. The singing of a canary, most people believe, is beautiful; however, it can be distracting to one who wishes to rest.

5. History, one would think, ought to teach people not to make the same mistakes again.

6. The Vandyke beard, according to authorities, was named after Sir Anthony Van Dyck, a famous Flemish painter.

c 7. Only after reading a book either very carefully or more than once should a critic write a review.

8. Having animals for pets is troublesome; having no pets, sometimes lonely.

9. Moving holidays from the middle of the week to Friday or Monday, a recent national practice, gives workers more consecutive days without work.

10. While burning, cedar has a distinct, strong odor.

■ **Exercise 6**

Follow the instructions for Exercise 5.

1. The hippopotamus has a stout hairless body, very short legs, and a large head and muzzle.

2. The tarantula, a large hairy spider, looks frightening; it is not, however, highly venomous.

3. Before students can understand the principles of quantum physics, they must master simple algebra.

4. When the clock struck, the dog barked and awakened the baby, who began to cry.

5. While the mystery writer was composing his last novel, *The Tiger's Eye*, he received a note warning him not to write about anyone he knew in the Orient.

6. The race being over, the jockey who rode the winning horse turned to the owner and said, "Now, Mrs. Astor, you have the money and the trophy."

7. The hungry prospector turned from the window, looked into his cabinet, and saw that he still had some tomato ketchup, dried white beans, and beef jerky.

8. Old encyclopedias, back issues of *National Geographic*, and outdated textbooks were all that remained at the close of the book sale, an eagerly awaited annual event.

9. Route 280, known as "the world's most beautiful freeway," connects San Francisco and San Jose.

10. Atlanta, Georgia, is lower in latitude than Rome, Italy. Miami, furthermore, is not as far south as the equatorial zone, is it?

■ **Exercise 7**

Add necessary commas.

1. Attempting to save money as well as time, some shoppers go to the grocery store only once a month; others, however, go almost daily.

2. The menu included beets, carrots, and radishes, for the chef was fond of root foods.

3. However the travelers followed the worn, outdated city map, they always returned to the same place.

4. The last selection on the program, a waltz by Strauss, brought the most applause, I believe.

5. High over the mountain clouds looked dark ominous.

6. Disappointed but still optimistic the singer packed her suit-case and headed home to Dover Delaware.

7. The red woolen mittens were sold right away but the expen-sive carved decoys attracted few buyers.

8. Edward Friar Ph.D. was awarded his honorary degree on June 1 1947 in Fulton Missouri.

9. Yes friends the time has come for pausing not planning.

10. With a major snowstorm on the way people should stock up on bread milk and eggs shouldn't they?

21 Unnecessary Commas *no ,*

Do not use commas excessively.

Placing commas at all pauses in sentences is not a correct practice.

21a Do not use a comma to separate subject and verb, verb or verbal and complement, or an adjective and the word it modifies.

NOT

The guard with the drooping mustache**,** snapped to attention.

Some students in the class admitted**,** that they had not read**,** "Mending Wall."

The stubborn, mischievous**,** child refused to respond.

Two commas may be used to set off a phrase or a word between subject and verb.

The malamute**,** an Alaskan work dog**,** can survive extraordinarily cold weather.

21b Do not use a comma to separate two compound elements, such as verbs, subjects, complements, or predicates.

He *left* the scene of the accident and *tried* to forget that it had happened.

21c Do not use a comma before a coordinating conjunction joining two dependent clauses.

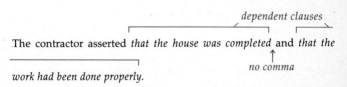

The contractor asserted *that the house was completed* and *that the work had been done properly.*

21d Do not use a comma before *than* in a comparison or between compound conjunctions like *as . . . as, so . . . as, so . . . that.*

no comma
↓

John Holland was more delighted with life on the Continent than he had thought he could be.

21e Do not use a comma after *like* and *such as.*

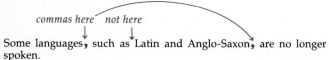

commas here   not here

Some languages, such as Latin and Anglo-Saxon, are no longer spoken.

A comma is not used **before** *such as* (as above) when the phrase is restrictive.

21f Do not use a comma with a period, a question mark, an exclamation point, or a dash. These marks stand by themselves.

no comma
↓

"Did you get the job?" her roommate asked.

21g A comma may be used after a closing parenthesis, but not before an opening parenthesis.

no comma

After a time of unemployment and despondency (nearly six months), the worker went back to the old job from which he had resigned.

comma

21h A comma is not used to set off coordinating conjunctions. A comma is not required after short introductory adverbial modifiers. (See **20d.**)

no comma

But some people are excessively tolerant.

OPTIONAL

After a hearty laugh, the class again became quiet.

21i Do not use commas to set off restrictive clauses, phrases, or appositives. (See **20e.**)

— *no commas* —

People who live in glass houses should not throw stones.

21j Do not use a comma between adjectives that are not coordinate. (See **20c.**)

— *no comma*

The old work horse stopped.

■ **Exercise 8**

Circle all unnecessary commas, and be prepared to explain your decisions.

1. Soccer is a popular sport in Great Britain, where it is sometimes called, football.

2. The secretary bird is so named, because, on its crest, it has feathers that resemble quill pens.

3. Restaurants, that serve excellent food at modest prices, are always popular among local people, though tourists seldom know about them.

4. Many children's games, such as, kick the can, hide and seek, and marbles, are not played much anymore, because children are more interested in television and mechanical toys.

5. Ticket holders standing at the end of the line, worried that they would not find seats, or that the only available seats would be too far forward in the theater.

6. Although the composer had indicated that the piece was to be played adagio, (slowly), the conductor, sensing the audience's boredom, increased the tempo.

7. Communities near large airports have become increasingly aware that noise pollution can be just as unpleasant as impurities in the air or in streams.

8. Once, huge movie houses were fashionable, but now most of these palaces are like dinosaurs, extinct giants, curious reminders of the past.

9. The Olympic runner was disqualified after he ran out of his lane, but he would not have won a gold medal anyway.

10. The accountant vowed that he would never work for the millionaire again and that he would go back to his small firm.

22 Semicolons ;

Use a semicolon between independent clauses not joined by coordinating conjunctions (*and, but, or, nor, for, so, yet*) and between coordinate elements with internal commas.

Omitting a semicolon between independent clauses may result in a comma splice or a fused sentence. (See **2**.)

22a Use a semicolon between independent clauses not connected by a coordinating conjunction.

WITH NO CONNECTIVE

For fifteen years the painting was stored in the attic; even the artist forgot it.

WITH A CONJUNCTIVE ADVERB

A specialist from the museum arrived and asked to examine it; *then* all the family became excited.

See **20f** for use of commas with conjunctive adverbs.

WITH A SENTENCE MODIFIER

The painting was valuable; *in fact,* the museum offered ten thousand dollars for it.

See **20f** for use of commas with sentence modifiers, such as *on the other hand, for example, in fact, in the first place.*

22b Use a semicolon to separate independent clauses that are long and complex or that have internal punctuation.

In many compound sentences either a semicolon or a comma can be used.

COMMA OR SEMICOLON

Moby-Dick, by Melville, is an adventure story, *(or ;)* and it is also one of the world's greatest philosophical novels.

SEMICOLON PREFERRED

Ishmael, the narrator, goes to sea, he says, "whenever it is a damp, drizzly November" in his soul; and Ahab, the captain of the ship, goes to sea because of his obsession to hunt and kill the great albino whale, Moby Dick.

22c Use semicolons in a series between items that have internal punctuation.

> The old farmer kept a variety of poultry: chickens, for eggs and Sunday dinners; turkeys, for very special meals; and peacocks, for their beauty.

22d Do not use a semicolon between elements that are not coordinate.

FAULTY

dependent clauses   *independent clause*

After the tugboat had signaled to the barge twice; it turned toward

the wharf.   ↑ *use* **,**

■ **Exercise 9**

Circle unnecessary semicolons and commas, and insert necessary ones. Write C by sentences that are correct.

1. The map shows the road heading east toward town;therefore,

   we are going in the wrong direction, or we are on the wrong

   road.

2. The stipulations of the agreement were⊙that each company

   would keep its own name, that profits would be evenly divided, and, that no employees would lose their jobs; because of the merger.

3. An advanced civilization is guided by enlightened self-interest; however, it is also marked by unselfish, good will.

4. The sound of the banjo drifted up from the floor below; it blended with the chatter of typewriters; and the droning of business conferences.

5. A chocolate cake was just part of the man's contribution to the bake sale; he also made a lemon, meringue pie.

6. The hallway was long, and dark; and at the end of it hung a dim, obscure painting representing a beggar; in eighteenth-century London.

7. The mutineers defeated the loyal members of the crew; took command of the ship; and locked the captain and other officers in the brig.

8. The storm knocked down the power lines, leaving the town dark; uprooted trees, leaving the streets blocked; and forced water over the levee, leaving the neighborhoods near the river flooded.

9. Fortune telling still appeals to many people; even when they realize it is superstitious nonsense, they continue to patronize charlatans, like palm readers.

10. The making of pottery, once a necessary craft as well as an art, has again become popular; and hundreds of young people, many of them highly skillful, have discovered the excitement of this art.

23 Colons :

Use a colon as a formal mark of introduction.

23a Use a colon before quotations, statements, and series that are introduced formally.

> Some of the buildings on the tour are unusual: antebellum two-storied homes, built mainly in the 1840s; smaller houses, which have long open hallways; and stores, some of which have two stories with porches.

A colon may be used to introduce a quotation formally.

> The warden began with a sharp reminder: "Gentlemen, you are now almost free; but some of you will not remain free long."

23b Use a colon between two independent clauses when the second explains the first.

Music communicates : it is an expression of deep feeling.

23c Use a colon before formal appositives, including those introduced by such expressions as *namely* and *that is.*

One factor is often missing from modern labor : pleasure in work.
The author made a difficult decision : he would abandon the manuscript.

NOTE: The colon comes before *namely* and similar expressions, not after.

The author made a difficult decision : namely, that he would abandon the manuscript.

23d Use a colon after the salutation of a formal letter, between figures indicating hours and minutes, and in bibliographical entries.

Dear Dr. Tyndale :   12 : 15 P.M.   Boston : Houghton, 1929
PMLA 99 (1984) : 75

23e Do not use a colon after a linking verb or a preposition.

NOT AFTER LINKING VERB
                        no colon
                           ↓
Some chief noisemakers **are** automobiles and airplanes.

no colon
NOT AFTER PREPOSITION ↓
> His friend accused him **of** wiggling in his seat, talking during the lecture, and not remembering what was said.

24 Dashes —

Use a dash to introduce summaries and to indicate interruptions, parenthetical remarks, and special emphasis.

NOTE: In typing, a dash is made by two hyphens (--) with no space before or after it.

FOR SUMMARY
> Attic fans, window fans, air conditioners——all were ineffective that summer.

FOR SUDDEN INTERRUPTIONS
> She replied, "I will consider the——No, I won't either."

FOR PARENTHETICAL REMARKS
> Three horses came from the water——a fourth had disappeared—— and struggled up the bank.

FOR SPECIAL EMPHASIS
> Great authors quote one book more than any other——the Bible.

25 Parentheses   ( )

Use parentheses to enclose a loosely related comment or explanation, figures that number items in a series, and references in documentation.

The frisky colt (it was not a thoroughbred) was given away.

The prospector refused to buy the land because (1) the owner had no clear title, (2) it was too remote, and (3) it was too expensive.

A reference in documentation:

Link does not agree (153). [See **48i.**]

A parenthetical sentence within another sentence has no period or capital, as in the first example above. A freestanding parenthetical sentence requires parentheses, a capital, and a period.

                            capital   *period here*
                               ↓   ↓
At the moment all flights are late. (The weather is bad.) Listen for further announcements.

26 Brackets [ ]

Use brackets to enclose interpolations within quotations.

In the opinion of Arthur Miller, "There is no more reason for falling down in a faint before his [Aristotle's] *Poetics* than before Euclid's geometry."

Parenthetical elements within parentheses are indicated by brackets ([ ]). Try to avoid constructions that call for this intricate punctuation.

27 Quotation Marks " "

Use quotation marks to enclose the exact words of a speaker or writer and to set off some titles.

Most American writers and publishers use double quotation marks (". . .") except for internal quotations, which are set off by single quotation marks ('. . .'). (See **27b**.)

27a Use quotation marks to enclose direct quotations and dialogue.

DIRECT QUOTATION

At a high point in *King Lear,* the Duke of Gloucester says, "As flies to wanton boys are we to the gods."

NOTE: Do not use quotation marks to enclose indirect quotations.

He said that the gods regard us as flies.

In dialogue a new paragraph marks each change of speaker.

DIALOGUE

"What is fool's gold?" asked the traveler who had never before been prospecting.

"Well," the geologist told him, "it's pyrite."

NOTE: Do not use quotation marks to enclose prose quotations that are longer than four lines. Instead, indicate the quotation by blocking—indenting ten spaces from your left margin and single spacing.

Unless your instructor specifies otherwise, poetry of four lines or more should be double-spaced and indented ten spaces. Retain the original divisions of the lines.

If you would keep your soul
From spotted sight or sound,
Live like the velvet mole;
Go burrow underground.

Quotations of three lines of poetry or less may be written like the regular text—not set off. Use a slash (with a space before and after) to separate lines:

> Elinor Wylie satirically advises, "Live like the velvet mole; / Go burrow underground."

27b Use single quotation marks to enclose a quotation within a quotation.

> The review explained: "Elinor Wylie is ironic when she advises, 'Go burrow underground.' "

27c Use quotation marks to enclose the titles of essays, articles, short stories, short poems, chapters (and other subdivisions of books or periodicals), dissertations (see pp. 357–363), episodes of television programs, and short musical compositions.

> D. H. Lawrence's "The Rocking-Horse Winner" is a story about the need for love.
>
> One chapter of *Walden* is entitled "The Beanfield." (For titles of books, see **30a**.)

27d On your paper, do not use quotation marks around its title.

27e Do not use quotation marks to emphasize or change the usual meanings of words or to justify slang, irony, or attempts at humor.

no

The beggar considered himself a "rich" man.

no

The old politician's enemies hoped that he would "croak."

Quotation marks do not give specialized or unusual definitions to words. They do not effectively add new meanings.

27f When you indicate a quotation by blocking (see **27a** and the model research paper, pp. 380–381), use quotation marks exactly as they appeared in the quoted passage.

Do not add quotation marks to show that you are quoting the entire passage. Blocking does that.

27g Follow established conventions in placing other marks of punctuation inside or outside closing quotation marks.

Periods and **commas** in American usage are placed *inside:*

> All the students had read "Lycidas."
> "Amazing," the professor remarked.

Semicolons and **colons** are placed *outside:*

> The customer wrote that she was "not yet ready to buy the first edition"; it was too expensive.

A **question mark** or an **exclamation point** is placed *inside* quotation marks only when the quotation itself is a direct question or an exclamation. Otherwise, these marks are placed *outside*.

> He asked, "Who is she?" (Only the quotation is a question.)
> "Who is she?" he asked. (Only the quotation is a question.)
> Did he ask, "Who is she"? (The quotation and the entire sentence are questions.)
> Did he say, "I know her"? (The entire sentence asks a question; the quotation makes a statement.)
> She screamed, "Run!" (Only the quotation is an exclamation.)
> Curse the man who whispers, "No"! (The entire statement is an exclamation; the quotation is not.)

After quotations, do not use a period or a comma together with an exclamation point or a question mark.

NOT
"When?", I asked.

BUT
"When?" I asked.

For parentheses with quotations and page numbers in documentation, see pp. 363–365.

28 End Punctuation .?!

Use periods, question marks, or exclamation points to end sentences and to serve special functions.

28a Use a period after a sentence that makes a statement or expresses a command.

Some modern people claim to practice witchcraft.

Water the flowers.

The gardener asked whether the plant should be taken indoors.
(This sentence is a statement even though it expresses an indirect
question.)

28b   Use periods after most abbreviations.

Periods follow such abbreviations as Mr., Dr., Pvt., Ave., B. C.,
A. M., Ph. D., e. g., and many others. In British usage periods are
often omitted after titles (Mr).

Abbreviations of governmental and international agencies
often are written without periods (FCC, TVA, UNESCO, NATO,
and so forth). Usage varies. Consult your dictionary.

A comma or another mark of punctuation may follow the period after an abbreviation, but at the end of a sentence only one
period is used.

After she earned her M. A., she began studying for her Ph. D.

But if the sentence is a question or an exclamation, the end punctuation mark follows the period after the abbreviation.

When does she expect to get her Ph. D.?

28c   Use three spaced periods (ellipsis dots) to show an
omission in a quotation.

Notice the quotation on p. 158 and how it can be shortened with
ellipsis marks.

He [the Indian] had no written record other than pictographs, and his conqueror was not usually interested, at the time, in writing down his thoughts and feelings for him. The stoic calm of his few reported speeches and poems gives only a hint of the rich culture that was so soon forgotten.

ROBERT E. SPILLER

ELLIPSIS

*marks not necessary at
beginning of quotation*

*one period to end sentence
and three for ellipsis*

The Indian "had no written record other than pictographs. . . . The stoic calm of his . . . speeches and poems gives only a hint of the rich

three periods for ellipsis in sentences

culture. . . ."

28d   A title has no period, but some titles include a question mark or an exclamation point.

The Sound and the Fury   "What Are Years?"
Westward Ho!   *Ah! Wilderness*

28e   Use a question mark after a direct question.

Do teachers file attendance reports?
Teachers do file attendance reports? (a question in declarative form)

Question marks may follow separate questions within an interrogative sentence.

Do you recall the time of the accident? the license numbers of the cars involved? the names of the drivers?

NOTE: A question mark within parentheses shows that a date or a figure is historically doubtful.

Pythagoras, who died in 497 B.C. (?), was a philosopher.

28f Do not use a question mark or an exclamation point within parentheses to indicate humor or sarcasm.

NOT
The comedy (?) was a miserable failure.

28g Use an exclamation point after a word, a phrase, or a sentence to signal strong exclamatory feeling.

Wait! I forgot my lunch!
What a ridiculous idea!
Stop the bus!

Use exclamation points sparingly. After mild exclamations, use commas or periods.

NOT
Well! I was discouraged!

BUT
Well, I was discouraged.

■ **Exercise 10**

Supply quotation marks as needed in the following passage, and in-sert the sign ¶ where new paragraphs are necessary.

Alex Tilman, young, vigorous, and alert, walked briskly beside the little stream. As he neared a pond, he thought of Thoreau's essay "Walking" and the calm that pervaded nature. An old man was fishing with a pole on the bank of the pond. ¶ (optional) Knowing that fishermen dislike noisemakers, Alex strolled quietly up to him and said, "How's your luck today? ¶ "Oh, about like every other day, except a little worse, maybe. ¶ "Do you mean you haven't caught anything? ¶ "Well, a couple of bream. But they're small, you know. Before I left home my wife said to me, 'If you don't catch any siza ble fish today, you might as well give it up.' And I'm beginning to wonder if she hasn't got something there. ¶ Alex watched the water for a little while, now and then stealing a glance at the un-shaved fisherman, who wore baggy breeches and a faded old flannel shirt. Then he dreamily said, "Well, I guess most people don't really fish just for the sake of catching something. ¶ The old gentleman looked up at him a little surprised. His eyes were much brighter and quicker than Alex had expected. "That's right," he said, "but, you know, that's not the kind of wisdom you hear these days. You new around here, son?"

"Yes. My wife and I just bought the old Edgewright place."

"Oh! Well, maybe you can come fishing with me sometime. I'm usually here about this time during the day."

Alex was not eager to accept the invitation, but he was moved by a sudden sympathy. "Yes. Maybe. Say, if you need any work, I might be able to find something for you to do around our place. My wife and I are trying to get things cleaned up."

A slight smile came over the man's face, and he said warmly, "Much obliged, but I've got more work now than I know what to do with. So I come out here and hum 'Lazy Bones' and fish."

On the way back to his house, Alex asked a neighbor who that old tramp was fishing down by the pond.

"Tramp!" his friend repeated. "Good heavens, man, that was no tramp. That was Angus Morgan, one of the wealthiest men in the country."

■ **Exercise 11**

Add quotation marks where needed; circle unnecessary ones. Also make all necessary changes in punctuation.

1. "Failure is often necessary for humanity," the speaker said. Without failure, he continued, how can we retain our humility and know the full sweetness of success? For, as Emily Dickinson said, Success is counted sweetest / By those who ne'er succeed.

2. Madam, said the talent scout, I know that you think your daughter can sing, but, believe me, her voice makes the strangest sounds I have ever heard. Mrs. Audubon took her daughter Birdie by the hand and haughtily left the room wondering how she could ever have been so stupid as to expose her daughter to such a common person.

3. After dinner, Grandmother said, I'm going to teach you a poem that I learned when I was a little girl. It's called The Wind and it begins like this I saw you toss the kites on high / And blow the birds about the sky.

4. The boy and his great-uncle were "real" friends, and the youngster listened intently when the old man spoke. "Son," he would say, 'I remember my father's words: You can't do better than to follow the advice of Ben Franklin, who said, "One To-day is worth two To-morrows."

5. To demonstrate that the English language is always "changing," the teacher said that each student should come up with: a list of expressions, such as "boom box," "courseware," and "golden parachute," not found in the dictionary used in class.

6. A recent report states the following: "The marked increase in common stocks indicated a new sense of national security; however, the report seems to imply "that this is only one of many gauges of the country's economic situation."

7. Chapters in modern novels rarely have any titles at all, especially "wordy" ones like the title of Chapter 51 in *Vanity Fair* (1848): "In which a Charade Is Acted Which May or May not Puzzle the Reader."

8. One of Mark Twain's most famous letters, addressed to
   ⌒Andrew Carnegie,⌒ reads as follows:

   "You seem to be in prosperity. Could you lend an ad-
   mirer $1.50 to buy a hymn-book with? God will bless you. I
   feel it; I know it. So will I⌒

   "N.B.—If there should be other applications, this one
   not to count⌒." "

9. In a ⌒postscript,⌒ Mark Twain added, "Don't send the hymn-
   book; send the money; I want to make the selection myself."
   He signed the letter simply "Mark."

10. The hermit thought the question⌒odd,⌒ but he replied, "You
    ask me, 'Why do you live here?' I ask you why you do not live
    here."

MECHANICS

29 Manuscript and Letter Form *ms*

Follow correct manuscript form in papers and business letters.

29a Papers

Paper

typing: white, 8½ by 11 inches
longhand: ruled
not: onionskin, spiral, legal size

Lines

typing: double-spaced
longhand: skip every other line (or follow your teacher's instructions)

Title

centered with extra space between title and text

Margins

ample and regular at bottom and top—at least one inch on each side

Page numbers

Arabic numerals (2, *not* II) in upper right corner except on first page (omit or center at bottom of page)

Example of correct manuscript form

About 1½ inch margin   Up Attic ⟵———————— *Center*

⌐— *Indent 5 spaces*   ⟵———————— *Triple Space*

↓ It is no topsy-turvy figure of speech to say that the roots of the

⌐—*2 spaces after periods*

old American home were in the attic. ▼There beneath the oak or chestnut

⌐—*2 hyphens no spaces for dash*

rafters were stored in endless profusion—▼and confusion—▼the records of

a family's life, perhaps for a century. On a bright summer day the attic

was unbearably hot and buzzed with flies; in winter it chilled you with

a stale cold. But on rainy days it was a fascinating place to explore by

the hour while the rain made a soft, soothing roar on the roof, and

sounds from the domestic world below came up smothered and unreal. The

roof of the old house where my boyhood was spent was adorned with a

cupola, which in turn was adorned with colored glass windows, a different

color for each point of the compass. Steep stairs led up to it from the

attic, and through the four windows you looked out upon four different

and strange worlds. The total unreality of a world all green, or all

red, or all blue, was never-to-be-too-much savored, but the all-yellow

world was a little terrifying, as if some ominous storm were brewing.

If Emerson's house had been equipped with such a cupola he would not

have had to recommend that clumsier argument for idealism--stooping down

and looking at a familiar landscape between your legs.

From the foot of the steep stairs to enchantment--or idealism--

there stretched out in all directions until they vanished under the low

eaves every sort of object saved from the long process of living in the

house below. There were, for instance, horsehair trunks lined with old

Leave ample margin at   ↑   *Page number for first page*
bottom of page | 1⟵——— *on bottom line (optional)*
                             ↓

Walter Prichard Eaton, "Up Attic."

29b Business letters

In writing a business letter follow conventional forms. All essential parts are included in the example on pp. 169–170. Type if possible: single-space, with double-spacing between paragraphs. Paragraphs may begin at the left margin without indentation in block form, or they may be indented.

Try to learn both the title and the name of the addressee. Opinions vary about the best custom when the name, title, or sex of the person is unknown. If the sex of the addressee is known but the name is not, use *Dear Sir* or *Dear Madam*. If the sex is not known, use *Dear Sir or Madam*. Or omit the salutation entirely. When a woman's marital status is unknown or when she prefers it, use *Ms*.

Business letters are usually written on stationery measuring 8½ by 11 inches. Fold horizontally into thirds to fit a standard-sized business envelope. For smaller envelopes fold once horizontally and twice the other way. (See page 170.)

Indented form of letter

                                        141 Oakhurst Drive, Apt. 2A
                                        Singleton, Ohio 54567
                                        March 1, 19--

Mr. Freeman O. Zachary, Manager
Personnel Department
Keeson National Bank
P. O. Box 2387
Chicago, Illinois 34802

Dear Mr. Zachary:

    I am writing to ask if you will have an opening this coming summer
for someone of my qualifications. I am finishing my sophomore year at
Singleton State College, where I intend to major in economics and
finance. I have been active in several extracurricular activities,
including the Spanish Club and the Singleton Players.

    Although I have no previous experience in banking, I am eager to
learn, and I am willing to take on any duties you feel appropriate.
Chicago is my home town, so I am especially anxious to find summer employment there. I will be in Chicago for spring vacation from March 20
to 26 and available for an interview. In addition, I shall be pleased
to furnish you with letters of recommendation from some of my professors here at Singleton State and with a transcript of my college
record. I appreciate your consideration, and I look forward to hearing
from you.

                                        Sincerely yours,

                                        Audrey De Veers

                                        Audrey DeVeers

Audrey DeVeers
141 Oakhurst Drive, Apt. 2A
Singleton, OH 54567

                    Mr. Freeman O. Zachary, Manager
                    Personnel Department
                    Keeson National Bank
                    P. O. Box 2387
                    Chicago, IL 34802

Blocked form of letter

Address of writer ————————→ 141 Oakhurst Drive, Apt. 2A
                                Singleton, Ohio 54567
Date ————————————————————→ March 1, 19--

Mr. Freeman O. Zachary, Manager ←——— *Name and title of addressee*
Personnel Department
Keeson National Bank
P. O. Box 2387   ←——————— *Full address*
Chicago, Illinois 34802

Dear Mr. Zachary: ←——————————— *Salutation and name. Use a colon.*

I am writing to ask if you will have an opening this coming summer for
someone of my qualifications. I am finishing my sophomore year at
Singleton State College, where I intend to major in economics and
finance. I have been active in several extracurricular activities,
including the Spanish Club and the Singleton Players.

Although I have no previous experience in banking, I am eager to learn,
and I am willing to take on any duties you feel appropriate. Chicago
is my home town, so I am especially anxious to find summer employment
there. I will be in Chicago for spring vacation from March 20 to 26 and
available for an interview. In addition, I shall be pleased to furnish
you with letters of recommendation from some of my professors here at
Singleton State and with a transcript of my college record. I appreciate your consideration, and I look forward to hearing from you.

Sincerely yours,   ←———————————————— *Complimentary close*

Audrey De Veers ←—————————————— *Signature, handwritten*

Audrey DeVeers   ←—————————————— *Name, typed*

Folding the letter

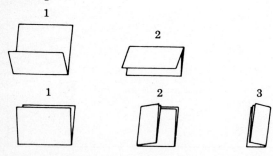

30 Underlining for Italics   *ital*

Underline titles of independent publications (books, magazines, newspapers), and underline *occasionally* for emphasis.

Italic type slants *(like this)*. Underline each word individually (<u>like this</u>), or underline words and spaces (<u>like this</u>).

30a Underline titles of books (except the Bible and its divisions), periodicals, newspapers, motion pictures, paintings, sculptures, musical compositions, television and radio programs, plays, and other works published separately.

Be precise: watch initial articles *(A, An, The)* and any punctuation.

BOOKS
> <u>Adventures</u> <u>of</u> <u>Huckleberry</u> <u>Finn</u> (*not* <u>The</u> <u>Adventures</u> . . .)
> <u>An</u> <u>American</u> <u>Tragedy</u> (*not* <u>The</u> <u>American</u> <u>Tragedy</u>)

PERIODICALS
> <u>The</u> <u>Atlantic</u> and the <u>American</u> <u>Quarterly</u>

NEWSPAPERS
> <u>The</u> <u>New</u> <u>York</u> <u>Times</u> or the New York <u>Times</u>

MOTION PICTURES
> <u>Citizen</u> <u>Kane</u>

MUSICAL COMPOSITIONS
> Bizet's <u>Carmen</u>
> Beethoven's <u>Mount of Olives</u> (*but not* Beethoven's Symphony No. 5)

PLAYS
> <u>The Cherry Orchard</u>

30b Underline names of ships and trains.

> the <u>Queen Elizabeth II</u>   the U.S.S. <u>Hornet</u>   the <u>Zephyr</u>

30c Underline foreign words used in an English context, except words that have become part of our language.

Consult a dictionary to determine whether a word is still considered foreign or has become part of the English language.

French
↓

> He claimed extravagantly to have been <u>au courant</u> since birth.

BUT
Some words that may seem foreign have become a part of the English language.

> faux pas, amigo, karate

30d Underline words, letters, and figures being named.

The word <u>puppy</u> usually has delightful connotations.
Don't forget to dot your i's.

NOTE: Occasionally quotation marks are used instead of underlining.

30e Avoid frequent underlining for emphasis.

Do not sprinkle a page with underlinings, dashes, or exclamation points. Writing is seldom improved by mechanical tricks.

30f On your paper, do not underline its title.

■ **Exercise 1**

Underline words as necessary in the following sentences. Put an X over words unnecessarily underlined.

1. An <u>earthquake</u> is an <u>awesome</u> natural phenomenon.
   or **The Los Angeles Times**
2. The Los Angeles <u>Times</u> announced the arrival of the ship

   <u>Tropical Explorer</u>.

3. The author's last novel, <u>The Green Summer</u>, was reviewed in
   or **The Philadelphia Inquirer**
   the Philadelphia <u>Inquirer</u>.

4. The painting is titled <u>Arrangement in Gray and Black</u>.

5. The lımousine [x] was used in a motion picture entitled The Years of Hope.

6. The motion picture The Killers is based on a short story by Hemingway.

7. Jack London's short story "To Build a Fire" is published in the latest edition of the anthology America's Great Tales.

8. The periodical Harper's has an article on the modern opera Streets of the City.

9. He made his i's with little circles over them instead of dots. [x]

10. While on the train The Northern Star, she saw a large moose.

31 Spelling *sp*

Spell correctly; make a habit of checking your dictionary.

Spelling is troublesome in English because many words are not spelled as they sound (*laughter, slaughter*); because some pairs and triplets sound the same (*capital, capitol; there, they're, their; to, too, two*); and because many words are pronounced with the vowel sound "uh," which gives no clue to spelling (*sensible, capable, defiant*).

Many misspellings are due to the omission of syllables in habitual mispronunciations *(accident-ly* for *acciden-tal-ly)*; the addition of syllables *(disas-ter-ous* for *disas-trous)*; or the changing of syllables *(prespiration* for *perspiration)*.

There are no infallible guides to spelling in English, but the following are helpful.

ie or *ei*?

> Use *i* before *e*
> Except after *c*
> Or when sounded as *a*
> As in *neighbor* and *weigh*.

WORDS WITH *IE*
believe, chief, field, grief, piece

WORDS WITH *EI* AFTER *C*
receive, receipt, ceiling, deceit, conceive

WORDS WITH *EI* SOUNDED AS *A*
freight, vein, reign

EXCEPTIONS TO MEMORIZE
either, neither, leisure, seize, weird, height

Drop final silent e?

DROP *When suffix begins with* *a vowel*		KEEP *When suffix begins with* *a consonant*	
curse	cursing	live	lively
come	coming	nine	ninety
pursue	pursuing	hope	hopeful
arrange	arranging	love	loveless
dine	dining	arrange	arrangement

TYPICAL EXCEPTIONS
courageous
noticeable
dyeing (compare *dying*)
singeing (compare *singing*)

TYPICAL EXCEPTIONS
awful
ninth
truly
argument

Change y to i?

CHANGE *When y is preceded by a consonant*		DO NOT CHANGE *When y is preceded by a vowel*	
gully	gullies	valley	valleys
try	tried	attorney	attorneys
fly	flies	convey	conveyed
apply	applied	pay	pays
party	parties	deploy	deploying

When adding -ing

try	trying
fly	flying
apply	applying

Double final consonant?

If the suffix begins with a consonant, do not double the final consonant of the base word *(man, manly)*.

If the suffix begins with a vowel:

DOUBLE
When final consonant is preceded by single vowel

Monosyllables

pen	penned
blot	blotted
hop	hopper
sit	sitting

DO NOT DOUBLE
When final consonant is preceded by two vowels

despair	despairing
leer	leering

Words ending with two or more consonants preceded by single vowel

jump	jumping
work	working

Polysyllables accented on last syllable		*Polysyllables not accented on last syllable after addition of suffix*	
defér	deferring	defér	déference
begín	beginning	prefér	préference
omít	omitting	devélop	devéloping
occúr	occurring	lábor	lábored

Add s or es?

ADD *S*		ADD *ES*	
For plurals of most nouns		*When the plural is pronounced as another syllable*	
girl	girls	church	churches
book	books	fox	foxes
For nouns ending in o *preceded by a vowel*		*Usually for nouns ending in* o *preceded by a consonant (consult your dictionary)*	
radio	radios	potatoes	
cameo	cameos	heroes	
		BUT	
		flamingos *or* flamingoes	
		egos	

NOTE: The plurals of proper names are generally formed by adding *s* or *es* (*Darby*, the *Darbys*; *Jones*, the *Joneses*).

Words frequently misspelled

Following is a list of over two hundred of the most commonly misspelled words in the English language.

absence	acquitted	amateur
accidentally	advice	among
accommodate	advise	analysis
accumulate	all right	analyze
acquaintance	altar	annual

apartment
apparatus
apparent
appearance
arctic
argument
arithmetic
ascend
athletic
attendance
balance
beginning
believe
benefited
boundaries
Britain
business
calendar
candidate
category
cemetery
changeable
changing
choose
chose
coming
commission
committee
comparative
compelled
conceivable
conferred
conscience
conscientious
control
criticize
deferred
definite
description
desperate
dictionary
dining
disappearance
disappoint

disastrous
discipline
dissatisfied
dormitory
eighth
eligible
eliminate
embarrass
eminent
encouraging
environment
equipped
especially
exaggerate
excellence
exhilarate
existence
experience
explanation
familiar
fascinate
February
fiery
foreign
formerly
forty
fourth
frantically
fulfill or fulfil
generally
government
grammar
grandeur
grievous
height
heroes
hindrance
hoping
humorous
hypocrisy
immediately
incidentally
incredible
independence

inevitable
intellectual
intelligence
interesting
irresistible
knowledge
laboratory
laid
led
lightning
loneliness
maintenance
maneuver
manufacture
marriage
mathematics
may
maybe
miniature
mischievous
mysterious
necessary
ninety
noticeable
occasionally
occurred
omitted
opportunity
optimistic
parallel
paralyze
pastime
performance
permissible
perseverance
personnel
perspiration
physical
picnicking
playwright
possibility
practically
precede
precedence

preference	recommend	sophomore
preferred	reference	specifically
prejudice	referred	specimen
preparation	repetition	stationary
prevalent	restaurant	stationery
privilege	rhythm	statue
probably	ridiculous	studying
professor	sacrifice	subtly
pronunciation	salary	succeed
prophecy	schedule	successful
prophesy	secretary	supersede
quantity	seize	suppose
quiet	separate	surprise
quite	sergeant	temperamental
quizzes	severely	tendency
recede	shining	their
receive	siege	thorough
recognize	similar	through

■ **Exercise 2**

In each of the following groups of words one, two, or three are misspelled. The others are correct. Put an X over incorrectly spelled words.

       x   x
1. lizard, blizard, gizard, wizard, sizzler

                  x   x
2. accommodate, acumulate, comming, blooming, ramming

  x   x
3. percieve, believe, recieve, achieve, conceive

              x   x   x
4. mountain, villian, protein, maintainance, certian

                      x   x   x
5. credence, precedence, balence, existance, independance

  x   x   x
6. tallys, valleys, bellys, modifys, fancies

  x   x   x
7. defys, relays, conveyes, carries, dirtys

8. obedience, modifyer, complience, applience, guidance

9. incredible, detectable, delectible, dependible, reversible

10. sensable, receivable, edable, likible, noticeable

32   Hyphenation and Syllabication -

Use a hyphen in certain compound words and in words divided at the end of a line.

Two words not listed as an entry in a dictionary are usually written separately *(campaign promise.)*

32a   Consult a dictionary to determine whether a compound is hyphenated or written as one or two words.

HYPHENATED	ONE WORD	TWO WORDS
drop-off	droplight	drop leaf (noun)
white-hot	whitewash	white heat
water-cool	watermelon	water system

32b   Hyphenate a compound of two or more words used as a single modifier before a noun.

HYPHEN	NO HYPHEN AFTER NOUN
She is a *well-known* executive	The executive is *well known*.

A hyphen is not used when the first word of such a group is an adverb ending in *-ly*.

HYPHEN	NO HYPHEN
a *half-finished* task	a *partly finished* task

32c Hyphenate spelled-out compound numbers from *twenty-one* through *ninety-nine*.

32d Divide a word at the end of a line according to conventions.

Monosyllables

Do not divide.

thought   strength   cheese

Single letters

Do not put a one-letter syllable on a separate line:

NOT
a-bout   might-y

Prefixes and suffixes

May be divided.

separ-able   pre-fix

Avoid carrying over a two-letter suffix.

    bound-ed   careful-ly

Compounds with hyphen

Avoid dividing and adding another hyphen.

    self-satisfied

NOT
    self-satis-fied

▪ Exercise 3

Underline the correct form for the words indicated. Use a dictionary when needed.

1. (Healthcare, Health-care, Health care) costs are (rapidlyin-creasing, rapidly-increasing, rapidly increasing).

2. The (thunderstorm, thunder-storm, thunder storm) drove people off the (golfcourse, golf-course, golf course) into the (justopened, just-opened, just opened) (clubhouse, club-house, club house).

3. The (foxhound, fox-hound, fox hound) was (welltrained, well-trained, well trained) not to chase rabbits.

4. The (twentyone, twenty-one, twenty one) dancers did not know how to (foxtrot, fox-trot, fox trot).

5. Several words in the paper were hyphenated at the end of lines: a-round, almight-y, al-most, self-in-flicted, marb-le.

33 Apostrophes '

Use the apostrophe for the possessive case of many nouns, contractions, omissions, and some plurals.

Use 's for the possessive of nouns not ending in *s*.

SINGULAR
child's, man's, deer's, lady's, mother-in-law's

PLURAL
children's, men's

Use 's for the possessive of singular nouns ending in *s*.

Charles's, Watts's, Dickens's, waitress's, actress's

NOTE: When a singular noun ending in *s* is followed by a word beginning with *s*, use only the apostrophe, not *'s*.

the actress' success, Dickens' stories

Use ' without *s* to form the possessive of plural nouns ending in *s*.

the Joneses' car, the Dickenses' home, waitresses' tips

Use 's to form the possessive of indefinite pronouns.

anybody's, everyone's, somebody else's, neither's

NOTE: Use no apostrophe with personal pronouns like *his, hers, theirs, ours, its* (meaning "of it"). *It's* means "it is."

Use 's with only the last noun for joint possession in a pair or a series.

> the architect and the builder's plan (The two jointly have one plan.)
> the architect's and the builder's plans (They have different plans.)

Use ' to show omissions or to form contractions.

> the roaring '20's, o'clock, jack-o'-lantern
> we'll, don't, can't, it's (meaning "it is")

Use 's to form the plural of numerals, letters, and words being named.

> three 7's (but *three sevens*), four *a*'s, six *the*'s

■ Exercise 4

Underline the words that contain correctly used apostrophes.

1. sheeps' wool, deer's horns, cats' eyes, a cat's eyes
2. the youths' organization, the women's club, the womens' club
3. the childrens' books, a childs' books, the two boys' books
4. the Beatles's songs, the Davises's vacation, Dennis's notebook
5. the sled that is her's, ours', theirs, somebody's else
6. wasnt, wasn't, two *m*s, three *n*'s
7. three *why*'s, four *hows*
8. one o'clock, two oclock, three opossums

9. Mary and Martin's store (together they own one store)

   Mary's and Martin's stores (each owns a store)

10. our's, ours', its', it's (for *it is*)

34 Capital Letters   *cap*

Use a capital letter to begin a sentence and to designate a proper noun (the name of a particular person, place, or thing).

Capitalize the first word of a sentence, the pronoun *I*, and the interjection *O*.

> How, O ye gods, can I control this joy?

Capitalize first, last, and important words in titles, including the second part of hyphenated words.

> *Across the River and into the Trees*
> "The Man Against the Sky"
> "After Apple-Picking"

NOTE: Articles (*a, an, the*), short prepositions, and conjunctions are not capitalized unless they begin or end a title.

Capitalize first words of direct quotations.

> The instructions warned, "Do not immerse in water."

Capitalize titles preceding a name.

> Professor Garcia

Capitalize the title of the head of a nation.

> The President is not expected to arrive today.

Capitalize titles used specifically as substitutes for particular names.

> Lieutenant Yo pleaded not guilty; the Lieutenant was found innocent.

NOTE: A title not followed by a name is usually not capitalized.

> The treasurer gave the financial report.

Titles that are common nouns that name an office are not capitalized.

> A college president has more duties than privileges.
> A lieutenant deserves a good living allowance.

Capitalize degrees and titles after a name.

> Jeffrey E. Tyndale, Ph.D., J.D.
> Abraham Lincoln, Attorney at Law

NOTE: Do not capitalize names of occupations used as appositives or as descriptions.

> Abraham Lincoln, a young lawyer from Springfield, took the case.

Capitalize words of family relationship used as names when not preceded by a possessive pronoun or the word *the*.

USED AS NAMES
After Father died, Mother carried on the business.

BUT

>   After my father died, my mother carried on the business.

Capitalize proper nouns but not general terms.

PROPER NOUNS	GENERAL TERMS
Plato, Platonic, Platonism	pasteurize
Venice, Venetian blind	a set of china
the West, a Westerner	west of the river
the Republican Party	a republican government
the Senior Class of Ivy College	a member of the senior class
Clifton Street	my street, the street
the Mississippi River	the Mississippi and Ohio rivers
the Romantic Movement	the twentieth century

Capitalize months, days of the week, and holidays.

>   April, Friday, the Fourth of July, Labor Day

NOTE: Do not capitalize seasons and numbered days of the month unless they name holidays.

>   spring, the third of July

Capitalize B.C. (used after numerals: 31 B.C.), A.D. (used before numerals: A.D. 33), words designating the Deity, religious denominations, and sacred books.

>   in 273 B.C.
>   the Messiah, our Maker, the Trinity, Yahweh, Allah, Buddha, Jesus
>   "Praise God from Whom all blessings flow."
>   Catholic, Protestant, Presbyterian
>   the Bible, the Koran

NOTE: Pronouns referring to the Deity are usually capitalized.

>   From Him all blessings flow.

Capitalize names of specific courses.

>   I registered for Sociology 101 and Chemistry 445.

NOTE: Do not capitalize studies (other than languages) that do not name specific courses.

>   I am taking English, sociology, and chemistry.

35   Abbreviations   *ab*

Avoid most abbreviations in formal writing.

Spell out names of days, months, units of measurement, and (except in addresses) states and countries.

Friday (*not* Fri.)	pounds (*not* lbs.)
February (*not* Feb.)	Sauk Centre, Minnesota (*not* Minn.)

Do not use note-taking or shortcut signs such as *w/* for *with* and *&* for *and* in formal writing.

ACCEPTABLE ABBREVIATIONS
Washington, D.C.

BEFORE NAMES
Mr., Mrs., Ms., Messrs., Mmes., Dr., St. *or* Ste. (for *Saint,* not *Street*), Mt., Rev. (but only with a first name: *the Rev. Ernest Jones,* not *Rev. Jones*)

AFTER NAMES
M.D. (and other degrees), Jr., Sr., Esq.

FOR MANY AGENCIES AND ORGANIZATIONS (WITHOUT PERIODS)
    TVA, NAACP, FBI

WITH DATES AND TIME
    B.C. and A.D. (with dates expressed in numerals, as *500 B.C.*), A.M.
    and P.M. or a.m. and p.m. (with hours expressed in numerals, as *4:00
    A.M.* or 4:00 a.m.)

36 Numbers *num*

Spell out numbers that can be written in one or two words.

    twenty-three, one thousand

Use figures for other numbers.

    123   1¹³⁄₁₆ $1,001.00

NOTE: Newspapers and government publications generally use
figures for numbers above ten.

EXCEPTIONS: Never use figures at the beginning of a sentence.
Spell out the number or recast the sentence.

Use numerals for figures in sequences.

    One polar bear weighed 200 pounds; another, 526; the third, 534.

Use figures for dates, street numbers, page references, percent-
ages, and hours of the day used with A.M. or P.M.

USE FIGURES

July 3, 1776 (*not* 3rd)
1010 State Street
See page 50.
He paid 15 percent interest.
The concert begins at 6 P.M.
   (or 6:00 P.M.)

SPELL OUT

the third of July
Fifth Avenue
The book has fifty pages.

The concert begins at
   six o'clock.

■ Exercise 5

*Supply capitals as needed below. Change capital letters to lower case
as necessary.*

1. "David," said mother, "I would like to borrow your copy of
   $\overset{\text{M}}{ }$ $\overset{\text{I}}{ }$
   War $\overset{\text{a}}{A}$nd Peace while you are home for the $\overset{\text{h}}{H}$olidays."

2. During the $\overset{\text{s}}{S}$pring, the student worked as a $\overset{\text{c}}{C}$heckout
   $\overset{\text{c}}{C}$lerk at a nearby $\overset{\text{K}}{k}$ mart.

3. Captain Kaplan, $\overset{\text{U}}{u}$nited States $\overset{\text{A}}{a}$rmy, arrived on $\overset{\text{W}}{w}$ednesday
   to find that he was late for the tour of $\overset{\text{B}}{b}$uddhist temples.

4. When she registered for $\overset{\text{c}}{C}$hemistry, $\overset{\text{M}}{m}$artha was told that she
   would need to take Algebra 101.

5. Alfred Curall, $\overset{\text{M D}}{m.d.}$, attended the meeting of the American
   Medical $\overset{\text{A}}{a}$ssociation and returned home before $\overset{\text{T}}{t}$hanksgiving
   $\overset{\text{D}}{d}$ay.

           W   c   n   c

6. Out West, Cowboys were numerous in the Nineteenth Century.

                                                B.C.   **A.D.**

7. Augustus Caesar, who was born in 63 ~~b.c.~~ and died in ~~a.d.~~
                                              t
   14, is a character in Shakespeare's Tragedy *Antony and Cleo-*

   patra.

                                                    A

8. Though the printer lived for a while on Magoni Avenue, he
             D
   moved to Detroit last August.

           v   p

9. The Salk Vaccine has all but eliminated the dangers of Polio,
                            m   j
   according to an article in a Medical Journal.

                                  l

10. She wanted to become a Lawyer, she explained, because she
                                        l   m
   saw a direct connection between the Law and Morals.

■ **Exercise 6**

Place an X by the following that are not acceptable in formal writing,
a ✓ by those that are acceptable.

✓ 1. May thirteenth
x 2. Twelve thirteen Jefferson Street
x 3. Jefferson Ave.
x 4. Mister and Mrs. Smidt
x 5. seven P.M.
✓ 6. six thousand votes
x 7. Minneapolis, Minn., on 3 June 1940
x 8. Eng. 199 in the Dept. of English

✓ 9. Page 10 in Chapter 11
✗ 10. Geo. Smith
✗ 11. William Adams, Junior
✓ 12. 300 B.C.
✗ 13. Friday and Saturday, May 16 & 17
✗ 14. 10 pounds, 9 oz.
✗ 15. five hundred and ten bushels
✗ 16. December 24th, 1985
✓ 17. $4.98 a pound
✗ 18. handle w/care
✓ 19. five million dollars
✓ 20. Friday, June 13

DICTION AND STYLE

37 Standard English and Style   *d*

Use Standard English. Conform to established usage. Make your speech and writing appropriate to the content and to the situation.

Standard English is the generally accepted language of educated people in English-speaking countries. Though it varies in usage and in pronunciation from one country or region to another (indicated by labels such as *U.S.* or *Brit.* in dictionaries), it is the standard that is taught in schools and colleges.

Nonstandard English consists of usages, spellings, and pronunciations not usually found in the speech or writing of educated people. Read the entry labels in a dictionary to determine when a word is nonstandard. The presence of a word in a dictionary does not make it always appropriate and correct.

Diction is the choice and use of words. Consult the explanatory material in your dictionary for definitions of the labels it employs (for example, *Slang, Dialect, Vulgar, Poetic, Informal, Obsolete*).

Informal or **colloquial** language (terms used almost interchangeably) is appropriate in certain situations, **though not usually in college papers. Contractions**—*don't, isn't,* and so forth—are informal. **Colloquial** does not mean **dialect or local language.**

37a   Using a dictionary

Dictionaries, which are good sources of information about language, record current and past usage. In minor matters they do not always agree.

Most brief paperback dictionaries provide too little information to be appropriate for college students. Particularly useful at the college level are the following desk dictionaries:

The American Heritage Dictionary. Boston: Houghton Mifflin Company.

The Random House College Dictionary. New York: Random House.

Webster's New Collegiate Dictionary. Springfield, Mass.: G. & C. Merriam Company.

Webster's New World Dictionary of the American Language. Cleveland: William Collins Publishers, Inc.

Webster's II: New Riverside University Dictionary. Boston: Houghton Mifflin Company.

Know how to look up a word, a word group, and many other kinds of information in your dictionary. You do not need to know all the different methods used by different dictionaries. Instead, select a good one and study carefully its explanations and systems. Read the entry on pp. 196–197 for the word *double* as given in *The American Heritage Dictionary* and study the explanatory material in red. Use this example as a guide. (A similar chart is included in the prefatory material of *Webster's New Collegiate Dictionary*.)

Style refers to the way writers express their thoughts in language. Effective writing always involves the choice of words and expressions, the arrangement of words, and variety in the patterns of sentences. The ways in which similar ideas are expressed can have vastly different effects, and many of the distinctions are a matter of style. Writing can be whimsical, poetic, terse, flippant, imaginative, literal, and so on. Develop the habit of noticing the personality of what you read and what you write. Your style should be appropriate to your subject, to your audience, and to your own character.

Dictionary Entry

Dictionaries provide the kinds of information indicated here in several ways. Other information (synonyms, variants, capitalizations, and so on) appears in many entries. Find the explanations you need in any dictionary.

① Boldfaced main entry   ② Dot indicating division between syllables   ③ Phonetic spelling for pronunciation (dictionaries place a pronunciation key at the bottom of each page)   ④ Accented syllable   ⑤ Abbreviation for part of speech—adjective   ⑥ Illustrative example   ⑦ Words or abbreviations in red blocks indicate terms that label specialized or technical meanings.   ⑧ Part of speech—noun. Note that the numbers start over when the part of speech changes.   ⑨ Part of speech —verb   ⑩ Forms of the verb—past tense and past participle, present participle, third-person singular ⑪ Kind of verb—transitive (see section **5** in this book)   ⑫ Kind of verb—intransitive (see section **5** in this book)   ⑬ Phrasal verb (used in *AHD* to mean verb plus adverb *or* preposition) ⑭ Part of speech—adverb   ⑮ Idioms (see **37f** in this book)   ⑯ Usage label (see **37, 37b-d** in this book)   ⑰ Etymologies are given in square brackets. Some dictionaries give the etymology early in the entry.   ⑱ A noun derived from the main entry

① ②   ③ ④ ⑤   ⑥

dou·ble (dŭb′əl) *adj.* **1.** Twice as much in size, strength, number, or amount: *a double dose.* **2.** Composed of two like parts: *double doors.* **3.** Composed of two unlike parts; dual: *a double meaning.* **4.** Accommodating or designed for two: *a double sleeping bag.* **5. a.** Acting two parts: *a double role.* **b.** Characterized by duplicity; deceitful: *speak with a double tongue.* **6.** *Bot.* Having many more than the usual number of petals, usually in a crowded or overlapping arrangement: *a double chrysanthemum.* —*n.* **1.** Something increased twofold. **2. a.** A duplicate of another; counterpart. **b.** An apparition; wraith. **3.** An actor's understudy. **4. a.** A sharp turn in running; reversal. **b.** An evasive reversal or shift in argument. **5. doubles.** A game, such as tennis or handball, having two players on each side. **6.** *Baseball.* A two-base hit. **7. a.** A bid in bridge indicating strength to one's partner; request for a bid. **b.** A bid doubling one's opponent's bid in bridge thus increasing the penalty for failure to fulfill the contract. **c.** A hand justifying such a bid. —*v.* **-bled, -bling, -bles.** —*tr.* **1.** To make twice as great. **2.** To be twice as much as. **3.** To fold in two. **4.** To duplicate; repeat. **5.** *Baseball.* **a.** To cause the scoring of (a run) by hitting a double. **b.** To advance or score (a runner) by hitting a double. **6.** *Baseball.* To put out (a runner) as the second part of a double play. **7.** To challenge (an opponent's bid) with a double in bridge. **8.** *Mus.* To duplicate (another part or voice) an octave higher or lower or in unison. **9.** *Naut.* To sail around: *double a cape.* —*intr.* **1.** To be increased twofold. **2.** To turn sharply backward; reverse: *double back on one's trail.* **3.** To serve in an additional capacity. **4.** To replace an actor in the execution of a given action or in the actor's absence. **5.** *Baseball.* To hit a double. **6.** To announce a double in bridge. —*phrasal verb.* **double up. 1.** To bend suddenly, as in pain or laughter. **2.** To share accommodations meant for one person. —*adv.* **1. a.** To twice the extent; doubly. **b.** To twice the amount: *double your money back.* **2.** Two together: *sleeping double.* **3.** In two: *bent double.* —*idioms.* **on** (or **at**) **the double.** *Informal.* **1.** In double time. **2.** Immediately. **see double.** To see two images of a single object, usually as a result of visual aberration. [ME < OFr. < Lat. *duplus.*] —**dou′ble·ness** *n.* ⑱

37b Generally, avoid slang. *sl*

Too often slang is a popular rubber stamp that only approximates exact thought. The expression "He's a jerk" does not communicate exactly. It has no precise meaning. It suggests only that he is in some vague way unattractive.

Slang expressions in student papers are usually out of place. They are particularly inappropriate in a context that is otherwise dignified.

> In the opinion of some students, the dean's commencement address *stunk*.
>
> When Macbeth recoiled at the thought of murder, Lady Macbeth urged him not to *chicken out*.

Some slang words are so recent or localized that many people will have no idea of the meaning.

Although slang can be offensive, it is sometimes colorful. Some words that once were slang are now considered Standard English. "Jazz" in its original meaning and "dropout" were once slang; and because no other word was found to convey quite the same social meanings as "date," it is no longer slang. As a rule, however, you should avoid words still considered slang, not only because they are too modern for conservative ears and eyes or because they are offensive to stuffy people, but also because they are generally not as precise or as widely known as Standard English.

37c Avoid dialect. *dial*

Regional, occupational, or ethnic words and usages should be avoided except when they are consciously used to give a special flavor to language.

There is no reason to erase all dialectal characteristics from talk and writing. They are a cultural heritage and a source of richness and variety, but in general communication avoid expressions that are local or substandard.

37d Avoid archaic words. *archaic*

Archaisms (*oft* for "frequent" and *yond* for "yonder") are out-of-date words and therefore inappropriate in modern speech and writing.

■ **Exercise 1**

In class, discuss usage in the following sentences.

1. Teen-agers is just as hip as they ever was, but a lot of them keep their doings quiet.
2. The speedsters heard on their ears that smokey was only three miles away on the blacktop.
3. The hairdresser was shook up because the shoppe had been sold.
4. The teller was instructed to tote the bread back to the vault and to follow the boss to his office.
5. Late payments always gross out sourpuss bill collectors.
6. What cleared him was that the pigs discovered the loot in his friend's suitcase.
7. Ere the rain ceased, the group of tourists were besprinkled, but their enthusiasm was not dampened.
8. He couldn't do nothing without the supervisor's giving him the eyeball and coming down hard on him.
9. The dispatcher reckoned that the plane'd arrive betimes, provided of course that the runways was not congested.
10. The award went to a little-known actress who played good the part of an erstwhile beauty with no brains in her noggin.

37e Do not use a word as a particular part of speech when it does not properly serve that function.

Many nouns, for example, cannot also be used as verbs and vice versa. When in doubt, check the part of speech of a word in a dictionary.

NOUN FOR ADJECTIVE
occupation hazard

VERB DERIVED FROM NOUN FORM
suspicioned

VERB FOR NOUN
good *eats*

VERB FOR ADJECTIVE
militate leader

ADJECTIVE FOR ADVERB
sing *good*

For words that are used inexactly in meaning (rather than function), see **37i.**

37f Use correct idioms.   *id*

An **idiom** is a construction with its own distinct form and meaning. Taken literally, the individual words may seem to mean something entirely different from their meaning in the complete expression. Expressions such as "catch the eye" and "by and large" are strange and puzzling unless their idiomatic meanings are known. Idioms come automatically to one who knows the language well, but they may cause serious difficulties to others.

Be sure that you are using all the words correctly in an idiomatic expression, for one wrong word will make the whole expression a glaring error with an inexact meaning.

Most errors in idioms result from using a preposition and a verb that do not ordinarily belong together.

UNIDIOMATIC	IDIOMATIC
according with	according to
capable to	capable of
conform in	conform to (*or* with)
die from	die of
ever now and then	every now and then
excepting for	except for
identical to	identical with
in accordance to	in accordance with
incapable to do	incapable of doing
in search for	in search of
intend on doing	intend to do
in the year of 1976	in the year 1976
lavish with gifts	lavish gifts on
off of	off
on a whole	on the whole
outlook of life	outlook on life
plan on	plan to
prior than	prior to
similar with	similar to
superior than	superior to
try and see	try to see
type of a	type of

See **49**. Dictionaries list idiomatic combinations for many words and give their exact meanings. See ⑮ on pp. 196–197.

Some word combinations besides those with prepositions are not idiomatic:

The scientists could not *make insights into* the cause of the accident. (Use *understand*.)

The automobile engine has not been started *since* about twenty years. (Use *for*.)

Fair-weathered friends may be true enemies. (Use *fair-weather*.)

■ **Exercise 2**

Select a verb that is the common denominator in several idioms, such as carry (carry out, carry over, carry through, *and so forth*). Look it *up in a dictionary. Study the idioms and be prepared to discuss them in class. Does the change of a preposition result in a different meaning? A slight change in meaning? No change?*

■ **Exercise 3**

Point out the incorrect prepositions and supply the correct ones in the following sentences.

1. All delegates to the meeting were committed <u>for</u> [to] a plan for peace.

2. The jury acquitted him <u>by</u> [of] the charge of loitering.

3. The candidate maintained that he had complied <u>to</u> [with] every one of the laws.

4. The hiker said that he was incapable <u>to</u> [of] going on.

5. The professor stated that his good students would conform <u>with</u> [to] any requirement.

6. The employees complained <u>with</u> [to] the manager because of their long hours.

7. Many vitamins are helpful <u>to</u> [in] preventing diseases.

8. The lecturer took exception <u>about</u> [to] the questioner's final point.

On
9. Upon the whole, matters could be much worse.

in
10. Let us rejoice for the knowledge that we are free.

37g   Avoid specialized vocabulary
in writing for the general reader.   *tech*

All specialists, whether engineers, chefs, or philosophers, have
their own vocabularies. Some technical words find their way into
general use; most do not. The plant red clover is well known, but
not by its botanical name, *Trifolium pratense*.

Specialists should use the language of nonspecialists when
they hope to communicate with general readers. The following
passage, for instance, would not be comprehensible to a wide
audience.

> The neonate's environment consists in primitively contrasted per-
> ceptual fields weak and strong: loud noises, bright lights, smooth
> surfaces, compared with silence, darkness and roughness. The be-
> havior of the neonate has to be accounted for chiefly by inherited
> motor connections between receptors and effectors. There is at this
> stage, in addition to the autonomic nervous system, only the sensori-
> motor system to call on. And so the ability of the infant to discrimin-
> ate is exceedingly low. But by receiving and sorting random data
> through the identification of recurrent regularity, he does begin to
> improve reception. Hence he can surrender the more easily to single
> motivations, ego-involvement in satisfactions.
>
> JAMES K. FEIBLEMAN,
> *The Stages of Human Life: A Biography of Entire Man*

Contrast the above passage with the following, which is on the
same general subject but which is written so that the general
reader—not just a specialized few—can understand it.

Research clearly indicates that an infant's senses are functional at birth. He experiences the whack from the doctor. He is sensitive to pressure, to changes in temperature, and to pain, and he responds specifically to these stimuli. . . . How about sight? Research on infants 4–8 weeks of age shows that they can see about as well as adults. . . . The difference is that the infant cannot make sense out of what he sees. Nevertheless, what he sees does register, and he begins to take in visual information at birth. . . . In summary, the neonate (an infant less than a month old) is sensitive not only to internal but also to external stimuli. Although he cannot respond adequately, he does take in and process information.

IRA J. GORDON,
Human Development: From Birth Through Adolescence

The only technical term in the passage is *neonate;* unlike the writer of the first passage, who also uses the word, the second author defines it for the general reader.

Special vocabularies may obscure meaning. Moreover, they tempt the writer to use inflated words instead of plain ones—a style sometimes known as *gobbledygook* or *governmentese* because it flourishes in bureaucratic writing. Harry S Truman made a famous statement about the presidency: "The buck stops here." This straightforward assertion might be written by some bureaucrats as follows: "It is incumbent upon the President of the United States of America to uphold the responsibility placed upon him by his constituents to exercise the final decision-making power."

37h Avoid triteness and clichés.
Strive for fresh and original expressions.   *trite*

Clichés are phrases and figures of speech that were once fresh and original but have been used so much that they have lost their effectiveness. Avoid extravagance, but be original enough so that your words have the freshness of a newly typed page rather than the faint tracings of a carbon copy.

Study the following twenty phrases as examples of triteness. Avoid pat expressions like these.

words cannot express
each and every
Mother Nature
sober as a judge
other side of the coin
slowly but surely
in this day and age
few and far between
last but not least
interesting to note

method in their madness
straight from the shoulder
first and foremost
hard as a rock
in the final analysis
sweet as sugar
the bottom line
all walks of life
easier said than done
better late than never

37i Be exact. Use words in their precise meanings. *exact*

Misuse of a word so that it does not convey exactly the intended meaning produces confusion. Preciseness requires knowledge of idiom and a good vocabulary. Check a dictionary whenever you have the slightest question. Misuse of *preservation*, for example, for *conservation* would cause misunderstanding. The italicized words in the following sentences are used inexactly.

The new rocket was *literally* as fast as lightning. (*Figuratively* is intended. Use *seems to be.*)

The captain of the team was *overtaken* by the heat. (The proper word is *overcome.*)

Words that are similar in sound but different in meaning can cause the writer embarrassment and the reader confusion.

A wrongful act usually results in a guilty *conscious.* (*conscience*)

The heroine of the novel was not embarrassed by her *congenial* infirmity. (*congenital*)

As the sun beams down, the swamp looks gray; it has only the unreal color of dead *vegetarian. (vegetation)*

A hurricane *reeks* havoc. *(wreaks)*

Displaced persons sometimes have no *lengths* with the past. *(links)*

Words sometimes confused because they sound alike are *climatic* for *climactic, statue* for *stature* (or vice versa), *incidences* for *incidents,* and *course* for *coarse.* Nonwords should never be used: *interpretate* for *interpret,* and *tutorer* for *tutor.*

Sometimes a fancy word seems effective when it is actually inexact in meaning, such as "scenario of the poem" for "story told in the poem." *Scenario* more exactly means "outline."

Inexactness and ambiguity result when a word in a phrase can be perceived in either of two ways; for instance, "perception of the judge" can refer to the understanding *by* the judge of the case or to the understanding *of* the judge by a lawyer.

■ **Exercise 4**

Point out clichés and inexact words and expressions in the following sentences.

1. It goes without saying that the value of a college education cannot be measured in money, but tuition is high as a kite.
2. The meal was fabulous, and the service was fantastic.
3. Although the model claimed she wanted to marry a strong, silent type, she tied the knot with a man who could talk the horns off a billygoat.
4. Holidays always repress some people.
5. On the outskirts of the small town a sign was erected that renounced that this was the home of the one and only Fitz Fritzsimmons.
6. The survivor was weak as a kitten after eight days on the ocean, but his overall condition was unbelievable.

7. The brothers were as different as night and day, but each drank like a fish.
8. The eager young attorney jumped to her feet and cried, "That is irrevelant and immaterial."
9. At the retirement dinner the corporation president toasted the old engineer and told him that his daily presents in the building would be soarly missed.
10. As he looked back, the farmer thought of those mornings as cold as ice when the ground was hard as a rock and when he shook like a leaf as he rose at the crack of dawn.

37j Add new words to your vocabulary. *vocab*

Good writers know many words, and they can select the precise ones they need to express their meanings. A good vocabulary displays your mentality, your education, and your talents as a writer.

In reading, pay careful attention to words you have not seen before. Look them up in a dictionary. Remember them. Recognize them the next time you see them. Learn to use them.

■ **Exercise 5**

Underline the letter identifying the best definition.

1. *contingency:* (a) series (b) important point (c) possible condition (d) rapidly
2. *aegis:* (a) sponsorship (b) eagerness (c) foreign (d) overly proper
3. *summit:* (a) highest point (b) total amount (c) heir (d) exhibition
4. *magnanimity:* (a) state of wealth (b) excellent health (c) strong attraction (d) generosity

5. *credibility:* (a) debt (b) kindness (c) knowledge (d) believability
6. *gullible:* (a) capable of flight (b) flexible (c) easily tricked (d) intelligent
7. *patent:* (a) obvious (b) long-suffering (c) omen (d) victim
8. *audible:* (a) capable of being heard (b) overly idealistic (c) easily read (d) tasty
9. *adamant:* (a) without measure (b) unyielding (c) fragrant (d) judicial decision
10. *travesty:* (a) long journey (b) congested traffic (c) scaffolding (d) mockery
11. *innate:* (a) void of sense (b) inborn (c) applied (d) digestible
12. *acrimonious:* (a) bitter (b) ritualistic (c) hypocritical (d) massive
13. *insurgents:* (a) deep cuts (b) rebels (c) music makers (d) physicians
14. *duress:* (a) fancy dress (b) with quickness (c) stress (d) penalty
15. *flagrant:* (a) odorous (b) conspicuously bad (c) beaten (d) delicious
16. *substantive:* (a) substantial (b) in place of (c) religious (d) hardheaded
17. *imprudent:* (a) unwise (b) lacking modesty (c) ugly (d) incapable of proof
18. *solicitous:* (a) seeking sales (b) without energy (c) heroic (d) concerned
19. *valid:* (a) butler (b) favorable (c) desirable (d) founded on truth
20. *charlatan:* (a) robe (b) quack (c) high official (d) strong wind

■ **Exercise 6**

Underline the letter identifying the best definition.

1. *impetus:* (a) egomaniac (b) incentive (c) ghost (d) perfectionist
2. *dire:* (a) terrible (b) bare (c) final (d) dishonest

3. *subpoena:* (a) below ground (b) in disguise (c) legal summons (d) unspoken
4. *commentary:* (a) explanations (b) military store (c) grouch (d) headland
5. *prodigy:* (a) extraordinary person (b) wasteful person (c) lover of children (d) musician
6. *vacillate:* (a) oil (b) repair (c) waver (d) empty
7. *peer:* (a) an equal (b) an ideal (c) an emotion (d) intense
8. *poignant:* (a) housecoat (b) fruitful (c) hostile (d) piercingly effective
9. *spurious:* (a) brimming over (b) pricking (c) not genuine (d) affectionate
10. *perennial:* (a) continuing (b) circus show (c) circular (d) filial
11. *contend:* (a) incantate (b) appease (c) compete (d) look after
12. *scapegoat:* (a) one being sought (b) one taking blame for others (c) one who looks stupid (d) one guilty of crime
13. *pomposity:* (a) heaviness (b) splendor (c) scarcity (d) self importance
14. *banal:* (a) commonplace (b) fatal (c) aggressive (d) tropical
15. *parameter:* (a) restatement (b) expansion (c) limit (d) device for measuring sound
16. *acute:* (a) appealing (b) severe (c) average (d) unorthodox
17. *vibrant:* (a) blunted (b) double (c) irritating (d) energetic
18. *presume:* (a) guess (b) judge (c) know (d) take for granted
19. *gesture:* (a) demonstration (b) internal disorder (c) joke (d) court clown
20. *veracity:* (a) boldness (b) speed (c) great anger (d) truthfulness

■ **Exercise 7**

Place the number on the left by the appropriate letter on the right.

1. heady	**12**	a.	exaggeration
2. reciprocate	**13**	b.	customary
3. dispiriting	**2**	c.	repay

4. literally		**17**	d.	a ranking
5. consecrate		**15**	e.	imitation
6. bolster		**16**	f.	basic
7. ideology		**4**	g.	in actuality
8. anticipate		**10**	h.	unreal
9. incorrigible		**11**	i.	opposition
10. fantastic		**1**	j.	impetuous
11. antagonism		**14**	k.	a showing forth
12. hyperbole		**18**	l.	one who comes before
13. conventional		**19**	m.	twist
14. manifestation		**9**	n.	not reformable
15. mimicry		**3**	o.	disheartening
16. seminal		**8**	p.	foresee
17. hierarchy		**5**	q.	make sacred
18. predecessor		**7**	r.	set of beliefs
19. distort		**20**	s.	maze
20. labyrinth		**6**	t.	support

■ **Exercise 8**

Select the word or phrase that most exactly defines the italicized word in each sentence.

1. An *obdurate* attitude seldom leads to prosperity. (egotistical, hardhearted, wasteful, false)
2. He felt it his *prerogative* to speak out. (turn, responsibility, right, nature)
3. The speech was marked by *vapid* expressions. (inspiring, dull, vigorous, sad)
4. The *renowned* singer performed in the small town. (famous, unknown, opera, talented)
5. *Gluttony*, explained the slim traveler, was not one of his faults. (hitchhiking, stagnation, overeating, speeding)
6. The banker's *salient* traits were frugality and kindness. (prominent, best, hidden, lacking)

7. Imagining himself a great statesman, he was the prime minister's *lackey*. (assistant, <u>servile follower</u>, hair groomer, moral superior)
8. The *laconic* old woman stood out among the group of excited young men. (<u>untalkative</u>, diseased, depressed, evil)
9. Not all those who took part in the robbery were *depraved*. (needy, <u>evil</u>, prepared, punished)
10. The gem was pronounced an *authentic* emerald. (<u>genuine</u>, artificial, rare, expensive)

■ **Exercise 9**

Follow the instructions for Exercise 8.

1. The judge found the defendant's answer *incredible*. (highly impressive, wonderful, <u>not believable</u>, awful)
2. A *transcript* was made of the tapes. (recording, <u>written copy</u>, mockery, extension)
3. To discuss the matter further would be to *obfuscate* it. (avoid, <u>obscure</u>, criticize, clarify)
4. I *deplore* the method used to recover the gems. (praise, understand, <u>regret</u>, follow)
5. The poem was composed by an *anonymous* author. (dead, foreign, excellent, <u>unknown</u>)
6. Finding the essay *provocative*, she discussed it with her tutor. (<u>stimulating</u>, disgusting, prolonged, offensive)
7. The child *reluctantly* joined her brother in the swimming pool. (rapidly, <u>hesitantly</u>, joyfully, playfully)
8. *Platitudes* can quickly destroy the effectiveness of a lecture. (catcalls, stutterings, <u>stale truisms</u>, bad jokes)
9. A *sorcerer* was said to be the king's only companion. (healer, valiant warrior, jester, <u>wizard</u>)
10. Make the report as *succinct* as possible. (colorful, <u>concise</u>, long, accurate)

■ **Exercise 10**

Dictionaries disagree about the levels of particular words. Read the preliminary pages in your dictionary, and study the labels that it applies to particular words. Webster's New Collegiate Dictionary uses fewer and less restrictive labels than other college dictionaries. Without your dictionary, put by ten of the following words the labels that you believe they should have. Then look up each word and determine which label it has.

   If a word is not labeled, it is considered formal.

1. flat out (at top speed)
2. deck (data-processing cards)
3. gussied up
4. on deck (present)
5. movie
6. ain't
7. cram (to gorge with food)
8. tube (subway)
9. tube (television)
10. phony
11. bash (a party)
12. bash (a heavy blow)
13. enthused
14. pigeon (a dupe)
15. balloon (to rise quickly)
16. freak (an enthusiast)
17. squeal (to betray)
18. deck (a tape deck)
19. wimp
20. on the level

38 Wordiness *w*

Omit needless words.

Conciseness increases the force of writing. Do not pad your paper merely to obtain a desired length or number of words.

USE ONE WORD FOR MANY

   The love letter was written by somebody who did not sign a name. (13 words)

   The love letter was anonymous (*or* not signed). (5 or 6 words)

USE THE ACTIVE VOICE FOR CONCISENESS (SEE **5**)
> The truck was overloaded by the workmen. (7 words)
> The workmen overloaded the truck. (5 words)

REVISE SENTENCES FOR CONCISENESS
> Another element that adds to the effectiveness of a speech is its emotional appeal. (14 words)
> Emotional appeal also makes a speech more effective. (8 words)

AVOID CONSTRUCTIONS WITH *IT IS* . . . AND *THERE ARE* . . . .
> *There are* some conditions *that* are satisfactory. (7 words)
> Some conditions are satisfactory. (4 words)

> *It is* truth *which* will prevail. (6 words)
> Truth will prevail. (3 words)

DO NOT USE TWO WORDS WITH THE SAME MEANING (TAUTOLOGY)
> basic and fundamental principles (4 words)
> basic principles (2 words)

Study your sentences carefully and make them concise by using all the preceding methods. Do not, however, sacrifice concreteness and vividness for conciseness and brevity.

CONCRETE AND VIVID
> At each end of the sunken garden, worn granite steps, flanked by large magnolia trees, lead to formal paths.

EXCESSIVELY CONCISE
> The garden has steps at both ends.

■ **Exercise 11**

Express the following sentences succinctly. Do not omit important ideas.

1. The kudzu plant is a plant that was introduced into America from Japan in order to prevent erosion and the washing away of the land and that has become a nuisance and a pest in some areas because it chokes out trees and other vegetation.

   Kudzu, which was introduced into America from Japan in order to prevent erosion, has become a nuisance in some areas because it chokes out other plants.

2. The cry of a peacock is audible to the ear for miles.

   The cry of a peacock is audible for miles.

3. The custom which once was so popular of speaking to fellow students while passing by them on the campus has almost disappeared from college manners and habits.

   The once-popular custom of speaking to fellow students on the campus has almost disappeared.

4. There are several reasons why officers of the law ought to be trained in the law of the land, and two of these are as follows. The first of these reasons is that policemen can enforce the law better if they are familiar with it. And second, they will be less likely to violate the rights of private citizens if they know exactly and accurately what these rights are.

   Officers should know the law so that they can enforce it better and avoid violating the rights of citizens.

5. Although the Kentucky rifle played an important and significant part in getting food for the frontiersmen who settled the American West, its function as a means of protection was in no degree any less significant in their lives.

   Although the Kentucky rifle played an important part in getting food for the frontiersmen, its protective function was just as significant.

6. Some television programs, especially public television programs, assume a high level of public intelligence and present their shows to the public in an intelligent way.

   Some public television programs assume an intelligent audience and present their shows accordingly.

7. It is not possible that any large American chestnut trees survived the terrible blight of the trees in the year of 1925.
   No large American chestnut trees survived the terrible blight of 1925.

8. The pilot who will fly the plane is a cautious man, and he foresees unusual flying conditions.
   The pilot is a cautious flyer.

9. It is a pleasure for some to indulge in eating large quantities of food at meals, but medical doctors of medicine tell us that such pleasures can only bring with them unpleasant results in the long run of things.
   The joys of overeating, doctors say, can have only unpleasant results.

10. The essay consists of facts that describe vividly many aspects of the work of a typical stockbroker. In this description the author uses a vocabulary that is easy to understand. This vocabulary is on neither too high a level nor too low a level, but on one that can be understood by any high school graduate.
    In simple language the essay describes vividly many aspects of the work of a typical stockbroker.

39 Repetition   *rep*

Avoid redundancy—excessive repetition of words and sounds. Repeat for emphasis rarely and carefully.

Unintentional repetition is seldom effective. Avoid by using synonyms and pronouns and by omitting words.

39a Do not needlessly repeat words.

REPETITIOUS

> The history of human flight is full of histories of failures on the part of those who have tried flight and were failures.

IMPROVED

> The history of human flight recounts many failures.

Do not revise by substituting synonyms for repeated words too often.

WORDY SYNONYMS

> The history of human flight is full of stories of failures on the part of those who have tried to glide through the air and met with no success.

39b Do not needlessly repeat sounds.

REPEATED SOUNDS

> The biologist again *checked* the *charts* to determine the *effect* of the poison on the *insect.*

IMPROVED

> The biologist again studied the charts to determine the effect of the poison on the moth.

39c Repeat only for emphasis or for clarity.

Effective repetition of a word or a phrase may unify, clarify, or create emphasis, especially in aphorisms or poetry.

Searching without knowledge is like *searching* in the dark.
"Beauty is truth, truth beauty." (John Keats)

■ **Exercise 12**

Rewrite the following passage. Avoid wordiness and undesirable repetition.

~~One of the pleasing things that all~~ Peoples of all lands have [and ages]

always enjoyed ~~since the earliest dawning of civilizations is the~~

~~pleasure of listening to the~~ melodious strands of music, [, which] ~~Music,~~

~~wrote some great poet,~~ [some great poet has said] can soothe the savage beast and make

~~him or her~~ [it] calm. ~~A question may arise in the minds of many,~~ [Some younger people, however, may be listening]

~~however, as to~~ ~~whether some of our members of the younger~~ [too frequently to their favorite music.]

~~generation may not be exposing themselves too frequently to~~

~~music they like and listen to almost constantly.~~

~~To me, the answer to the above question is just possibly in~~ [Nearly every day, for example, one meets a young person who lis-]

~~the affirmative, and the evidence that I would give would be in~~ [tens to music]

~~the form of a figure that we see nearly every day. This is the fig-~~

~~ure, usually a young person but not always, of a person with a~~

~~radio or stereo headset who is listening to music~~ while doing

some ~~such~~ activity that ~~used to~~ [should] occupy ~~all of one's~~ [his or her full] attention and

Sometimes a person in the library looks through books while

time. ~~In the library of a college such a figure is now sometimes to~~

wearing a headset.

~~be seen looking through books with a headset on his or her head.~~

of this sort

Some ~~of these~~ music lovers ^ seem incapable of ~~even~~ taking a walk

and enjoying

~~to enjoy~~ the beauty of nature. ~~without their headsets.~~

If we enjoy good music,

~~If music is good and if we enjoy it, the reader may now ask,~~

it as   as modern

what is wrong with listening to ~~music more~~ frequently ~~than we~~

electronics enables us to do? It is not old-fashioned to believe that

~~used to be able to listen to music thanks to the present modern~~

those who spend much of their time with headsets on are missing

~~improvements and developments in the electronic medium? It~~

other important and pleasurable sensory experiences—the sounds of

~~may seem old-fashioned and out-of-date to object to headsets~~

birds and even just the quiet of the morning. Further, it is hard to think

~~just because we did not once have them and they are relatively~~

while the ear is piped full of music. Time that should be used for think-

~~new on the scene. What is important, here, however, is the point~~

ing is also lost—time when we develop and mature intellectually. All

~~that those who spend so much of their time with headsets on are~~

kinds of music, even rock, have an important place, but music should

~~missing something. They may be getting a lot of music, but they~~

not be allowed to exclude too many other valuable experiences.

~~are missing something. What they are missing can be classified~~

~~under the general heading of other important and pleasurable~~

~~sensory experiences that they could be experiencing, such as~~

~~hearing the sounds that birds make and just enjoying the quiet~~

~~that morning sometimes brings. In addition to this, it is hard to~~

~~think while music is being piped into the ear of the listener. We~~

~~lose time, therefore, that should by all rights be reserved for~~

~~thinking and contemplation, which is to say, that time when we all~~

~~develop and mature intellectually. Music, all kinds of music, even~~

~~rock music, has an important place in the lives of humankind, but~~

~~let us not so fall in love with its seductive appeal that beckons us~~

~~that we let it intrude upon the territory of other valuable and es-~~

~~sential experiences.~~

40 Abstract and General Words *abst*

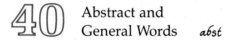

Do not write abstractly or vaguely. Choose specific and concrete words.

Abstract writing may communicate little information or even cause misunderstanding.

Words that pinpoint meaning form the basis of the most exact and the best writing. To describe a sofa as **pleasing** is to be less precise than to say it is **comfortable.** Specific words say what you think. They do not permit disputable or ambiguous meanings.

NOT SPECIFIC
    She complained that *things* prevented her from studying.

SPECIFIC

She complained that *conversations with her friends* prevented her from studying.

Concreteness is relevant in all kinds of writing: a college catalogue; a business letter; instructions on how to put together a gas grill; a speech; a paper; art, fiction, or poetry.

■ Exercise 13

The following ten words or phrases are general. For any five of them substitute four specific and concrete words. Do not let your substitutions be synonymous with each other.

EXAMPLE

    tools   claw hammer, screwdriver, monkey wrench, saw

1. associations
2. rural (or urban) buildings
3. people who are failures
4. works of art
5. terrains
6. nuts (or vegetables, or meats, or breads)
7. missives
8. educational institutions above the second year of college
9. foot races
10. ways to walk

■ Exercise 14

Write your personal definition of one of the following abstract terms in a paragraph of about two hundred words. Give concrete instances from your experience.

education

family

maturity

pride

era

41 Connotation   *con*

Choose words with connotations appropriate to tone and content.

Many words carry special associations, suggestions, or emotional overtones—**connotations.** What *dog* suggests besides the literal *four-legged carnivore* is connotation, which can be pleasant or unpleasant. To one person *dog* may suggest friendship; to another, once attacked by a dog, the word may connote terror.

A good writer uses connotations to evoke planned emotional reactions. To suggest sophistication, the writer may mention a *lap dog;* to evoke the amusing or the rural, *hound dog.* To make a social or moral judgment, the writer may call someone a *cur.* Consider the associations aroused by *canine, pooch, mutt, mongrel, puppy,* and *watchdog.* Even some breeds arouse different responses: *bloodhound, shepherd, St. Bernard, poodle.*

Denotations of words are precise meanings, the exact definitions given in dictionaries. Words that are denotative synonyms may have very different connotative overtones. Consider the following:

drummer—salesperson—field representative
slender—thin—skinny

Be sure that your words give the suggestions you wish to convey.
A single word with the wrong connotation can easily spoil a passage. President Lincoln once said in a speech:

> Human nature will not change. In any future great national trial,
> compared with the men of this, we shall have as weak and as strong,
> as silly and as wise, as bad and as good.

Notice how substituting only a few words ruins the consistent
high tone of the passage, even though the meanings of the substitutes are close to those of the original.

> Folks will not change. In any future great national trial, compared
> with the men of this, we shall have as weak and as strong, as silly
> and as wise, as crooked and as good.

■ Exercise 15

*The ten words or phrases in the left column below name a subject.
The right column gives a word referring to that subject. For each word
in the right column, list a close synonym that is much more favorable
in connotation and another that is less favorable.*

1.	weight	**stout**
2.	intelligence	**sense**
3.	writing style	**intelligible**
4.	food	**edible**
5.	degree of value	**economical**
6.	personality	**fairly agreeable**
7.	physical skill	**coordinated**
8.	exactness of measurement	**close enough**
9.	efficiency	**competent**
10.	beauty	**attractive**

42 Figurative Language *fig*

Avoid mixed and inappropriate figures of speech. Use fresh figures.

Figures of speech compare one thing (usually abstract) with another (usually literal or concrete). Mixed figures associate things that are not logically consistent.

MIXED

> These corporations lashed out with legal loopholes. (You cannot *strike* with a *hole*.)

Inappropriate figures of speech compare one thing with another in a way that violates the mood or the intention.

INAPPROPRIATE

> Shakespeare is the most famous brave in our tribe of English writers. (It is inappropriate and puzzling to compare Shakespeare to an Indian brave and a group of writers to an Indian tribe.)

Use figurative comparisons (of things not literally similar) for vivid explanation and for originality. A simile, a metaphor, or a personification gives you a chance to compare or to explain what you are saying in a different way from the sometimes prosaic method of pure statement, argument, or logic.

METAPHORS (IMPLIED COMPARISONS)

> Though calm without, the young senator was a volcano within.
> Old courthouse records are rotting leaves of the past.

SIMILES (COMPARISONS STATED WITH *LIKE* OR *AS*)

> Though calm without, the young senator was like a volcano within.
> Old courthouse records are like rotting leaves of the past.

■ **Exercise 16**

Explain the flaws in these figures of speech.

1. The new race car flew once around the track and then limped into the pit like a sick horse into its stable.
   Comparing a machine first to a bird and then to a horse is a flawed mixture.
2. The speaker's flamboyant oration began with all the beauty of the song of a canary.
   The volume, pitch, and rhythm of an oration are not embodied well in a sound like the song of a canary.
3. Crickets chirped with the steadiness of the tread of a marching army.
   The pounding of a marching army does not describe the sounds of crickets well.
4. The warm greetings of the students sounded like a horde of apes rushing through a jungle.
   Mannerly human responses are not well expressed in the simile of rushing apes.
5. He nipped the plan in the bud by pouring cold water on all suggestions.
   Nipping (cutting) is not similar to pouring a cold liquid.

■ **Exercise 17**

Compose and bring to class two fresh and appropriate figures of speech.

■ **Exercise 18**

Find two figures of speech in your reading and show how they are mixed or especially appropriate or inappropriate.

43 Flowery Language *fl*

Avoid ornate and pretentious language.

Flowery language is wordy, overwrought, and artificial. Often falsely elegant, it calls attention to itself. In the hope that such language will sound deep and wise, some inexperienced writers substitute it for naturalness and simplicity.

PLAIN LANGUAGE	FLOWERY LANGUAGE
The year 1981	The year of 1981
Now	At this point in time
Lawn	Verdant sward
Shovel	Simple instrument for delving into Mother Earth
A teacher	A dedicated toiler in the arduous labors of pedagogy
Reading a textbook	Following the lamp of knowledge in a textual tome
Eating	Partaking of the dietary sustenance of life
Going overseas	Traversing the ever-palpitating deep

PAPERS

44 Writing Papers

A good paper usually evolves through four basic stages: initial thinking (planning), preliminary writing, revising, and final writing. The same classifications are used for papers as for paragraphs—argument, process, definition, and so forth—so the explanation of paragraph types on pp. 286–291 applies to papers as a whole.

44a Select a good subject.

Although on certain occasions your instructor may assign you a topic, you often will have the responsibility for finding your own. The mental processes through which a writer finally arrives at a good subject for a paper are complex and somewhat mysterious. Writers themselves may not be able to look back and trace with accuracy the specific mental steps that led to the discovery of their subjects. At times a writer labors to come up with something to write about, staring at the blank page or computer screen and wondering where all the ideas have gone. At other times a good subject just seems to pop into the mind without much thought, but it may have been hiding in some deep recess, waiting for its chance to come forward.

Experienced writers know that the most crucial time in the composing process often occurs when a subject is being formed. This period of preparation, sometimes called **prewriting,** is of inestimable importance, whether it covers a short span or a relatively long one. It is a time when you should let your mind play freely over areas of your experience and interest. In doing so you are engaging in an activity called **brainstorming.**

Brainstorming begins with opening up the mind to sudden flurries of ideas. Hard judgments can be suspended until later.

This mental activity is often associated with unexpected inspiration, but with some practice you can initiate and control this method of getting ideas for writing. Learn first to open your mind to all possibilities for topics and second to keep your attention on ideas as they appear rather than allowing your mind to wander away from them. As ideas appear rapidly, some will be immediately appealing. Some will not appeal to you personally more than a moment; some will be too big; others, too skimpy; some will not be appropriate for the kind of assignment. Others will momentarily seem fresh and then turn stale. Retain the promising ones; reject the rest.

Many a good idea for a paper has been lost—that is, forgotten—because it was not recorded when it emerged. You cannot depend on even a sharp and reliable memory to retain fleeting ideas. Therefore, develop the habit of **journal jotting.** Some of the world's greatest writers early in their careers begin the practice of keeping a journal and having it available at all times so that they can write down thoughts that can later be developed. Unless you want to make the entries extensive, you need not do so; jot down just enough to make sure you can remember a promising idea at a later time.

44b   Break the subject down.

Almost as soon as you think of something you want to write about, you should mentally break the subject down into parts, list aspects of it, draw together in clusters those areas that are related, and generally probe for ways of arriving at the points you will want to make in your paper. Some writers prefer to begin writing immediately in order to get something down on paper or on a word processor; they like to allow their thoughts to come during the process of composing. Whichever method suits you, you can use some of the techniques described below, which have been shown to be helpful during this formative stage of composition.

Listing

You may find it helpful to list various points suggested by your general subject. At this stage you do not need to be concerned with their order or final relevance. In fact, you will probably list more points than you will want to make in your paper. The purpose of listing, and of other prewriting strategies, is to get your thoughts on paper and to stimulate further thinking.

Suppose a student is interested in current advertising and has decided to write a paper on some aspect of this subject. He or she might list the following thoughts:

1. Recent advances in ways of presenting products
2. Doctors and attorneys who advertise
3. Selling by mail
4. News commentators who also deliver commercials
5. Opportunities in this field for high-paying positions
6. May be the most competitive of all fields at present
7. Government control of advertising—is it a good idea?
8. For successful firms, is advertising really necessary?
9. Effects of disagreeable advertisements on sales
10. Artistic content of some television advertisements
11. Talk shows that allow guests to plug latest motion picture or book
12. Deceptiveness in methods of advertising
13. Advertisements in newspapers that are made to look like news items
14. Appeals for money on religious programs
15. False advertising
16. The high cost of television advertising
17. Dangers of disguised advertising—brings on loss of trust
18. Ethics—question of whether still important to those who control advertising
19. Advertising and mind control
20. Subliminal messages

The writer has randomly listed almost everything that came to mind—too much for a paper of average length. The list is a good start, however, in exploring the subject of advertising.

Clustering

Relationships among several ideas are often easier to understand when you project them graphically. In **clustering** you draw a diagram rather than write. Just as graphs and maps are useful alternatives to words, this technique of invention and development can aid in revealing connections among ideas. Begin by writing down your principal subject and circling it. Then as sub-ideas come to you, jot them down, circle them, and draw connecting lines to reveal relationships that you have perceived.

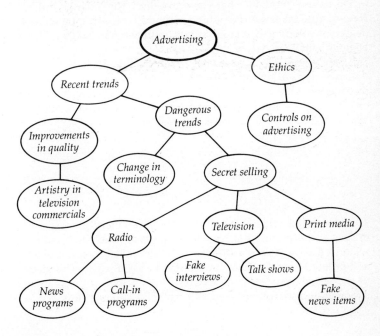

A large blackboard is ideal for this kind of exercise when you are developing a subject, working through a mental puzzle. You can erase frequently and substitute new ideas. If a blackboard is not available, you can achieve much the same effect with pencil and paper. However you do it, clustering enables you to view the subject from different perspectives and to see graphically how the composite parts are related.

Freewriting

Some writers prefer not to begin writing before they have given their subject a good deal of thought and planning; others find that the discovery process can occur during the act of writing. The problem is how to get started. One way is to begin by expressing in words any thoughts that come to mind. This activity, called **freewriting,** takes a writer where whims dictate. At some point a degree of coherence emerges out of fragmentation; related ideas begin to appear.

Freewriting usually does not produce a first draft. It is a preliminary step—the written form of brainstorming. It is a way of discovering what you want to write about as you write, a way of overcoming the inhibitions some people experience when they view a blank sheet of paper or a blank screen.

44c Find the center.

The ideas made available through the preliminary processes of finding and exploring a subject for its parts are likely to be somewhat in disarray. They will need to be examined closely, culled, and ordered to make them contribute to a good paper. This stage of the writing process is necessary if the finished paper is to be coherent and sharply focused, not rambling and pointless.

Before you can shape your ideas into a cohesive argument, however, you must determine precisely what it is you wish to say. Each paper should have a clear center from which all the details and illustrations radiate. If you do not determine the heart of the matter before you really begin writing your paper, you will fail to present your ideas well.

When you pin the central idea down, you can usually express it in a single sentence, called the **thesis statement.** Many instructors require you to compose a specific and concise statement and to include it in your first or second paragraph in order to give your readers (and yourself) a good sense of direction.

A thesis statement tells in a few words what your argument *is*, not what your argument is *about*.

NOT

> The purpose of this paper is to reveal a dangerous trend in modern advertising, selling disguised as something else. (A description, not a thesis statement.)

NOT

> The media should be careful that all advertisements are aboveboard. (A thesis statement, but not a good one because it is not specific enough.)

BUT

> Advertising in the guise of news or personal commentary represents a disturbing trend in radio, television, and the print media.

44d Organize effectively.

What to put where can be a problem—although sometimes the blocks fall naturally into place after you have thought through the subject. You may or may not need an outline, depending on the extent to which the development process has already unfolded in your mind. It is a good idea to set out with some sort of plan, though, even if you require only a brief one. Three of the most common kinds of outlines are described below.

Scratch outline

This is the simplest kind of outline: a list of points to make, in order but without subdivisions. It is a quick way to organize your thoughts and to remind yourself of their order while you are writing. For brief papers, those written in class, and essay examinations, a scratch outline often suffices. You might use the following points for a scratch outline of a paper entitled "Secret Selling":

> some positive aspects of modern advertising
> a negative factor—secret selling
> in radio, television, and newspapers
> what should be done about it

Topic outline

The topic outline is a formal, detailed structure to help you organize your materials. Observe the following conventions:

1. Number the main topics with Roman numerals, the first subheadings with capital letters, and the next with Arabic numbers. If further subheadings are necessary, use a, b, c and (1), (2), (3).

```
    I. ...........................................................................................
       A. ......................................................................................
          1. .................................................................................
             a. ..............................................................................
                (1) ........................................................................
                (2) ........................................................................
             b. ..............................................................................
          2. .................................................................................
       B. ......................................................................................
   II. ...........................................................................................
```

2. Use parallel grammatical structures.
3. Write down topics, not sentences.
4. Do not place periods after the topics.
5. Punctuate as in the example that follows.
6. Check to see that your outline covers the subject fully.
7. Use specific topics and subheadings arranged in a logical, meaningful order.
8. Be sure that each level of the outline represents a division of the preceding level and has a smaller scope.
9. Avoid single subheadings. If you have a Roman numeral I, you should also have a II, and so forth.

INCORRECT
  I. Current advertising in the media
     A. Recent improvements   ⟵ *B. Another subheading is needed.*
 II. Advertising in the guise of news

Here is an example of a topic outline with a title, a thesis statement, and a series of orderly and carefully developed topics:

Secret Selling

Thesis statement: Advertising in the guise of news or personal commentary represents a disturbing trend in radio, television, and the print media.

  I. Current advertising in the media
     A. Recent improvements
     B. Change in terminology
 II. Advertising in the guise of news
     A. Radio
        1. News commentators
        2. Talk-radio hosts
     B. Television
        1. Popular talk shows
        2. Advertisements with talk-show format
     C. Print media

III. Dangers of secret selling
    A. Increasing deceptiveness
    B. Growing public distrust

Sentence outline

The sentence outline is an extensive form of preparation for writing a paper. More thinking goes into it than into a scratch or topic outline, but the additional effort usually enables you to keep tight control over your writing. The sentence outline follows the same conventions as the topic outline, but the entries are expressed in complete sentences. Place periods after sentences in a sentence outline.

Secret Selling

Thesis statement: Advertising in the guise of news or personal commentary represents a disturbing trend in radio, television, and the print media.

  I. Because of keen competition in the marketplace, advertisers are constantly searching for more effective and more imaginative ways to present their products.
    A. Many of these ways constitute advances in creative advertising.
    B. A less positive tendency is suggested by a change in terminology to refer to commercial presentations.
 II. One alarming trend is the frequent failure to identify the act of selling for what it is.
    A. Radio appears to lend itself especially well to secret selling.
      1. News commentators sometimes do not indicate when they have stopped giving news and started selling a product.
      2. Hosts on talk-radio programs are on occasion guilty of mixing opinions with advertisements.
    B. Disguised advertising is also evident on television.
      1. Popular talk shows allow guests to discuss their latest movies, books, and enterprises—a form of undercover advertising.
      2. Recently, half-hour and hour programs that resemble interviews or talk shows but are actually efforts to sell a specific product have appeared.

    C. Newspapers and magazines have a rule that advertisements must be identified as such, but ingenious methods are being used to blur the once-clear line between news and commercial selling.
III. Secret selling is a dangerous form of advertising.
    A. It could become even more deceptive in the future.
    B. Because of it, the public might finally come to distrust all advertising.

44e Adapt your writing to your audience.

Prepare yourself to reach your audience effectively. Consider the following questions. How much information do members of the audience have on the subject you are dealing with? What is their average level of education? Are they likely to have strong opinions one way or the other on the topic? What lines of work or study are they engaged in as a rule? Do they fall into a definite age group? Writers who ignore such important considerations are inviting rejection. Mark Twain learned the necessity of carefully matching writing with audience when he composed and delivered a humorous but rather crude series of caricatures to an audience of distinguished and highly dignified New England writers whom he greatly admired and did not wish to insult. The performance was received with stony silence by the offended audience, and Mark Twain regretted his misjudgment for life.

Although your instructor may ask you to write for specialized audiences, usually papers are composed with *general readers* in mind: educated adults who do not have highly specialized vocabularies and who are interested in a wide variety of general subjects. To keep their attention, you must be intelligent, interesting, rational, and clear. Writing a paper is an act of communication, not merely an exercise or an opportunity for self-expression.

Resist the temptation to write solely for an individual professor. Frustrated students who complain that they do not know what their professors want in a paper can often avoid this needless exercise in trial and error by concentrating on a general audience. If you compose with only your professor in mind, you might write somewhat over your head or employ obscure or flowery language.

Audience awareness helps you to become a better judge of your own writing and consequently to revise more successfully. By learning to read your writing as your audience will, you can communicate with greater clarity and grace.

■ Exercise 1

Think of an experience in which you felt that you were wronged or in which you wronged someone: something involving a store, an automobile repair shop, a restaurant, an insurance company, or the like. Then write about this experience three times, with three audiences in mind: (1) close friends; (2) managers, supervisors, or owners of the business; (3) readers of a large local newspaper. All three writings may be in the form of letters.

44f Sustain an appropriate tone.

Tone derives from attitude. If you are displeased, you can show that attitude through your choice of words. If you are amused and wish to pass that attitude on to your audience, you can do so by creating a humorous tone. Enthusiasm, urgency, fear, objectivity, displeasure, playfulness, skepticism—all can be conveyed effectively, but first you have to determine precisely what attitude you wish to communicate. Trouble occurs when a writer is uncertain what tone to take and suddenly switches unthinkingly from one attitude to another, as in the following example.

Art critics have the power to make or break young painters. Their word is especially influential among collectors and wealthy investors who deal in art. If a few of these better-known critics praise a given artist, he or she can rise almost overnight from struggling anonymity to wealthy repute. Conversely, all it takes is a negative opinion from them to doom an aspiring artist. Do these critics exercise their enormous power responsibly? They care only for themselves. *Shift* They are shameless frauds who invent nonsense about art and pass *in* it off as the truth. They are arrogant and effete impostors who de- *tone* serve to be whipped.

At the beginning of the passage, emotions are under control and the tone is coolly objective. Then the tone changes abruptly as an angry outburst destroys what could otherwise be a convincing argument. If the writer had decided ahead of time to make indignation the prevailing tone of the essay, he or she could have written indignantly but thoughtfully and effectively. As it is, the writing is ineffectual because the sudden shift in tone confuses readers.

Whatever tone you choose, sustain it carefully; do not shift back and forth from one attitude to another. In general, avoid flippancy and sarcasm. Flippancy in writing is often the mark of immaturity. Sarcasm is difficult to sustain without creating hostility.

44g Before writing the final version, compose a draft.

A rough draft is a necessary step toward a finished paper. Writers who go directly from an outline to what they consider the final copy usually produce a much less effective paper than they could have otherwise. Do not worry about how you are expressing your ideas in your draft; simply get them down first. After that you can make improvements.

Read the following draft of a paper on "Secret Selling":

Secret Selling

Advertisers face keen competition in the marketplace these days. Therefore, advertisers are constantly searching for more efficient, more imaginative, and more creative ways to present their various products. Due to this tendency to find new avenues of approach, a tendency is developing to present advertisements, not as attempts to sell but as attempts to inform. For example, many television programs have stopped calling their commercial announcements by the name of commercials or referring to the commercials as "a word from our sponsor" and are labelling them "messages." A message is news. Usually eagerly awaited. This change in terminology is significant. Not all that is happening in advertising is progressive and encouraging. As in almost every endeavor, "progress" is accompanied by certain unsavory activities.

Advertisements sometimes blend in to such an extreme extent, that it may be difficult to tell what is selling and what is telling. I find it alarming that they fail to identify an act of

2

selling as an act of selling. Advertising in the guise of news or personal commentary represents a disturbing trend in radio, television, and the print media.

Before mentioning a certain product by name, a news commentator may indicate that some new discovery has been made or at last a great need has been met, making the advertisement sound a lot like a news item. So this same voice that has just been bringing the news and commenting on events will launch into the advocacy of a brand of roach poison, or a new kind of sunglasses without giving us any notification that he has started on a commercial. Now if this commentator happens to be well known, prominent, and widely trusted for giving accurate details and for exercing sound judgment, the public is more likely to buy the product. The commentator has unfairly used his prestige to sell something, and he is doing it as if he is still giving the news. So radio appears to lend itself especially well to the art of secret selling. Those who host call-in programs on radio have also been known to indulge in this form

3

of selling. After acquiring a wide audience of admirers who respect their opinions, these talk-radio
hosts then endorse products as if they are endorsing ideas.

For many years, popular talk shows on television have partially paid guests for their appearances by allowing them to plug their latest movie,
book or whatever. They make this sound like current events but it is actually disguised advertising. Another development has been shows that have
appeared recently that are like talk shows, but
they are not. They use the same format but they
center the entire discussion on some single topic--
like the latest developments in hair loss or skin
care. So-called "authorities" answer questions
posed by the so-called "host" and sometimes telephone calls coming in from the home viewing
audience are allowed. It looks just like a legit-
imate interview or talk show, but the whole thing
is a mere set-up for the sole purpose of selling
things like preparations to restore hair loss or to
prevent wrinkled skin.

4

The print media is just as bad. Although they have a rule that advertisements must be identified as advertisements, they get around this with ingenious methods in order to make the advertisements look like news. A newspaper advertisement may carry a headline that very much resembles one designating an important story. Sometimes these are in very large black letters. The body of the article may be almost identical with that of a news item and may even include a by-line. What is in actuality an attempt to push, say, a certain brand of home computers looks like news about how modern technology recently made an enterprising person rich and famous. If the article did not have a thin black border around it with the scarcely noticeable words "paid advertisement" printed near it, then it would not be much different in its appearance from reports of world events.

Much is wrong with secret selling. But chiefly the problem with it is that it is just not what it appears to be, it is just plain deception at its base. At this point in time the wary consumer can

5

usually spot attempts at secret selling, but if the
trend goes on for much longer, and the line between
genuine news or educational material breaks down
even further, trust will eventually break down
between the public and its suppliers. Secret selling should therefore be identified for what it is--
a form of deception--and prohibited as such.

44h Revise the draft.

Even though you may be pleased with what you have written in
the draft, do not regard it as final before scrutinizing it carefully.
Look first for the big problems—those in focus, organization, development, and so forth. If you learn to read your own work with
an editor's eye, you will almost always find material you wish to
delete or move. You may spot statements that badly need more
development or illustration. Occasionally you will need to throw
away an entire draft and begin over.

Notice how the writer has made major revisions in the first
paragraph of the paper on "Secret Selling."

Secret Selling

Advertisers face keen competition in the marketplace these days. Therefore, advertisers are constantly searching for more efficient, more imaginative, and more creative ways to present their various products. Due to this tendency to find new avenues of approach, a tendency is developing to present advertisements, not as attempts to sell but as attempts to inform. For example, many television programs have stopped calling their commercial announcements by the name of commercials or referring to the commercials as "a word from our sponsor" and are labelling them "messages." A message is news. Usually eagerly awaited. This change in terminology is significant. Not all that is happening in advertising is progressive and encouraging. ~~As in almost every endeavor, "progress" is accompanied by certain unsavory activities.~~

In recent years television commercials have become so creative and entertaining that many are widely praised and appreciated. Advertisements on radio stations, in magazines, and in newspapers are also generally attractive and often technically sophisticated.

To introduce advertisements, announcers frequently say, "And now for these messages."

After major revisions (sometimes called **global revisions**), you can turn to the fine-tuning of the writing process—correcting errors in spelling, punctuation, and mechanics and making changes that clear up problems with repetition, diction, and so forth. Below is the first paragraph of "Secret Selling" with the student's final revisions.

Secret Selling

Because of ~~Advertisers face~~ keen competition in the marketplace, ~~these days,~~ ~~Therefore,~~ advertisers are constantly searching for more efficient, *and* more imaginative, ~~and more creative~~ ways to present their ~~various~~ products. In recent years television commercials have become so creative and entertaining that many are widely praised and appreciated. Advertisements on radio stations, in magazines, and in newspapers are also generally attractive and often technically sophisticated. Not all that is happening in ~~advertising~~ *this area, however,* is progressive and encouraging. ~~Due to this tendency to find new avenues of approach,~~ *a* ~~a~~ tendency is developing to present advertisements, not as attempts to sell but as *efforts* ~~attempts~~ to inform. For example, many television programs have stopped calling their commercial announcements by *that* ~~the~~ name ~~of commercials~~ or refer-

ring to ~~the commercials~~ *them* as "a word from our sponsor"

and are ~~labelling~~ *labeling* them "messages." To introduce

advertisements, announcers frequently say, "And now

for these messages." A message is news, *U*sually

eagerly awaited. This change in terminology is

significant.

After revising and before submitting your paper, read it over two or three times, at least once aloud. Listen for annoying repetitions. Compare the finished copy of the paper on "Secret Selling" on pp. 250–253 to the draft on pp. 240–244.

You will find the following checklist helpful during the process of writing and revising as well as just before turning in your paper.

Checklist

Title

The title should accurately suggest the contents of the paper.

It should attract interest without being excessively novel or clever.

It should not be too long.

NOTE: Do not underline the title of your own paper, and do not put quotation marks around it.

Introduction

The introduction should be independent of the title. No pronoun or noun in the opening sentence should depend for meaning on the title.

It should catch the reader's attention.

It should properly establish the tone of the paper as serious, humorous, ironic, or otherwise.

It should include a thesis statement which declares the subject and the purpose directly but at the same time avoids worn patterns like "It is the purpose of this paper to. . . ."

Body

The materials should develop the thesis statement.

The materials should be arranged in logical sequence.

Strong topic sentences (see **44c**) should clearly indicate the direction in which the paper is moving and the relevance of the paragraphs to the thesis statement.

Technical terms should be explained.

Paragraphs should not be choppy.

Adequate space should be devoted to main ideas. Minor ideas should be subordinated.

Concrete details should be used appropriately. Insignificant details should be omitted.

Transitions

The connections between sentences and those between paragraphs should be shown by appropriate linking words and by repetition of parallel phrases and structures. (See **46h**.)

Conclusion

The conclusion should usually contain a final statement of the underlying idea, an overview of what the paper has demonstrated.

The conclusion may require a separate paragraph; but if the paper has reached significant conclusions all along, such a paragraph is not necessary for its own sake.

The conclusion should not merely restate the introduction.

Proofreading

Allow some time, if possible at least one day, between the last draft of the paper and the final, finished copy. Then you can examine the paper objectively for wordiness, repetition, incorrect diction, misspellings, faulty punctuation, choppy sentences, vague sentences, lack of transitions, and careless errors.

44i Learn from your mistakes.

The process of composition is not complete until you have carefully examined your paper after it is returned to you, looked up your errors in this book and in a dictionary so that you understand how to correct them, and revised along the lines suggested by your instructor. Learn from your mistakes so that the same problems do not turn up in future papers.

Model paper

Secret Selling

Because of keen competition in the marketplace, advertisers are constantly searching for more efficient and more imaginative ways to present their products. In recent years television commercials have become so creative and entertaining that many are widely praised and appreciated. Advertisements on radio stations, in magazines, and in newspapers are also generally attractive and often technically sophisticated. Not all that is happening in this area, however, is progressive and encouraging. A tendency is developing to present advertisements not as attempts to sell but as efforts to inform. For example, many television programs have stopped calling their commercial announcements by that name or referring to them as "a word from our sponsor" and are labeling them "messages." To introduce advertisements, announcers frequently say, "And now for these messages." A message is news, usually eagerly awaited. This change in terminology is significant.

2

More alarming is the failure to identify at all the act of selling for what it is. Advertisements sometimes blend in to such an extent that it may be difficult to tell what is selling and what is telling. Advertising in the guise of news or personal commentary represents a disturbing trend in radio, television, and the print media.

Radio appears to lend itself especially well to secret selling. At times the same voice that has been bringing the news and commenting on events will launch into the advocacy of a brand of roach poison or a new kind of sunglasses without any notification that a commercial presentation has begun. Before mentioning a product by name, the commentator may indicate that some new discovery has been made or that at last a great need has been met, making the advertisement sound like a news item. If this person happens to be well known and widely trusted for giving accurate details and for exercising sound judgment, the public is more likely to buy the product. Those who host call-in programs on radio also indulge frequently in this form of selling. After acquiring a wide audience

3

of admirers who respect their opinions, these talk-radio hosts then endorse products on their programs as if they are endorsing ideas.

For many years, popular talk shows on television have paid guests low fees for their appearances but allowed them to speak of their latest motion picture, book, or commercial undertaking (whether it be a line of suits or wigs). This information is introduced as current events, but in fact it is disguised advertising. Recently, half-hour and hour programs that use the talk-show format have appeared in which the entire discussion centers on a single topic, such as the latest developments in research on hair loss or skin care. So-called authorities answer questions from the host and sometimes telephone calls from the viewing audience. In appearance these are public information events, but they are set up for the sole purpose of selling preparations to restore hair or to prevent wrinkled skin.

Although newspapers and magazines require advertisements to be identified as such, ingenious methods are presently used to blur the once clear

4

line between news and commercial selling. A newspaper advertisement may carry a headline that very
much resembles that designating an important story.
The body of the article may be almost identical
with that of a news item and may even include a by-
line. What is actually an attempt to sell, say, a
certain brand of home computers looks like news
about how modern technology recently made an enterprising person rich. If the article did not have a
thin black border around it with the scarcely
noticeable words "paid advertisement" printed near
it, it would not differ in appearance from reports
of world events.

The problem with such camouflaged advertising
is that it appears to be something that it is not.
Its base is deception. At present the wary consumer
can usually spot attempts at secret selling, but if
the trend continues and the line between genuine
news or educational material and advertising becomes
ever fainter, then trust between the public and its
suppliers will eventually break down. Secret selling should therefore be identified for what it is--
a form of deception--and prohibited.

44j   Composing and revising on a word processor

Many of the writing techniques discussed in this chapter—for example, freewriting and listing—can be effectively practiced on a personal computer with a word processing system. Indeed, some writers find it easier to initiate the flow of ideas on a word processor than to do so on a typewriter or with pen and paper. Thoughts can be recorded on the screen and discarded or retained quickly and easily. The current popularity of word processors is based not merely on their ability to save time; more important, they enable people to engage in the process of creating without interrupting the flow of mental current, as other methods of writing can.

If you are used to writing drafts of papers in longhand or on a typewriter, you probably have a built-in resistance to throwing away sheets of paper and beginning all over again, recopying, retyping. The awareness of inconvenience often acts as a psychological barrier to thorough revisions of drafts. With a word processor you can insert words, sentences, and paragraphs, make minor or extensive changes in wording, delete passages, and revise in other ways with an ease undreamed of a few years ago. You should use this ability to cultivate the habit of more thorough revising.

If you do not have access to a word processor or if you prefer not to use one, do not feel hopelessly disadvantaged or backward. You can increase and maintain your effectiveness as a writer with the traditional, time-proven methods. Word processors will not make you more intelligent or imaginative. They are superb tools, but like all tools they have their limitations. A word processor can revolutionize the somewhat arduous procedure of revising, but at the same time it can make it more difficult for you to create an effective organization for your paper. Users often complain that proofreading on screen is difficult, and almost every devotee of computers has a story about how valuable material has been irretrievably lost because of a brief interruption in the supply of electricity.

Recent innovations bring solutions but can create new problems. A spelling checker on a word processor, for example, can help you produce a correctly spelled paper, but it may discourage you from looking up words in a dictionary and thus act as a barrier to your becoming a better speller. Recently a prominent journalist complained that he has become so fascinated with the wonders of his time-saving computer that he wastes hours and hours of valuable time experimenting with it. A word processor can help you significantly but only as long as you use it rather than allow it to use you.

Subjects for papers

Keep a notebook of items that you think may be useful to you as possible subjects and materials for papers. Some suggestions follow, but many will need narrowing or refining.

Government Sponsored
   Lotteries
Survival Training
Living for the Future
Escalation of Medical Costs
Daydreaming
True Beauty
Peer Pressure
Egotism—Its Results
The Teenager in Current
   Films
Old Photographs
Fair Journalism
Return to the Country
Political Cartoons
The New Music
Divorce
Freedom vs. Responsibility

Taking Risks
Living for the Moment
Living in the Past
Helping Others
Handling Disappointment
Laughter as Medicine
The Illusion of Equality
Three Types of Drivers
Dieting
The Inner City
Bad Teaching
Abortion
Television Commercials
Invasion of Privacy
Working in a Political
   Campaign
Homelessness
Educating the Parent

The Pursuit of Pleasure
Gestures and Body Language
From Outer Space
A Deserted House
Repaying Victims of Crime
Exploring Caves
The Scientific Attitude
The Emergency Room
An Intense Emotional
    Experience

Camping Out
Future of Our National Parks
Censorship
Varieties of Greed
Credit Cards: The Plastic
    Economy
Welfare
Acting in a Play
Superficial Fashion Trends

Part of finding a subject for your paper is establishing a point of view. Note how each of the following groups presents three points of view on the same subject. In selecting a topic, you may choose one of the statements below or take a stand on an issue of your own choosing.

1. A. Each generation passes on to its children a better world.
   B. Each generation passes on to its children a world in worse condition than it was before.
   C. The condition of the world, everything considered, is always just about the same.

2. A. The best way to win an argument is never to let the opponent talk much.
   B. Silence wins the most arguments.
   C. In any argument, say just a little, but say it well.

3. A. A democracy is obligated to give every person an education.
   B. Educational institutions and agencies should carefully supervise admissions according to talent and abilities.
   C. Colleges should not bother to educate students who are below average in intelligence or learning.

4. A. Optimism and belief in progress have long characterized most American thought.
   B. Optimism and belief in progress have greatly declined in the last two decades.

C. Modern problems make it necessary for Americans who strongly believe in optimism and progress to temper their views.

5. A. If technology is allowed to advance without any interference from environmental interest groups, it will advance far enough to restore any environmental damage.
   B. It is impossible for technology to continue to develop at its present pace without irreparably damaging the environment.
   C. It is possible for technology to develop in such a way that any adverse effect on the environment is minimal.

6. A. Credit buying has been the ruin of the middle class.
   B. Credit buying has made demand strong and hence our economy strong.
   C. Although middle-class families should watch their credit buying, purchases of homes and cars strengthen certain industries and allow families to enjoy these products for many years without great financial harm.

ACCURATE THINKING AND WRITING

45   Logic and Accuracy   *log*

In speech or in writing, convey your thinking accurately and
clearly. Do not talk or write in a way that misleads or gives false information or conclusions. Present facts without error, reach logical
conclusions from facts, and state conclusions clearly. In an argument, admit uncertainties and concede the possible merits of opposing points of view.

The two most common forms of reasoning are **inductive** and
deductive. Which of these forms you use determines your method
of writing—the order, sequence, kind of beginning, procedure, and
presentation of the conclusion.

Inductive thinking

Inductive thinking and writing begins with specifics, then draws
conclusions from this evidence.

 I. Substance of the reasoning—information derived from experiments,
    examples, cases, related facts, statistics, and other specific data
II. Conclusions—general principles derived from the materials examined

Deductive thinking

Deductive writing follows a pattern of thinking almost exactly
opposite that of inductive writing. It begins with a general principle (usually stated near the beginning) and shows how the principle prevails in particular instances.

 I. Statement of the principle, truth, or rule
II. Applications to examples, cases, new situations, specific aspects of
    large problems, and other particular instances

Both inductive thinking and deductive thinking are tested and questioned by those to whom the conclusions are presented. Of an inductive thinker, one asks whether the facts are true, whether the exceptions have been noted, whether the selection of materials is representative, whether the conclusions are truly and accurately drawn from the data, whether the conclusions are stated precisely or exaggerated. Of a deductive thinker, one asks whether the given principle is impartial truth or mere personal opinion, whether it is applied to materials relevantly, whether the conclusion is accurate according to the principle, and whether exceptions have been noted.

With good motives and bad, with honesty and with deceit, different thinkers reach different conclusions derived from the same data or from the same principles. Learn to discriminate between sound and illogical reasoning. Indeed, when you write, you must constantly question your own reasoning. Watch for errors in thinking, which are called **logical fallacies.**

45a Use accurate information. Check the facts.

Facts can be demonstrated. They form the bases of judgments. Distinguish carefully between the facts and the judgments derived from them, and then explain how one comes from the other.

Errors, whether of fact, ignorance, or dishonesty, make the reader suspicious and lead to distrust. An otherwise compelling argument crumbles when just one or two facts are shown to be wrong. The following statements contain factual errors.

MISINFORMATION PRESENTED AS FACT

Columbus was indisputably the first European to step on the North American continent.

>   *In fact:* Some historians assert that other Europeans, especially
>   Vikings, came to America before Columbus.
>   Some historians believe Columbus never set foot on the
>   North American mainland.

Hot water will freeze faster than cold water when placed in a
freezer.

>   *In fact:* Physicists state that cold water freezes faster. (However,
>   water that has been heated and has cooled will freeze
>   more quickly than water that has not been heated.)

45b   Use reliable authorities.

Not all so-called or self-proclaimed specialists are reliable. Do not
accept everything in print as authoritative. Consider the following criteria in evaluating authorities:

1. When was the work published? (An old publication may contain superseded information.)
2. Who published the work? (University presses and well-estab-
   lished publishing houses employ informed consultants,
   whereas others may not.)
3. Does the work have a reputation for reliability? (For example,
   how has it been evaluated by other authorities in annotated
   bibliographies and in reviews?)
4. Is the presumed authority writing about his or her own field?
   (An atomic scientist may not be an expert on the life and writings of Shakespeare.)
5. Are the language and the tone reasonable, or does the authority attempt to persuade by using ornate rhetoric or slanted
   words and terms?
6. Does the authority show objectivity by admitting the existence
   of facts that seem contradictory?
7. Does the authority distinguish fact from opinion?

45c Avoid sweeping generalizations. Allow for exceptions.

Avoid exaggerations. Do not make statements about *everyone* or *everything* or *all* when you should refer to *some* or *part*. Do not be too inclusive. Such writing can be naive or deceitful. Do not convey wrong information about exceptions to a general principle.

EXCESSIVE GENERALIZATION
    Poor people do not get fair trials in courts.

FAIRER
    Poor people *often* do not get fair trials in courts, in many cases because they cannot pay for good attorneys.

Generalizations about nationalities and race are often pernicious.

EXCESSIVE GENERALIZATION
    Russian athletes are the best in the world.

FAIRER
    Russian athletes have had extraordinary success in world competition.

Caution: You cannot avoid or justify exaggeration and excessive generalization by adding a phrase such as "in my opinion."

45d Use specific and adequate evidence to support your argument.

Depend on an adequate number of examples, statistics, polls of public opinion, and other accurate information. Gather your data from sources that you have chosen fairly and representatively. Determine and report how absolute your evidence is. It can be fact (compare sections **45a** and **45b**), or it can suggest probability. Indicate whether you are dealing with incontrovertible fact or probable opinion.

45e Stick to the point.

Be sure you have a point, and then do not wander off the subject. Test every sentence to see whether it has a place in the discussion and that it is not simply a digression or an extraneous comment.

First and last paragraphs of papers can be especially problematical if they begin or end at a point too far removed from the subject. Failure to focus the reader's attention on the main topic causes loss of power and conviction in writing.

For further help in sticking to the point and examples of failure to do so, see unity in paragraphs (pp. 276–278).

45f Recognize and admit conflicting views.

Be aware of information and opinions that seem to refute or qualify your views and conclusions. Deal with them fully and honestly. You can actually strengthen your case by taking opposing opinions into consideration.

45g Do not reason in a circle.

Reasoning in a circle (often called "begging the question") begins with an assumption—an idea that requires proof—and then asserts that principle without ever offering proof. It states the same thing twice.

> Universal education is necessary because everyone ought to have an education.
>
> Some brokers are ambitious simply because they wish to succeed.

45h Do not substitute appeals to emotion for appeals to reason.

Appeals to emotion ignore reasoning and attempt to convince without requiring reliable thinking. Labels attempt to shape an attitude by prejudice rather than logic.

Name-calling refers to the practice of labeling someone who does not share your views an idiot, for example. This is an argument against a person rather than one against a principle or a point of view.

Flattery attempts to persuade through excessive praise. The political candidate who tells the people that he knows they will vote for him because of their high intelligence is attempting to convince by flattering.

Snob appeal asserts that one should adopt a certain view because all the better people do. The use of athletes, beauty queens, or motion picture stars in advertising is a form of snob appeal.

Mass appeal attempts to persuade by asserting that everyone follows a certain pattern. One who does not follow the herd is said to be in error (*everyone ought* to go to college; *everyone ought* to own a home).

45i Draw accurate conclusions about cause and effect.

Exact causes of conditions and events are often difficult to determine, just as the effects of an action or a circumstance are. Consider all possible causes and effects.

A condition that precedes another is not necessarily the cause of it (technically, this kind of error is called *post hoc, ergo propter hoc*). Similarly, it does not necessarily follow that one condition in a relationship is logically the effect of another *(non sequitur)*.

> The defending champions lost the toss of the coin before the game; they could not expect to win this year.
>
> Because the writer is very young, the novel he has published is surely a bad book.

45j Be moderate.

Be temperate in your judgments and choice of words. Overstatement and overemphasis to make a point may irritate readers and arouse doubt or even disbelief. The temptation to exaggerate is natural, but moderation and even understatement convince where brashness and arrogance alienate.

45k Avoid the *either . . . or* fallacy (also called false dilemma).

Allow for adequate possibilities. When more than two choices exist, do not illogically assert that there are only two.

Either coauthors must do all their writing together, or they will not be able to write their book.

Children either do very well in school, or they remain illiterate.

45L Avoid illogicalities created by careless wording.

What is clear in a writer's mind can be confusing and illogical when it is expressed because of a careless choice of words.

INCORRECT

I was the last of my roommates to arrive home. (Logically, the writer is a roommate but not, as the sentence implies, his or her *own* roommate.)

CORRECT

I arrived home after all my roommates.

Frequently confusion and unintentional humor result from a passage by a writer who may be thinking but is not composing logically:

When I was barely seventeen, I became engaged. My father was happy and sad at the same time. My mother was just the opposite. (How can one be "the opposite" of "happy and sad at the same time"? What the writer probably means is that her father had mixed feelings about her engagement but her mother was strongly opposed to or strongly approved of it.)

Go over your writing carefully to be sure that you are stating your thoughts logically.

■ **Exercise 1**

Describe the weaknesses in content and thinking in each of the following sentences. Some sentences contain more than one kind of error. Write **C** *by sentences that reveal correct thinking.*
Principles for correct logic overlap, and errors in logic can be sometimes identified by more than one label.

1. The possession of wealth and property creates happiness.
   Inaccurate information; inadequate evidence; sweeping generalization

2. Poor people who have the necessities are free from worries and troubles.
   Inaccurate information; inadequate evidence; sweeping generalization

C 3. Poverty and the possession of wealth and property affect attitudes and emotional conditions.

4. Workers who are happy with their work are cheerful because they enjoy what they are doing.
   Reasoning in a circle

5. Evangelists who run for political office are hypocrites and liars.
   Lack of moderation; appeal to emotion

6. The new employee is bound to fail at his job; he has held three positions in the past six years.
   Sweeping generalization; inadequate evidence

7. Students should make all their own decisions.
   Sweeping generalization; conflicting views; lack of moderation.

8. The younger generation enjoys wild and raucous music, rebels angrily against traditions, refuses to exercise good manners, and generally acts unpleasant to older people.
   Lack of moderation; sweeping generalization

9. Once an amendment to the Constitution of the United States has passed, it becomes an unchangeable part of the document.
   Inaccurate information

10. Specialists and professors in the humanities have shown that the great amount of memory work required in college courses in some sciences does not really educate students well in scientific fields.
    Inaccurate information; unreliable authority; sweeping generalization

11. College students dress in an unusual way, either in the latest designer fashions or in threadbare and faded clothes.
    Inaccurate information; sweeping generalization; *either . . . or* fallacy

12. College graduates these days cannot read and write effectively and correctly.
    Sweeping generalization

13. Take the right kind of vitamins, and you can improve your physical health and capabilities as top Hollywood stars do.
    Inaccurate information; snob appeal

14. Jogging is the first real panacea discovered by humans. People who jog according to good practices can solve all major mental and physical problems.
    Sweeping generalization; lack of moderation

15. The athletics programs in college benefit every student.
    Sweeping generalization

16. Religious authorities and ministers should have the ultimate say even in civil and legal matters.
    Conflicting views

17. Three of four students in the class who spelled poorly had

hearing problems. Most misspellings are caused by bad hearing.
Sweeping generalization

18. Boys are good in mathematics and science; girls are good in English and fine arts.
    Inaccurate information; inadequate evidence

19. American medicine is far behind that in Russia because our doctors are interested only in money.
    Inaccurate information; lack of moderation; inadequate evidence

20. My professor must be a good scholar; she is a member of the Modern Language Association.
    Inaccurate information

PARAGRAPHS

46   Writing Paragraphs   ¶

Paragraphs civilize writing. Without them an essay is a wilderness of sentences in which it is easy to get lost. Writings without paragraph divisions are larger versions of fused sentences, which often frustrate or bewilder readers. It is necessary to know how and where to begin and end a paragraph just as it is necessary to know how and where to begin and end a sentence. A sentence is a group of words that expresses a complete thought; **a paragraph is a group of sentences that develops a single idea.** Paragraphing and thinking, then, are inseparable.

46a   Determine precisely the single idea you wish to develop in a paragraph.

To compose an effective paragraph, you need to sort out your thinking so that several ideas do not tumble about like garments in a clothes dryer. Select one appropriate thought to develop, and save others for other paragraphs. You may find useful some of the principles and methods discussed in connection with getting started on a paper (see **44a, b,** and **c**). For illustrations of paragraphs that develop a single idea and those that ineffectually include several, see **46c.**

46b   Express the central thought succinctly in a topic sentence that is effectively placed.   *ts*

What the thesis statement is to an entire paper (see pp. 233, 235), the **topic sentence** is to a paragraph. The topic sentence should be a clear, crisp statement of the central thought of the paragraph, and it should be placed where it will be most effective.

Sometimes you will need several attempts to produce a good topic sentence. As you write and revise, remember that you want a sentence that is precise and sharply focused. Below is a topic sentence from a paragraph about the advantages of reinstating the military draft.

> A great many young people, both men and women, are out of work, more each year it seems, and a good solution should be forthcoming for this severe problem.

The core idea of the paragraph—that the draft should be reinstated—is not even mentioned in this sentence. Notice the improvement in the following topic sentence:

> Reinstating the military draft could reduce America's unemployment.

Topic sentences, then, supply direction; other sentences in the paragraph add evidence, make refinements, and develop the main idea. The following paragraph illustrates this pattern:

Topic sentence

Body of paragraph, with specific evidence

A number of research studies substantiate the assumption that television interferes with family activities and the formation of family relationships. One survey shows that seventy-eight percent of the respondents indicated no conversation taking place during viewing except at specified times such as commercials. The study notes: "The television atmosphere in most households is one of quiet absorption on the part of family members who are present. The nature of the family social life during a program could be described as 'parallel' rather than interactive, and the set does seem to dominate family life when it is on." Thirty-six percent of the respondents in another study indicated that television viewing was the only family activity participated in during the week.

MARIE WINN,
"Family Life"

Topic sentences most often come at the beginning of paragraphs, as above, but they can appear anywhere. Place the topic sentence wherever it will be most effective. In the following paragraph, the topic sentence is placed after the first sentence for purposes of contrast:

> In the United States, companies show off by erecting tall buildings. In Japan, businessmen have another way of flaunting their wealth: building huge Buddha statues. In May, a taxi-company owner unveiled the latest, a 56-foot-high Buddha in Fukui. A few years ago an 80-foot statue went up in Aomori Prefecture.
>
> "Japan's Buddha Wars,"
> *Newsweek*

If you want to set up a point with which to contrast or argue or to create a sense of suspense before you introduce the main subject, the topic sentence can come even later. It is the third sentence in the following paragraph:

> Biologists may be accustomed to working on obscure beasts—ugly horseshoe crabs, prickly sea urchins, slimy algae. But anthropologist Grover Krantz of Washington State University has a problem of a different sort. He is studying, or trying to study, a creature no scientist has ever seen: the mysterious Sasquatch, or Bigfoot. [The rest of the paragraph discusses the nature of the research.]
>
> "Tracking the Sasquatch,"
> *Newsweek*

When you have several specific bits of evidence or examples that you intend to use in order to prove a point, it is sometimes effective to present the evidence first and to end the paragraph with your central idea. In the following paragraph, the topic sentence comes at the end:

> Sensible business people who deal in realities every day will often go out of their way on the street to avoid walking under a ladder. Diners in restaurants throw salt over their shoulders to ward off bad luck when they spill a little. A perfectly sane adult will knock on

wood to insure continued good fortune. Many people moan over broken mirrors because they believe that they are in for seven years of bad luck. <u>Superstitions still manifest themselves in the actions of many normal human beings.</u>

By practicing the various placements of topic sentences, you can increase your skills as an alert writer who does not compose paragraphs automatically in one monotonous pattern.

■ **Exercise 1**

Underline the topic sentences in the following paragraphs and be prepared to discuss the effectiveness of their placement.

1. <u>The world is shaped by gravity and the operations of nature depend on it.</u> After gathering the materials of the earth into a ball, it holds them together. Opposing the titanic convulsions of the young planet, it formed the mountains. It propels the rivers and streams. Gravity pulls the rain from the clouds and flattens the surface of the sea. It gives direction to the trunks of trees and the stems of flowers.

    HANS C. VON BAEYER,
    "Gravity"

2. The New York investment banking house of Morgan Stanley encourages people it is thinking of hiring to discuss the demands of the job with their spouses, girlfriends, or boyfriends —new recruits sometimes work 100 hours a week. The firm's managing directors and their wives take promising candidates and their spouses or companions out to dinner to bring home to them what they will face. <u>The point is to get a person who will not be happy within Morgan's culture because of the way his family feels to eliminate himself from consideration for a job there.</u>

    RICHARD PASCALE,
    Fortune

■ **Exercise 2**

Compose two paragraphs, one with the topic sentence at the begin-
ning and the other with the topic sentence in another position. Be pre-
pared to justify the placement of the topic sentences.

46c Unify. Relate each sentence in a paragraph to the
central idea.

Each sentence in an effective paragraph bears directly and obviously on the main point. Do not make your readers ponder and
strain before they can see connections. Even slightly irrelevant
material can throw the entire paragraph out of focus and leave
readers confused about the direction of the argument.

The following paragraph compares secrecy to fire, but after a
good topic sentence at the beginning, it includes three sentences
(in italics) that stray off the point.

> Secrecy is as indispensable to human beings as fire, and as
> greatly feared. *Of course, we all know that fear can be a terrible barrier*
> *to communication and is generally destructive itself. Nothing is more*
> *important to society than communication.* Both fire and secrecy en-
> hance and protect life, yet both can stifle, lay waste, spread out of
> control. *Naturally, gossip is also to be feared as one of the negative*
> *aspects of civilization.* Fire and secrecy can be good—as in guarding
> intimacy and nurturing—or bad—as in invading or consuming.

What starts out as a thoughtful and original comparison between
secrecy and fire soon sprawls into a commentary on fear, communication, and gossip. Below is the paragraph as it was actually
written. Notice its effective unity.

> Secrecy is as indispensable to human beings as fire, and as
> greatly feared. Both enhance and protect life, yet both can stifle, lay
> waste, spread out of all control. Both may be used to guard intimacy

or to invade it, to nurture or to consume. And each can be turned
against itself; barriers of secrecy are set up to guard against secret
plots and surreptitious prying, just as fire is used to fight fire.

SISSELA BOK,
Secrets

The paragraph below attempts to develop the central idea of
preserving our forests, but about halfway through, the writer
abruptly changes to the topic of beauty and thus destroys the coherence of the paragraph.

An encouraging sign in modern management of national re-
sources is the planting of trees systematically to replace those har-
vested. Large lumber companies have learned that it is in their best
interests to look to the future and not merely to get what they can at
the moment from the land. *Besides that, trees are beautiful and add
much to the pleasure of being in nature. Only God, as the poet so aptly
put it, can make a tree.* With modern tools and methods, whole forests can be destroyed in a fraction of the time that lumberjacks with
their axes and handsaws attacked the woods. It is more necessary
than ever, therefore, that conservation be a primary concern not
only of the general citizenry but also of industry.

If the two digressive sentences printed in italics were deleted, the
paragraph would be coherent and would communicate, as it
should, a single well-argued point.

Often it is not so easy to make a good paragraph from a
flawed one. Without planning and care, a paragraph can be
merely a random collection of thoughts with only a vague central
idea. The writer of the following paragraph seems not to have
thought through what he or she wanted to say before writing.

It is not an easy matter to be an only child. Children have dif-
fering characteristics, and some people say that infants have traits
that will remain throughout their lives. As people grow up, they find
that their views change, especially when they reach college. In order
to understand children, we need to treat them as individuals, not as
playthings. There is much truth in the saying that the child is the
parent of the adult. Some writers believe that children are more mature in important ways than adults. At any rate, children do feel
things keenly.

The sentences that make up the previous paragraph are not closely related and do not work toward the development of a thesis. Though it is on the general subject of children, it is so fragmented that it conveys disorder and confusion.

■ **Exercise 3**

Study the paragraph below and delete all extraneous material.

As the basic social unit, the family is as important today in America as it ever was, though perhaps in a different way. Family coherence was essential in the early days of the country to insure the survival of the individual members. They helped each other and protected each other. Today people need their families not so much to insure physical survival as to help them through the perils of modern times, especially through such psychological perils as loss of identity. ~~America is not all bad, however. It offers the greatest freedom of all countries for individual development. America is still the land of opportunity.~~ The family gives one a sense of belonging, a sense of the past. When all else seems severed, the family can be the anchor to sanity.

46d   Flesh out underdeveloped paragraphs.

Making a new paragraph after every two or three sentences, without regard to development and coherence, is nearly as distracting as having no paragraph divisions at all. Inexperienced writers often believe erroneously that the sole function of an indentation is to give the reader's eye a brief rest by breaking the monotonous flow of print. In most expository writing, underdeveloped paragraphs are like undernourished people: they are weak, unable to carry out their normal purposes. Make sure your paragraph divisions come only with new units of thought and that you have appropriately fleshed out an idea before going on to another one.

The following paragraphs on George Washington are ineffectively developed.

> In many ways, the version of George Washington we grew up on is accurate. He was an honest and personally unambitious politician.
>
> But history teachers rarely tell us about the complex character of the man.
>
> Most historians feel that he was not a great soldier; yet he was the luckiest man alive.
>
> He even survived the attacks of his mother. When he was president, she went so far as to state publicly that he was starving and neglecting her, neither of which was true.

Though interesting, these paragraphs are too underdeveloped to do their jobs. They are just strong enough to state the points. Then they leave the reader yearning for more details. Contrast them with the paragraphs below.

> In many ways, the version of George Washington we grew up on is accurate. He was an honest and personally unambitious politician, a devout patriot and a fearless soldier. Through circumstance, he becomes the lodestar for the swift-sailing Revolution. Even his enemies conceded that national success would have been impossible without him.
>
> But history teachers rarely tell us about the complex character of the man. Often moody and bleak, he did not like to be touched. When he became president, he required so much ritual and formality that it caused one observer to quip: "I fear we may have exchanged George the Third for George the First." Though he drank hard with the enlisted men, he was a tough disciplinarian, describing himself as a man "who always walked on a straight line."
>
> Most historians feel that he was not a great soldier; yet he was the luckiest man alive. He had two horses shot out from under him; felt bullets rip through his clothes and hat; and survived attacks by Indians, French and English troops, hard winters, cunning political opponents, and smallpox.

He even survived the attacks of his mother. When he was president she went so far as to state publicly that he was starving and
neglecting her, neither of which was true. Then, to twist the emotional knife, she tried to persuade the new government to pass a law
that future presidents not be allowed to neglect their mothers.

ADAPTED FROM DIANE ACKERMAN,
"The Real George Washington"

In a few kinds of writing, short paragraphs are acceptable
and expected. Newspapers, for example, generally use brief paragraphs because few details and little exposition are needed.
Sometimes it is effective to use a short paragraph amid longer
ones for emphasis. The length of a writing assignment to some
extent may influence the length of paragraphs. A paper of one
thousand words provides more room to develop full paragraphs
than a short assignment does.

■ **Exercise 4**

*Seven broad subjects for paragraphs are listed below. Choose the two
that you like best and select one aspect of each topic. On each subject,
first write a skimpy paragraph. Then write a paragraph of 125 to175
words with fuller development of the subject.*

television advertising
preventive medicine
nuclear energy
eating disorders
America's idea of success
a favorite recreation
study habits

46e Trim and tighten sprawling paragraphs.

A sprawling paragraph is the opposite of an underdeveloped one.
It needs trimming, and to do so you must exercise your mind. As

you write, keep alert to the length of your paragraphs. Very long paragraphs make it difficult for a reader to digest meaning easily. To reduce excessive length, you may find it necessary to reduce the scope of the topic sentence, but sometimes you can produce a more coherent, more sharply focused paragraph of effective length simply by discarding material. For example, all your details may be pertinent and interesting, but you may not need ten examples to illustrate your point; four or five may do it more efficiently.

46f Put the parts of a paragraph together in appropriate, coherent order. *coh*

Sentences can be arranged systematically in a number of ways. Certain effects are produced from certain orders of sentences, and what may be an appropriate arrangement for one kind of paper will not be for another. Paragraphs with no system of order are like motors with the parts haphazardly assembled: they function poorly or not at all. Study below the various patterns most often used to arrange sentences in a paragraph.

Time

In paragraphs organized by time, things that happen first usually come first in the paragraph. In many ways, this is the simplest system because chronology is a ready-made pattern. Paragraphs describing a process (how steel is made, how photographs are developed, and so forth) naturally are arranged sequentially. If you get steps out of order, the paragraph is confusing. Narratives usually begin at the first event and end with the last. In some instances, however, the writer may wish to create a special effect by describing a late event first and then coming back to the beginning.

The following paragraph is in strict chronological order.

At the beginning of the cruise, the ship's engines seemed noisy, but the captain considered this a minor problem. He consulted with the chief engineer, who politely but firmly told him that he was imagining things. On the third day out, smoke was reported in the engine room, and the captain prepared the crew before giving orders to abandon ship. Shortly before the announcement was to be made, however, a large freighter came into view. It was an Italian ship, and few aboard spoke English, but they quickly discerned the problem, gave full assistance, and took the passengers on board their ship. Soon the fire was out and the *Ocean Wind* was in tow. After the two days that it took to reach Miami, the passengers agreed that they had never had better food, better quarters, or more attentive hosts.

Space

Descriptive paragraphs are most frequently organized according to spatial progression. If you are describing a scene or a person, you move from detail to detail of what you have observed. As with time sequence, you must maintain the logical progression, in this instance the movement of the eye as it follows the object or scene. Getting sentences out of order may resemble counting 1, 2, 5, 4, 3 instead of 1, 2, 3, 4, 5. Notice how the paragraph below carries the eye from one wall of a room to another.

The right wall of the spacious office was covered completely with a mural of the most striking aspect. It was meant to represent a city skyline, but the buildings resembled giant trees in winter, and the color red prevailed everywhere. The rear wall was composed of one piece of glass from floor to ceiling overlooking the real skyline. The contrast was immediate, but one could also see that in a strange sense the buildings did, indeed, look like a surrealistic forest. The left wall was taken up with bookshelves filled with volumes of various shapes and sizes. A closer look revealed that the top four shelves contained all first editions of famous works. The lower four shelves, however, were given to books of only two kinds—writings on architecture and on the cultures of certain Pacific islanders.

NOTE: Paragraphs with sentences arranged by time or space sometimes do not have conventional topic sentences.

Climactic order (increasing importance)

Sentences that progress according to importance are arranged in **climactic order.** This is an effective structure, based on sequence of importance (not chronological sequence). If you place a lesser sentence (an anticlimax) at the end of a paragraph, you may create confusion or unintentional humor. The strategy in arranging climactically is not to put down your thoughts simply as they occur to you, but to list them first, order them according to their relative importance, and then form the paragraph. Notice how the final sentence in the following paragraph dramatically acts as a climax.

> How successful one is in obtaining peace of mind and fulfillment depends upon which path is followed. Gratification of the physical appetites is vigorously pursued by some people as if this were the true route to happiness. Others eschew such a primitive attempt and give themselves over to the accumulation of material wealth. Their rewards may be somewhat more long lasting, but their disappointment is inevitable, for money is notoriously lacking in the food that feeds the inner person. Having recognized this basic truth, other seekers aim at what they consider a higher goal—the acquisition of power and influence, in which they find challenge and excitement. Power admittedly brings more satisfaction to the ego than does money. Those most likely to find their way will do so not through physical gratification, money, or power, but through the development of self-understanding and self-esteem.

The topics that are ordered according to increasing importance (climactically) are the following: physical appetites, material wealth, acquisition of power and influence, self-understanding and self-esteem.

General to particular, particular to general

Paragraphs in which the sentences progress from a general statement to particular details are related to deductive reasoning, and those that progress from several details to a generalization about them are related to inductive reasoning (see **45**). Writers often compose a topic sentence and then support and explain it with details, reasons, and illustrations. This sequence moves from the general to the particular (see paragraph **A** below). The reverse order usually has the topic sentence at the end of the paragraph with particulars coming first (as in paragraph **B** below). A more frequent pattern moves from the general to the particular and back to the general again, as in illustration **C.**

(A)   Never was there a more outrageous or more unscrupulous or more ill-informed advertising campaign than that by which the promoters for the American colonies brought settlers here. Brochures published in England in the seventeenth century, some even earlier, were full of hopeful overstatements, half-truths, and downright lies, along with some facts which nowadays surely would be the basis for a restraining order from the Federal Trade Commission. Gold and silver, fountains of youth, plenty of fish, venison without limit, all these were promised.

DANIEL BOORSTIN,
Democracy and Its Discontents

(B)   Photocopying makes it possible for a researcher to reproduce a long passage instantly instead of laboriously copying it in longhand or dragging along the entire book so that the section can be copied later. Ball-point and felt-point pens, now used widely instead of old-fashioned ink pens, are economical, convenient, and generally neater. The wide variety of colors in these pens enables writers to distinguish notes on one subject from those on another. Word-processing machines allow the change of single words or the revision of a line or a passage long after the original typing. Transparent tapes are now available that can be written or typed on. A great number of conveniences have been developed for researchers and writers in the last few decades.

(C)   Mankind's most enduring achievement is art. At its best, it reveals the nobility that coexists in human nature along with flaws and evils, and the beauty and truth it can perceive. Whether in music or architecture, literature, painting or sculpture, art opens our eyes and ears and feelings to something beyond ourselves, something we cannot experience without the artist's vision and the genius of his craft. The placing of Greek temples like the Temple of Poseidon on the promontory at Sunion outlined against the piercing

blue of the Aegean Sea, Poseidon's home; the majesty of Michelan-
gelo's sculptured figures in stone; Shakespeare's command of language and knowledge of the human soul; the intricate order of Bach,
the enchantment of Mozart; the purity of Chinese monochrome pottery with the lovely names—celadon, oxblood, peach blossom, clair
de lune; the exuberance of Tiepolo's ceiling where, without the picture frames to limit movement, a whole world in exquisitely beautiful colors lives and moves in the sky; the prose and poetry of all the
writers from Homer to Cervantes to Jane Austen and John Keats to
Dostoevsky and Chekhov—who made all these things? We—our
species—did.

BARBARA TUCHMAN,
Thomas Jefferson lecture, Washington, D.C.

46g   Develop a paragraph by a method that will appropriately enable it to fulfill its function.

Each paragraph has its own distinctive identity, and yet it must
carry out its duty in the paper as a whole. Long-established practices may at times be helpful in planning and arranging your
thoughts.

Opening and closing paragraphs   *intro / conc*

Opening and closing paragraphs of a paper are often difficult to
write. The first paragraph is sometimes harder to compose than
the next several pages. It must attract interest, state the purpose
or thesis or argument, and then sometimes suggest the method of
development that will be used in the entire paper. If the first paragraph is dull, mechanical, or obscure, your reader may decide
immediately that the paper is not worth reading.

The concluding paragraph does not simply restate the opening paragraph. It does not add substantial new information not
discussed previously in the paper. Instead, it gives a brief over-

view of what the paper has shown and makes a final assessment of the importance and the originality of the paper in regard to its subject matter.

Methods of development

Many methods of development are useful in working with different kinds of content. Several particular kinds of paragraphs are discussed below.

Definition

Whether you are using a new word or a new meaning for an old one, a definition explains a concept. It avoids the problems that arise when two persons use the same term for different things. Be as specific as possible; exemplify. Avoid definitions that are uniquely your own (unless you are willing to be challenged). Definitions, of course, may be much more elaborate than those given in dictionaries. Avoid the expression "According to Webster. . . ."

> Romantic love may be described as an emotion; it is translated into behavior. A person in love wants to do something to or with his loved one. The behavior a couple settles upon comprises their love. The better the translation of emotion into behavior, the less residual emotion will remain. Paradoxically, then, people who love each other do not feel love for each other.
>
> ADAPTED FROM GEORGE W. KELLING,
> *Blind Mazes: A Study of Love*

Comparison and contrast

Two basic methods can be used in developing a paragraph by comparison and contrast: writing everything about one point and then everything about the other (XXXX YYYY) or writing about alternating points throughout the paragraph (XY XY XY XY). Either method can be effective, but in long and complex comparisons and contrasts the alternating method is generally better because it keeps both aspects in mind at the same time throughout.

The degree of comparison or of contrast can vary a great deal from one instance to another. You might write, for example, that there are a great many likenesses between two things but only one or two strong contrasts. Your organization, then, might be represented this way (with likenesses represented by X and contrasts by Y): XXXXXX YY. Or the reverse could be true, with a great many contrasts but one or a few striking likenesses. Whatever your methods of recounting comparisons and contrasts, be certain that they are represented appropriately.

> Hot water is the most satisfactory form of heat for the small greenhouse. The heat is more evenly distributed than in the case of steam heat and there is less danger of a sudden drop in temperature. And it is an accepted fact that practically all plants thrive better under a system of hot water heat than under steam heat. It is a more natural kind of heat and is more nearly like the heat of the sun. Hot water heat has the added advantage of being more economical than steam, as it is possible to maintain a very low fire in mild weather.
>
> JAMES BUSH-BROWN AND LOUISE BUSH-BROWN,
> *America's Garden Book*

Cause and effect

Generally a paragraph of this kind states a condition or effect and then proceeds by listing and explaining the causes. However, the first sentences may list a cause or causes and then conclude with the consequence, the effect. In either method of development, the writer usually begins with a phenomenon that is generally known and then moves on to the unknowns.

The following paragraph begins with an effect and proceeds to examine the causes.

> This close-knit fabric [of the city] was blown apart by the automobile, and by the postwar middle-class exodus to suburbia which the mass-ownership of automobiles made possible. The automobile itself was not to blame for this development, nor was the desire for

surburban living, which is obviously a genuine aspiration of many Americans. The fault lay in our failure, right up to the present time, to fashion new policies to minimize the disruptive effects of the automobile revolution. We have failed not only to tame the automobile itself, but to overhaul a property-tax system that tends to foster automotive-age sprawl, and to institute coordinated planning in the politically fragmented suburbs that have caught the brunt of the postwar building boom.

EDMUND K. FALTERMAYER,
Redoing America

Example

Some topic sentences state generalizations that may not seem clear or true without evidence and illustration. Proof can be provided by an extended example or several short examples. They must be accepted as true in themselves and as representative of the generalization. Examples can add concrete interest as well as proof.

> It was during this period that some of our most notable examples of garden art were produced: the great villas of Italy, the palace gardens of Spain, the vast plaisances of the French châteaux, the careful parterres of the Dutch, and the beautiful manor house gardens of England.

JAMES BUSH-BROWN AND LOUISE BUSH-BROWN,
America's Garden Book

Classification

Paragraphs that classify explain by arranging a number of things into groups and categories. Seeing the distinctions should lead to clear understanding of the component parts and then to understanding of the larger group or concept. Analysis explains one thing by naming its parts. Synthesis lists several categories and then puts them into a single concept or classification.

Modern pessimism and modern fragmentation have spread in three different ways to people of our own culture and to people across the world. *Geographically,* it spread from the European mainland to England, after a time jumping the Atlantic to the United States. *Culturally,* it spread in the various disciplines from philosophy to art, to music, to general culture (the novel, poetry, drama, films), and to theology. *Socially,* it spread from the intellectuals to the educated and then through the mass media to everyone.

FRANCIS A. SCHAEFFER
How Should We Then Live?

Analogy

An analogy is a figurative comparison; it explains one thing in terms of another. It is likely to be most effective when you can show a resemblance that is not generally recognized between two things that have so many differences that they are not ordinarily likened. In the paragraph below, for example, the writer convincingly reveals an analogy between the game of football and war.

A further reason for football's intensity is that the game is played like a war. The idea is to win by going through, around or over the opposing team and the battle lines, quite literally, are drawn on every play. Violence is somewhere at the heart of the game, and the combat quality is reflected in football's army language ("blitz," "trap," "zone," "bomb," "trenches," etc.). Coaches often sound like generals when they discuss their strategy. Woody Hayes of Ohio State, for instance, explains his quarterback option play as if it had been conceived in the Pentagon: "You know," he says, "the most effective kind of warfare is siege. You have to attack on broad fronts. And that's all the option is—attacking on a broad front. You know General Sherman ran an option through the South."

MURRAY ROSS,
"Football Red and Baseball Green"

Process

Several methods can be used in describing a process. Most processes are given in chronological order, step by step. The kind of writing should be adapted to the particular kind of process. The simplest perhaps is the type used in a recipe, usually written in the second person or imperative mood. The necessity here is to get the steps in order and to state each step very clearly. This process tells *how to do* something. It is more instruction than exposition.

Another kind of process is the exposition of *how something works* (a clock, the human nervous system). Here the problems lie in avoiding technical terms and intricate or incomprehensible steps in the process. This kind of process is explanation; the reader may at some time need to understand it or to use it.

Still another kind of process, usually written in the past tense, tells *how something happened* (how oil was formed in the earth, how a celebration or riot began). Usually a paragraph of this type is written in the third person. It is designed to reveal how something developed (once in all time or on separate occasions). Its purpose is to explain and instruct. The following paragraph explains one theory about the process that formed the moon. The distinct steps are necessary for explanation here just as they are for instruction in a paragraph that tells how to do something.

> There were tides in the new earth long before there was an ocean. In response to the pull of the sun the molten liquids of the earth's whole surface rose in tides that rolled unhindered around the globe and only gradually slackened and diminished as the earthly shell cooled, congealed, and hardened. Those who believe that the moon is a child of earth say that during an early stage of the earth's development something happened that caused this rolling, viscid tide to gather speed and momentum and to rise to unimaginable heights. Apparently the force that created these greatest tides the earth has ever known was the force of resonance, for at this time the period of the solar tides had come to approach, then equal, the period of the free oscillation of the liquid earth. And so every sun tide was given increased momentum by the push of the earth's oscillation, and each of the twice-daily tides was larger than the one before it. Physicists have calculated that, after 500 years of such monstrous, steadily increasing tides, those on the side toward the sun became

too high for stability, and a great wave was torn away and hurled into space. But immediately, of course, the newly created satellite became subject to physical laws that sent it spinning in an orbit of its own about the earth. This is what we call the moon.

RACHEL CARSON,
The Sea Around Us

46h Use transitional devices to show the relationships between the parts of your writing. *tr*

Transitional devices are connectors and direction givers. They connect content words to other words, sentences to sentences, paragraphs to paragraphs. Writings without transitions are like a strange land with no signs for travelers. Practiced writers assume that they should keep their readers informed about where a paragraph and a paper are going.

The beginnings of paragraphs can contribute materially to clarity, coherence, and the movement of the discussion. Some writers meticulously guide readers with a connector at the beginning of almost every paragraph. H. J. Muller, for example, begins a sequence of paragraphs about science as follows:

> In this summary, science . . .
> Yet science does . . .
> Similarly the basic interests of science . . .
> In other words, they are not . . .
> This demonstration that even the scientist . . .
> This idea will concern us . . .
> In other words, facts and figures . . .

CONNECTIVE WORDS AND EXPRESSIONS

but	indeed	likewise
and	in fact	consequently
however	meanwhile	first
moreover	afterward	next

CONNECTIVE WORDS AND EXPRESSIONS (CONTINUED)

furthermore	then	in brief
on the other hand	so	to summarize
nevertheless	still	to conclude
for example	after all	similarly

DEMONSTRATIVES

| this | that | these | those |

References to demonstratives must be clear (see p. 65).

OTHER PRONOUNS

| many | each | some | others | such | either |

Repeated key words, phrases, and synonyms

Repetitions and synonyms guide the reader from sentence to sentence and paragraph to paragraph.

Parallel structures

Repeating similar structural forms of a sentence can show how certain ideas within a paragraph are alike in content as well as structure. A sequence of sentences beginning with a noun subject or with the same kind of pronoun subject, a series of clauses beginning with *that* or *which,* a series of clauses beginning with a similar kind of subordinate conjunction (like *because*)—devices like these can achieve transition and show connection.

Excessive use of parallelism, however, is likely to be too oratorical, too dramatic. Used with restraint, parallel structures are excellent transitional devices.

The following paragraph on the subject of patriotism illustrates how various transitional devices can help create direction and coherence.

There is no reason why <u>patriotism</u> has to be so heavily asso-

ciated, in the minds of the young as well as adults, with military ex-

Synonym: citizenship for patriotism

ploits, jets, and missiles. <u>Citizenship</u> must include the <u>duty</u> to ad-

vance our ideals actively into practice for a better community,

connective word: And

country, and world if peace is to prevail over war. <u>And</u> <u>this</u> obliga-

synonym: obligation for duty   **demonstrative: this**

<u>tion</u> stems not just from a secular concern for humanity but from a

belief in the brotherhood of man—"I am my brother's keeper"—

that is common to all major religions. It is the classic confrontation:

repeated key word: patriotism

barbarism *vs.* the holy ones. If <u>patriotism</u> has no room for delibera-

tion, for acknowledging an individual's sense of justice and his relig-

ious principles, it will continue to close minds, stifle the dissent that

parallel structure:

has made us strong, and deter the participation of Americans <u>who</u>

who challenge in order to/   who question in order to

<u>challenge in order to</u> correct and <u>who question in order to</u> answer.

repeated key word: patriotism

We need only to recall recent history in other countries where <u>patri-</u>

<u>otism</u> was converted into an epidemic of collective madness and de-

parallel structure: A patriotism . . . asks/   A new

struction. <u>A patriotism</u> manipulated by the government <u>asks</u> only

patriotism requires

for a servile nod from its subjects. <u>A new patriotism requires</u> a think-

repeated key word: patriotism

ing assent from its citizens. If <u>patriotism</u> is to have a "manifest des-

tiny," it is in building a world where all mankind is our bond in

peace.

RALPH NADER,
"We Need a New Kind of Patriotism"

General exercises

■ **Exercise 5**

Write three paragraphs on any of the following subjects. Use at least two methods of development and two kinds of order (see pp. 281–291). Name the method you use in each paragraph.

1. Wisdom	5. Security
2. Boredom	6. Human rights
3. Poverty	7. Youth
4. Politics and sincerity	8. Carelessness

■ **Exercise 6**

Find three good paragraphs from three different kinds of writing: from a book of nonfiction, an essay, a review, or a newspaper article. Discuss how effective paragraphs differ in different kinds of writing.

■ **Exercise 7**

Find an ineffective paragraph in a book or article. Analyze it in a paragraph.

LITERATURE

47 Writing About Literature

Reading literature casually and hastily can be pleasurable, but a deep and careful probing brings a different kind of satisfaction. In writing about literature, students should express their reactions in a way that does justice to the richness and the complexity of the work. A good paper is not purely subjective although it does state the writer's opinions. It convinces others by solid evidence derived from the work.

A poem, a work of fiction, or a play does not mean whatever a reader wishes it to mean. Although works of literature can have more than one correct interpretation, some readings are truer than others to the art and meaning of the poem or story, and some criticisms can be shown to be erroneous.

47a Choose a literary work that interests you. Write about the feature of the work that interests you most.

Your instructor may assign you a particular work for a paper, or you may be allowed to choose for yourself. If you have any freedom of choice, select carefully. A bad selection will make success difficult even if you write well.

Give thought to your choice. You are likely to write a better paper, one that will glint with freshness, if you choose a **work new to you**, one that no one has ever taught to you and one that you have never written about before. As much as you can, search for the kind of topic you like. Look at familiar authors, famous authors whose works you have not read, works recommended to you by people who have tastes somewhat like yours. Look at shelves of books, lists of authors and works, stories and poems you have heard about but not read, new stories and poems by authors familiar to you, anthologies, collections. You are unlikely to write a good paper about a work that you regard as dull or mediocre. If a literary work contains no mystery for you at first, you are unlikely to explain it originally or interestingly to others.

Avoid shallow and obvious literature. If you read something that makes you think, "That is exactly what I have always known," you should doubt the originality of the author. If you think, "True, but I never thought of anything like that before," you may have a good selection on your hands. A work that interprets or explains itself will not leave much for you to write about. Good papers are often derived from literature that is somewhat puzzling and obscure during and immediately after the first reading. Additional readings and careful thought can produce surprises that give you something to write about.

If you like a work but do not yet see the best subject, list several. You might choose subjects such as these:

SETTING	An island in a flooding river
CHARACTER	A sudden change in the life or belief of a character
MOOD	Joy or sorrow—or both
ACCIDENT	The drastic effect of an unexpected event

There are as many possibilities in literature as there are in life.

Do not decide to write on a particular subject before you read the work. What you think will be a good subject based on some preconception may not be there at all. Find your subjects as you read the literature and as you think about it afterward. Let good subjects grow and develop; bad ones will disappear or fade away. The most surprising and significant topics may come to you when you least expect them—as you slowly wake in the morning, for example, or as you engage in some kind of physical activity.

The methods you use in choosing a topic and arranging ideas on papers on other subjects (see pp. 228–237) are likely to be useful in planning and writing papers about literature. List topics and subtopics; group them; arrange them; rearrange them; write whatever comes into your mind about them, whether it seems good or bad at the moment; write to keep the words going, even when what you are writing seems unimportant at the moment. Cross out. Put checkmarks by important points; draw arrows from ideas on one part of the page to related ideas on another part; photocopy parts of works; make notations of lines, passages, images, sentences. Write quickly for a time. Think and write slowly and carefully about crucial subjects. Stop writing and walk about. Use every physical and mental device you can think of to tease good thoughts out of your mind.

Be willing to give up ideas that are inferior. Expect surprises and twists and turns during the process of writing. Few papers are written like bullets speeding toward a single idea with a calculated aim; most of the time they act more like floods, gathering valuables and debris at the same time. After the first draft, you will be able to begin separating bad from good ideas.

47b Let the subject determine the kind of paper you write.

Writings about literature fall into several categories. A few of the more significant ones are explained below.

Interpretation

Most papers are interpretations, which derive mainly from a close study of the literary work. An interpretative paper identifies methods and ideas. Through analysis, the writer presents specific evidence to support the interpretation.

Distinguish carefully between the thinking of a character and that of the author. Unless an author speaks in his or her own voice, you can deduce what the author thinks only from the work as a whole, from effects of events in the plot, and from attitudes that develop from good or bad characters. Many works of literature depict a character whose whole way of life is opposite to the author's views. To confuse the character with the author in this kind of work is to make a crucial mistake. Sometimes it is clear immediately what an author thinks about the characters, but not always.

Review

A good review of a book or an article

1. identifies the author, the title, and the subject.
2. summarizes accurately the information presented and the author's argument.
3. describes and perhaps categorizes the author's methods.
4. provides support (with evidence and argument) for the good points and explains the author's mistakes, errors, misjudgments, or misinterpretations.
5. evaluates the work's accomplishments and failures.

Character analysis

A character sketch is a tempting kind of paper to write, but a good analysis of a character or an explanation of an author's methods of characterization is truly a difficult task. This kind of paper easily becomes a superficial summary in which the student fails to consider motivations, development, change, and interrelationships of characters. Meaningful interpretation of a character in a literary work may define something that the character does not know about himself or herself, traits that the author reveals only by hints and implications. For example, if you can show that a character clearly is an entirely different kind of person from what he thinks he is, you may be on the way to writing a very good paper.

Of course, a character analysis may *not* deal at all with *what the character is* but consider the *methods* the author uses to reveal the character. Body language and modes of speech, facial expressions or changes in mood, excessive talking or silence, and appearance are some of these methods. Remember that the author characterizes; the critic discusses the methods of characterization.

Setting

Often the time and place in which a work is set reveal important moods and meanings. Setting may help to indicate the manners and emotions of characters by showing how they interact with their environments. When you write about setting, you accomplish very little by merely describing it. Show what its functions are in the literary work.

Technical analysis

The analysis of technical elements in literature—imagery, symbolism, point of view, structure, prosody, and so on—requires special study of the technical term or concept as well as of the literary work itself. Begin by looking up the term in a good basic reference book, such as C. Hugh Holman's *A Handbook to Literature*. However, you should never be concerned with vocabulary and technical terms for their own sake. If you discover an aspect of a work that you wish to discuss, find the exact term for it by discussing it with your teacher, looking it up in a dictionary, and then studying it in a handbook or even an encyclopedia. Then determine what the technique does in the work you are writing about.

Combined approaches

Many papers combine different approaches. A thoughtful paper on imagery, for example, does more than merely point out the images, or even the kinds of images, in the literary work; it uses the imagery to interpret, analyze, or clarify something else as well —theme, structure, characterization, mood, relationship, recurrent patterns, and so on. Depending on the subject and the work you are writing about, many aspects can mingle to accomplish a single objective.

47c Give the paper a precise title.

Do not search for a fancy title at the expense of meaning. Authors of literary works often use figurative titles like *Death in the Afternoon* and *The Grapes of Wrath,* but you would be wise to designate your subject more literally. Be precise; state your subject in the title.

· Do not use the title of the work as your own title, as in "Robert Frost's 'Directive.' " Do not merely announce that you are writing about a work by calling your paper "An Analysis of Frost's 'Directive,' " or "An Interpretation of . . ." or "A Criticism of. . . ." The fact that you are writing the paper indicates that you are writing an analysis, a criticism, or something of the sort.

Stick to the topic named in the title. The topic sentence of every paragraph should point back to the title, the introduction, and the thesis statement.

47d Organize and develop the paper according to significant ideas.

Do not automatically organize your paper by following the sequence of the literary work. Sometimes the result of this order can be poor topic sentences, summary rather than analysis, mechanical organization, and repetitive transitional phrases.

Usually it is better to break up your overall argument into several aspects and to move from one of these to the next.

First sentences that provide mechanical and dull information do not encourage further reading. Avoid generality, as in the following sentence:

> T. S. Eliot, in his famous poem written in 1922, *The Waste Land*, expressed a theme that has been a frequent subject of works of literature.

Instead, you might try something like this:

> The relationship between the physical, mental, and spiritual health of a ruler of a nation and the condition of his people is a subject of T. S. Eliot's poem *The Waste Land*.

The first sentence states nothing of true significance; the second announces a particular topic to be explored.

Just as a paper should not begin mechanically, the parts should not contain mechanical first sentences and dull transitions. Your paragraphs will not attract readers if they use beginnings like these:

> "In the first stanza . . ."
> "In the following part . . ."
> "At the conclusion . . ."

First sentences of papers and paragraphs should entice readers like the smell of hot popcorn, rather than presenting the equivalent of rows of empty paper bags.

47e   Do not summarize and paraphrase excessively.

A certain amount of summarizing is usually necessary. To a slight extent, summary can involve interpretation. (See Section **48**.) But tell the story, quote, and paraphrase only enough to prove your point. Mere detailed summary is inadequate; summary must prove your argument, not be an end in itself. When you paraphrase, distinguish clearly between the author's thinking and your ideas about what he or she has written.

NOTE: When you do summarize, use the historical present tense. (See Section **4**.) Tell what *happens*, not what *happened*.

47f Think for yourself.

The purpose of your paper is to *state your opinions* and to *provide evidence*. If you find that you have no worthwhile opinions of your own about the meaning or the art of the work, find a literary work that stimulates your thought.

47g Write about the literature, not about yourself or your reading and writing processes.

In a paper, the difference between what you saw in a first reading and your insight after later readings is not usually important. Do not write about the process of discovery. Write about *what you discover*. Present only your final and considered views.

Generally, do not write about how others might read or misread the work. Omit such irrelevant information.

The writing process assumes that what you write is *your belief* unless you indicate otherwise. An occasional "I think" or "I believe" can be inconspicuous. But emphasizing that your attitudes are personal becomes a distraction. Avoid frequent use of the first-person pronouns *I* and *we*.

47h   Provide enough evidence to support your ideas.

Strike a proper balance between generalizations and detailed support of your points. Make a point, develop its specifics and ramifications, quote the work, and show how the point is supported by the quotation. Avoid long quotations.

Papers, and even paragraphs, usually should not begin with a quotation. Readers prefer to see what you have to say first. As a rule, do not conclude paragraphs with quotations either.

47i   Do not moralize.

Good criticism does not preach. Do not use your paper as a platform from which to state your views on the rights and wrongs and conditions of the world. A literary paper can be spoiled by an attempt to teach a moral lesson.

Begin your paper by introducing the work and your ideas about it as literature. If the author discusses morals, religion, or social causes, his or her literary treatment of these subjects is a proper topic. Do not begin your paper with your own ideas about the world and then attempt to fit the literature to them or merge your ideas with the author's. Think for yourself, but *think about the author's writing.*

47j   Acknowledge your sources.

Define the difference between what other critics have written and what you think. State your contribution. Do not begin papers or paragraphs with the names of critics and their views before you have presented your own ideas.

Develop your own thesis. Stress your views, not those of others. Use sources to show that other critics have interpreted the literature correctly, to correct errors in criticism that is otherwise excellent, to show that a critic is right but that something needs to be added, or to show that no one has previously written on your subject.

It is not a problem if no critic has written about the work or the point you are making unless your instructor requires you to have a number of sources. However, it is a serious error to state incorrectly that nothing has been written about your subject. Be thorough in your investigation.

For bibliographies of writings about literature, see **48b.** For information about plagiarism and documentation, see **48f** and **48g.**

Writing a paper about a poem

Suppose you have looked at a number of poems and chosen to write about Mary Oliver's "The Black Walnut Tree." The text of the poem is printed below. Read it through quickly. Read it again and think of or list topics you might want to discuss. Look at the questions that follow the poem. Study the poem as you think of the general questions and your own list of topics. At some stage in this process, write down answers, take notes, and prepare to write a critical paper.

The Black Walnut Tree

My mother and I debate:
we could sell
the black walnut tree
to the lumberman,

and pay off the mortgage.
Likely some storm anyway
will churn down its dark boughs,
smashing the house. We talk
slowly, two women trying
in a difficult time to be wise.
Roots in the cellar drains,
I say, and she replies
that the leaves are getting heavier
every year, and the fruit
harder to gather away.
But something brighter than money
moves in our blood—an edge
sharp and quick as a trowel
that wants us to dig and sow.
So we talk, but we don't do
anything. That night I dream
of my fathers out of Bohemia
filling the blue fields
of fresh and generous Ohio
with leaves and vines and orchards.
What my mother and I both know
is that we'd crawl with shame
in the emptiness we'd made
in our own and our fathers' backyard.
So the black walnut tree
swings through another year
of sun and leaping winds,
of leaves and bounding fruit,
and, month after month, the whip-
crack of the mortgage.

MARY OLIVER

Questions and topics for consideration

1. What is the significance of the two characters?
2. What are the roles of a mother and a daughter? Would two

sisters have the same meaning and poetic effect as characters?

3. The poem does not name the subjects of the women's talk. What are some of the possibilities?
4. What is the importance of the characters' fear that the tree may be destroyed by a storm?
5. Explain the women's concerns about the roots, the cellar drains, the leaves, the fruit (or nuts).
6. Interpret the "sharp and quick edge."
7. What is the meaning of digging and sowing?
8. Explain the daughter's dream about Bohemian fathers.
9. What does "emptiness" mean?
10. Explain the ending of the poem—the winds, leaves, and fruit and also the mortgage.
11. Consider the meaning of the tree, the character of the people, and the nature of their problems.
12. Why did the poet choose a black walnut tree? Why does the poem use the word *fruit* for nuts? Why would a lumberman be interested in a black walnut? (You may know the answer, or you may need to do research.)

■ **Exercise 1**

Using your answers to the questions above, write a paper about "The Black Walnut Tree."

Writing a paper about a work of fiction

Read the following short story carefully.

A Game of Catch
Richard Wilbur

Monk and Glennie were playing catch on the side lawn of the firehouse when Scho caught sight of them. They were good at it, for seventh-graders, as anyone could see right away. Monk, wearing a catcher's mitt, would lean easily sidewise and back, with one leg lifted and his throwing hand almost down to the grass, and then lob the white ball straight up into the sunlight. Glennie would shield his eyes with his left hand and, just as the ball fell past him, snag it with a little dart of his glove. Then he would burn the ball straight toward Monk, and it would spank into the round mitt and sit, like a still-life apple on a plate, until Monk flipped it over into his right hand and, with a negligent flick of his hanging arm, gave Glennie a fast grounder.

They were going on and on like that, in a kind of slow, mannered, luxurious dance in the sun, their faces perfectly blank and entranced, when Glennie noticed Scho dawdling along the other side of the street and called hello to him. Scho crossed over and stood at the front edge of the lawn, near an apple tree, watching.

"Got your glove?" asked Glennie after a time. Scho obviously hadn't.

"You could give me some easy grounders," said Scho. "But don't burn 'em."

"All right," Glennie said. He moved off a little, so the three of them formed a triangle, and they passed the ball around for about five minutes, Monk tossing easy grounders to Scho, Scho throwing to Glennie, and Glennie burning them in to Monk. After a while, Monk began to throw them back to Glennie once or twice before he let Scho have his grounder, and finally Monk gave Scho a fast, bumpy grounder that hopped over his shoulder and went into the brake on the other side of the street.

"Not so hard," called Scho as he ran across to get it.

"You should've had it," Monk shouted.

It took Scho a little while to find the ball among the ferns and dead leaves, and when he saw it, he grabbed it up and threw it toward Glennie. It struck the trunk of the apple tree, bounced back at an angle, and rolled steadily and stupidly onto the cement apron in front of the firehouse, where one of the trucks was parked. Scho ran hard and stopped it just before it rolled under the truck, and this time he carried it back to his former position on the lawn and threw it carefully to Glennie.

"I got an idea," said Glennie. "Why don't Monk and I catch for five minutes more, and then you can borrow one of our gloves?"

"That's all right with me," said Monk. He socked his fist into his mitt, and Glennie burned one in.

"All right," Scho said, and went over and sat under the tree. There in the shade he watched them resume their skillful play. They threw lazily fast or lazily slow—high, low, or wide—and always handsomely, their expressions serene, changeless, and forgetful. When Monk missed a low backhand catch, he walked indolently after the ball and, hardly even looking, flung it side-arm for an imaginary put-out. After a good while of this, Scho said, "Isn't it five minutes yet?"

"One minute to go," said Monk, with a fraction of a grin.

Scho stood up and watched the ball slap back and forth for several minutes more, and then he turned and pulled himself up into the crotch of the tree.

"Where you going?" Monk asked.

"Just up the tree," Scho said.

"I guess he doesn't want to catch," said Monk.

Scho went up and up through the fat light-gray branches until they grew slender and bright and gave under him. He found a place where several supple branches were knit to make a dangerous chair, and sat there with his head coming out of the leaves into the sunlight. He could see the two other boys down below, the ball going back and forth between them as if they were bowling on the grass, and Glennie's crew-cut head looking like a sea urchin.

"I found a wonderful seat up here," Scho said loudly. "If I don't fall out." Monk and Glennie didn't look up or comment, and so he began jouncing gently in his chair of branches and singing "Yo-ho, heave ho" in an exaggerated way.

"Do you know what, Monk?" he announced in a few moments. "I can make you two guys do anything I want. Catch that ball, Monk! Now you catch it Glennie!"

"I was going to catch it anyway," Monk suddenly said. "You're not making anybody do anything when they're already going to do it anyway."

"I made you say what you just said," Scho replied joyfully.

"No, you didn't, said Monk, still throwing and catching but now less serenely absorbed in the game.

"That's what I wanted you to say," Scho said.

The ball bounded off the rim of Monk's mitt and plowed into a gladiolus bed beside the firehouse, and Monk ran to get it while Scho jounced in his treetop and sang, "I wanted you to miss that. Anything you do is what I wanted you to do."

"Let's quit for a minute," Glennie suggested.

"We might as well, until the peanut gallery shuts up," Monk said.

They went over and sat cross-legged in the shade of the tree. Scho looked down between his legs and saw them on the dim, spotty ground, saying nothing to one another. Glennie soon began abstractedly spinning his glove between his palms; Monk pulled his nose and stared out across the lawn.

"I want you to mess around with your nose, Monk," said Scho, giggling. Monk withdrew his hand from his face.

"Do that with your glove, Glennie," Scho persisted. "Monk, I want you to pull up hunks of grass and chew on it."

Glennie looked up and saw a self-delighted, intense face staring down at him through the leaves. "Stop being a dope and come down and we'll catch for a few minutes," he said.

Scho hesitated, and then said, in a tentatively mocking voice, "That's what I wanted you to say."

"All right, then, nuts to you," said Glennie.

"Why don't you keep quiet and stop bothering people?" Monk asked.

"I made you say that," Scho replied, softly.

"Shut up," Monk said.

"I made you say that, and I want you to be standing there looking sore. And I want you to climb up the tree. I'm making you do it!"

Monk was scrambling up through the branches, awkward in his haste, and getting snagged on twigs. His face was furious and foolish, and he kept telling Scho to shut up, shut up, shut up, while the other's exuberant and panicky voice poured down upon his head.

"*Now* you shut up or you'll be sorry," Monk said, breathing hard as he reached up and threatened to shake the cradle of slight branches in which Scho was sitting.

"I *want*—" Scho screamed as he fell. Two lower branches broke his rustling, crackling fall, but he landed on his back with a deep thud and lay still, with a strangled look on his face and his eyes clenched. Glennie knelt down and asked breathlessly. "Are you O.K., Scho? Are you O.K.?," while Monk swung down through the leaves crying that honestly he hadn't even touched him, the crazy guy just let go. Scho doubled up and turned over on his right side, and now both the other boys knelt beside him, pawing at his shoulder and begging to know how he was.

Then Scho rolled away from them and sat partly up, still struggling to get his wind but forcing a species of smile onto his face.

"I'm sorry, Scho," Monk said. "I didn't mean to make you fall."

Scho's voice came out weak and gravelly, in gasps. "I meant —you to do it. You—had to. You can't do—anything—unless I want—you to."

Glennie and Monk looked helplessly at him as he sat there, breathing a bit more easily and smiling fixedly, with tears in his eyes. Then they picked up their gloves and the ball, walked over to the street, and went slowly away down the sidewalk. Monk punching his fist into the mitt, Glennie juggling the ball between glove and hand.

From under the apple tree, Scho, still bent over a little for lack of breath, croaked after them in triumph and misery, "I want you to do whatever you're going to do for the whole rest of your life!"

Some final hints on writing about literature

Read the work once carefully.

Decide on a subject generally.

Narrow the subject as much as you can before a second reading.

Ask yourself questions as you read the work a second time, a third, and so on.

Write down the answers to your questions.

Arrange the answers by topics.

Decide on a final approach, topic, title, and thesis.

Discard the erroneous answers to your questions.

Discard the irrelevant points. Choose the one you wish to discuss.

Select the best topics.

Put them in logical order.

Rearrange them as you carry out the creative process of thinking through the subject and writing the paper.

Revise as many times as necessary.

Do not display or emphasize technical terms, which may sometimes be as distracting as they are helpful. Your reader will not be impressed by attempts to show off. That is no substitute for straight thinking and clear writing.

Be sure early in the paper to name the work that you write about and the author (even though you may have this information in the title). Do not misspell the author's name—as often happens. Ernest Hemingway, for example, spelled his last name with only one *m*.

■ **Exercise 2**

Write down a list of questions about "A Game of Catch" like those about "The Black Walnut Tree." Make a list of topics for papers about Wilbur's story. Write a paper on "A Game of Catch" before you read the model paper that follows.

The Missing Glove in "A Game of Catch"

What happens when two boys are throwing a
baseball back and forth and a third boy shows up to
join them without the necessary glove is the subject of Richard Wilbur's short story "A Game of
Catch." He develops this situation in such a way
as to reveal indirectly one of life's recurrent
problems. The story is an account of a misfit.

Of utmost importance in the story is Scho's
missing glove. When he joins Monk's and Glennie's
"luxurious dance in the sun," as Wilbur calls their
game of catch, they notice immediately that he has
no glove. "'Got your glove?' asked Glennie after a
time. Scho obviously hadn't." If he had had a
glove, he might have been able to participate har-
moniously with others in this "dance in the sun,"
which broadly represents the game of life. Since
he has no glove, he cannot play the game well, and
his fellow players feel that he is spoiling it for
them. Therefore, they must find a way to exclude
him.

Life is a give-and-take affair, a fast-moving
game of skill with high rewards for those who can

play it well and who have the right equipment.
Monk and Glennie are such skillful players who use
their talents and their tools (glove and mitt) effectively. The ball they toss lands in "the round
mitt . . . like a still-life apple on a plate."
Coming into this game without a glove is like ap-
pearing in life without some necessary talent or
credential required by society for success. In
societies that look favorably on distinguished
family history, the criterion might be the right
background. In circles where racial bias is strong,
it might be the right color. It might be particular personality traits in societies where they are
highly regarded. The necessary equipment in this
sense is anything needed for acceptance and success.
Without it, one is a misfit and will suffer
exclusion.

How alienation can affect a person who lacks
some missing ingredient is the subject of the
second half of Wilbur's story. Having been denied
the opportunity to enjoy the fruit of life (the
baseball-apple), Scho attempts to rise above society
and to make himself superior to it. He climbs to

the top of a nearby apple tree so that he can sulk
and look down on those participating in the game of
catch. He pretends that he is now part of something
greater than the everyday affairs of life. Partially to annoy those who do not accept him and partly
to ease the pain of rejection in himself, he creates
from his seat in the apple tree a game of his own--
control of others. But he has no equipment for this
game either. He is not really superior to others.
He cannot actually make them do what he wants them
to do. All he can do is anger them with his arrogant claims of being able to control them and bring
about a conflict that results in injury to himself.
Even after he falls from the tree to the ground and
is suffering pain and misery, he will not give up
his own game--even though Monk and Glennie express
guilt and concern. At the end of the story, Glennie
and Monk "picked up their gloves and the ball,
walked over to the street and went slowly down the
sidewalk, Monk punching his fist into the mitt,
Glennie juggling the ball between glove and hand."
Scho, no longer in the "cradle" of the apple tree--
it having rejected him as society has--sits under

the tree and croaks "after them in triumph and
misery."

  "A Game of Catch," then, can be read on one
level as a psychological study of the misfit who,
missing the "glove"--that is, the requirements
needed to join in the fast-moving activities of
life and gain the respect of society--develops an
alternate game, one that puts him in conflict with
society and brings him violence, suffering, and a
misguided sense of self-importance. Wilbur blames
neither those who possess the tools to play well
nor the one whose glove is missing. The story
preaches no sermon but merely depicts with a touch
of sadness and compassion a situation all too
common in life.

■ **Exercise 3**

1. *Write a brief description of the methods, techniques, and subject of criticism in the model paper.*
2. *Suggest other topics for critical papers about Wilbur's story.*

■ **Exercise 4**

Write a critical paper about a short story assigned or approved by your instructor.

Writing a paper about a film

Most of the principles and suggestions presented in the chapter on writing about literature will help you in writing about films. You should always keep in mind, however, that film is a visual art with its own advantages and problems distinct from those of short stories, novels, poems, and even drama. In pursuing your project, be prepared to see the motion picture several times and to study parts of it in even more detail. A single viewing will seldom produce a perceptive and interesting paper.

The phases of your own composing and writing processes about films may vary considerably both in nature and in order. One possible way of proceeding is suggested in the following steps.

1. Select a film to write about *soon* after the paper is assigned. Choose a particular film because you have an interest in the subject matter or the film's reputation.
2. View the entire film on a video cassette recorder twice in order to determine its chief meanings and techniques. Jot down notes and random ideas.

3. From these notes and from brainstorming, arrive at a tentative topic, one narrow enough to cover in a few pages but important enough to relate to larger areas of interest.
4. Identify scenes in the film that pertain to the topic and review each of these several times while making notes.
5. After reviewing all your notes and thinking through the possibilities, decide whether the topic is promising.
6. Read generally about the film's subject, production, and merits. [Note: Research for particular assignments is often neither required nor prohibited. Follow your teacher's instructions in the use of secondary material.]
7. Organize an argument based on the contribution of your subject to such matters as the film's tone, characterization, and theme.
8. Write a rough draft.
9. Revise extensively, trying to achieve coherence as well as clarity and correctness.
10. Type the paper and proofread it carefully.

Model paper

Patton's Dog

When the film <u>Patton</u> was released in 1970, the public hailed it as one of the great motion pictures of modern times. The Academy of Motion Picture Arts and Sciences was impressed: <u>Patton</u> received seven academy awards, including those for best picture, best director (Franklin J. Schaffner), best actor (George C. Scott, though he refused it), and best screenplay. The script was written by Francis Ford Coppola, who, after doing extensive research on Patton's life, decided neither to glorify Patton nor to condemn him but to portray his complexity with understanding. To help do that, he introduced into the film a bull terrier, who played Patton's dog, Willie.

Though <u>Patton</u> has been the subject of extensive critical writing, the function of Patton's dog has gone largely unnoticed. The extent of Coppola's research into Patton's life is evident here. Patton really did have a white bull terrier named Willie that had originally belonged to a pilot in the RAF killed in combat. However, Coppola created eleven scenes with the dog to bring out comedy, character, and theme.

Before the debut of Willie, Patton is the focus of several scenes of action, such as in the battle of El Guettar. Moments later, he climbs out a window at his headquarters in North Africa to stand boldly in the path of two German planes strafing the city. Scenes like these steadily emphasize conflict and violence until a change of pace is needed. It comes in the form of comic relief named Willie. After Patton arrives in a staff car to give a speech for a women's organization, his aide, Colonel Codman, opens the door and Patton appears with Willie on a leash. Describing his new dog to Codman, Patton says: "Bred for combat. I'm gonna call him William--for William the Conqueror." As Patton and Codman walk toward the podium, Patton's dog begins to bark at a small dog belonging to one of the women. Patton says, "Watch this, Codman," who replies, "General, he'll kill that dog." Smilingly, Patton says, "Naw, I'll hold him." As the woman's dog begins to bark ferociously, Willie, "bred for combat," retreats in fear. The woman picks up her lap dog and walks toward Patton with an apology: "I'm terribly sorry, General. Did Abigail frighten your dog?" Patton reassures her with a polite but embarrassed smile, but when she leaves, he looks down disgustedly at his dog and says: "Your name isn't William; it's Willie." It is one of the truly comic moments in the film.

Willie's function as comic relief continues into the next scene, where positioning of the camera clearly illustrates how a film can create effects hardly possible in other art forms. Just as George C. Scott is about to deliver the speech Patton made to a gathering of British women, a speech that caused much consternation and seriously damaged the general's military career, the camera shifts abruptly to Willie looking sheepishly at Abigail, the same small dog that had terrorized him just a few moments before. She reacts to Willie's stare by barking at him, and Willie once again retreats in fear. The camera then shifts back to Patton as he makes his notorious prediction that America and Britain would be the sole rulers of the postwar world, with Russia left out of the picture. Willie's comic performance in this scene prevents it from becoming an all-too-early climax in a film about Patton's career, which still has a long way to go. In addition, Patton's speech, received with high seriousness at the time it was actually given, contains in historical perspective an element of the comic. The film underscores this aspect by associating the speech with Willie's humorous performance on the podium.

In addition to furnishing a much-needed comic ingredient, Patton's dog is invaluable as a foil to the general's character: Willie is constantly Patton's opposite. In the two scenes with Abigail as well as later in the film when he is badly startled by a cart pulled by horses, Willie manifests a trait that Patton finds intolerable: fearfulness. In fact, Patton was severely disciplined during World War II for slapping a soldier with battle fatigue, a condition that the general considered an excuse for cowardice. If Willie has no stomach for fighting, he also contrasts with his owner physically. George C. Scott projects Patton as aristocratically straight in posture and well coordinated in movements, while Willie is awkward

and lovingly clumsy. Unlike Patton, Willie seems
to have no enemies (except Abigail), and he is
friendly to all he encounters. He sits in the lap
of a sergeant while on a plane headed for France.
His manner appears to express kindness and perhaps
sympathy toward the American soldiers walking by
him as they go to rescue troops at Bastogne. In
contrast, Patton's demeanor is prideful as he
thinks of his troops--they are merely parts in his
war machine, noble and fine, but nevertheless ex-
pendable. Willie's mildness and good humor are
evident in a scene when he approaches his master,
tail wagging, in Patton's headquarters, but the
general has no time for such simple affection: he
is studying the art of war.

Although the dog serves generally to help
bring out Patton's commitment to war as a way of
life, Willie ironically is also an instrument
through which the warmonger is shown to have a
tender but sensitive side. For example, in a scene
where Patton is in his headquarters after the
liberation of Paris, he walks past Willie (sitting
like a human being in a chair) and pets him with

what seems genuine affection. Despite Willie's
failure to live up to his breeding as a fighter,
Patton--this man who thrives on fighting--keeps him
by his side, a startling fact that suggests effectively the general's great complexity.

Among other things, Patton is a motion picture
with a powerful but subtle theme, one that has
resounded through the ages: those whose values
endure are the peacemakers, not the conquerors.
Yet Patton is not a propagandistic or preachy film.
This underlying theme is unobtrusively developed
largely through a series of images and references
relating to the figure of the conqueror and, more
specifically, to the historical William the Conqueror. Patton originally called his dog William
the Conqueror because of his ardent admiration for
that great combatant. The film sustains a series
of allusions to William. For example, Patton at
one point is seen reading the History of the Norman
Conquest and formulating his battle plans in Europe
as he thinks of William's tactics. He imagines
himself to be in the line of the world's great conquerors; he even suspects that he is related to them

through reincarnation. But it is his love of war and warriors and his image of himself as a twentieth-century William the Conqueror that finally brings him down from the majestic if profane conqueror who opens the film with a speech to his troops to the dejected outcast of the final scene. There he walks behind his dog, Willie, as his voice off-screen describes nostalgically the receptions of ancient conquerors as they returned in victory to their cities. Only Patton and his dog are present in this last scene; Willie leads the way to suggest perhaps that the true conquerors in life are not the Pattons but the peace-loving meek. Ironically, Willie was the conqueror after all.

RESEARCH

48 Writing the Research Paper

Research is the act of gathering new information. The English word *research* derives from the Old French *recerche*, which means to seek out, to travel through. When you embark on research, you set forth on a sort of travel through lands that may be strange and fascinating. By making alert observations and asking astute questions, you have the opportunity to familiarize yourself with a new region.

You will profit greatly from getting your thinking straight at the very beginning of your project about why you are engaged in research. Your purpose should not be merely to find enough material on a subject to satisfy your instructor that you have used the library and know how to find, quote from, and cite sources. The *primary* reason for research is to learn enough about a subject to be able to write or speak about it knowledgeably. Research is necessary for you to know what you are talking about. You need to be honest and considerate toward those from whom you learn, however, and give them proper credit for the discoveries they have passed on to you. This section will help you to know when and how to do that.

After discovering new information on your subject and examining and evaluating various ideas, you will arrive at a crucial point. Your basic research is finished, but the project is not. A good research paper is not simply a series of paraphrases, citations, and quotations. Its heart is yours, not someone else's. You must formulate your own thesis, give your own slant to the subject, think through questions, and present some conclusions of your own. A research paper, then, embodies the results of exploration into your own thinking as well as into the thinking of others.

48a Choose a subject that interests you. Limit it to a manageable size.

Writing a research paper usually involves an extended period of time and a variety of activities and skills. If you get an early start (delay is deadly on a research project), give adequate consideration to potential topics, and choose one that captures your imagination and piques your curiosity, you will find the process not only instructive but also intriguing. Often it is helpful to set aside a period for thumbing through current periodicals. Ask your reference librarian to point out to you bibliographic guides such as *Hot Topics* and *Editorial Research Reports.* Make sure, however, that you carry out *controlled browsing,* for you can waste time if you do not keep constantly in mind that even at this stage you are doing research; you are searching for a good topic, not merely reading and looking randomly.

Choose a general subject area

Begin the process of selecting a topic by asking yourself what truly interests you. Perhaps you would like to learn more about photography, the fast-food industry, or the Roman Empire. The possibilities are infinite. Untie your imagination and let it roam freely. If nothing comes to mind and your browsing in magazines and a good encyclopedia produces no positive results, turn to a list of broad areas such as the following, decide on one you like, and then go on to narrow it down.

advertising	acting	law	business
religion	literature	art	oceanography
ecology	philosophy	history	government
science	anthropology	economics	medicine
geography	industry	sociology	archaeology
psychology	folklore	agriculture	education

Get more specific

Suppose you have chosen medicine for your general area. Naturally, you will need to focus on one aspect of this vast field. To help you decide on an aspect of the area you have selected on the list, draw a circle around it and then review the other entries on the list or think of more topics to determine which ones represent your secondary interests. Draw arrows from your primary area to the secondary ones, as in the example below.

advertising	acting	law	business
religion	literature	art	oceanography
ecology	philosophy	history	government
science	anthropology	economics	medicine
geography	industry	sociology	archaeology
psychology	folklore	agriculture	education

By associating a major area of interest with secondary (but vital) concerns, you move closer to a subject. For instance, think of aspects of medicine that involve law and sociology. After more thinking and general reading, a specific topic may emerge: "The Effect of Malpractice Suits on the Public's Image of the Physician."

With an entirely different set of interests, you might circle, say, *science* and then draw arrows to *history, geography, anthropology, archaeology,* and *ecology.* Many possibilities for a good topic exist in such a combination, but this procedure brings to light a pattern of interest that gets you closer to your final subject (which might be in this instance "What Happened to the Dinosaurs: A Continuing Debate"). The student who wrote the model paper on pp. 369–415 circled *oceanography,* then drew arrows to *psychology, science,* and *sociology.* Some hard thinking then resulted in a good subject, "The Dolphin Controversy."

Avoid inappropriate subjects

After you have tentatively selected a topic, trim it, refine it, and polish it into a definite title and then ask yourself the following questions about it.

1. *Is it too broad?* If you set out to write a research paper of two thousand words on "Religions of the World," the paper will probably be too general, undetailed, and shallow. You might be very much interested in "East Africa: 1824–1886," but this is the subject for a book or monograph. These are both good areas to work in, but general titles such as these show that further narrowing is badly needed before a workable subject is discovered.

2. *Is it too technical?* Consider this question from two angles: yours and your audience's. You may know a great deal about "Bronchial Morphometry in Odontocete Cetaceans," but an audience of general readers will not. Try to reconstitute your subject into one that will be more understandable to your readers.

3. *Does it promise more than it can deliver?* Examine your subject carefully to be sure that the promise implicit in the title can be fulfilled. For example, how could a research paper live up to the expectations created by a subject such as "Is There a God?" Even a topic that seems sufficiently limited and unspecialized can be inappropriate because it is overly ambitious.

4. *Is it too close to home?* Sometimes controversial issues create such an emotional response in the writer that a sustained, even tone is impossible. If volatile subjects such as abortion, television ministers, racism, and the Equal Rights Amendment cause you such anguish that you cannot be calm and objective about them, avoid them. Interest is one thing; subjective indulgence is another. Controversial questions currently in the news can be excellent and compelling topics for papers, but be certain that you are not so deeply involved that you will get carried away emotionally.

5. *Is it dull?* You must stand outside yourself to answer this question. You may be fascinated with "Four Types of Bathroom Tubs," but ask yourself if others will be. Usually you can relate what might be an uninteresting topic to other concerns and produce a promising subject. If for some reason you are intrigued with bathtubs, you might develop an imaginative subject by linking that interest with art ("The Bathtub in Postmodern Impressionism") or with psychology ("Psychological Implications of Modern Bathtub Designs").

48b Follow a search strategy for using the library.

Once you have determined your subject, you should compile a **working bibliography,** a list of publications pertinent to your topic. The items on this list should include only the author's name, the title, and any information you need in order to find the source in the library. Where to begin and how to proceed in your search are matters that require planning; otherwise, you can waste countless hours in random and fruitless excursions. Usually the best place to begin is the **reference room.** Your professors in this area are the reference librarians, indispensable professionals in any college or university library. They can save you time by suggesting shortcuts or other alterations in your search strategy; they can also direct you to helpful guides, such as the *Library of Congress Subject Headings*, which enables you to locate by subject materials in the catalog of the library.

Before you turn to the library's catalog, however, look up your subject in a general or specialized encyclopedia, dictionary, or other such reference work. This is often an excellent starting point because the entries are usually general enough to give you a

Subject Card

Subject (sometimes in red)

Library of Congress
call number

Author

Title of book

Pages and technical
data

Subject headings
under which this
book is listed

*Publication
information*

*Dewey decimal
call number*

QL737
C4M36

CETACEA

McNally, Robert, 1946-
So remorseless a havoc : of dolphins, whales, and men / by
Robert McNally ; illustrations by Pieter Arend Folkens. — 1st
ed. — Boston : Little, Brown, c1981.

xvi, 268 p. : ill. ; 24 cm.

Bibliography: p. 253-259.
Includes index.
ISBN 0-316-56292-0 : $12.95

1. Cetacea.   2. Whaling.   I. Title.

QL737.C4M36   1981   333.95'9—dc19   81-5958
                                              AACR 2   MARC

Library of Congress

Another Subject Card

QL737
C4M36   WHALING

      McNally, Robert, 1946-
         So remorseless a havoc : of dolphins, whales, and men / by
Robert McNally ; illustrations by Pieter Arend Folkens. — 1st
ed. — Boston : Little, Brown, c1981.

         xvi, 268 p. : ill. ; 24 cm.

         Bibliography: p. 253-259.
         Includes index.
         ISBN 0-316-56292-0 : $12.95

         1. Cetacea.   2. Whaling.   I. Title.

         QL737.C4M36   1981   333.95'9—dc19   81-5958
                                                AACR 2   MARC

     Library of Congress

Author Card

QL737
C4M36

      McNally, Robert, 1946-
         So remorseless a havoc : of dolphins, whales, and men / by
Robert McNally ; illustrations by Pieter Arend Folkens. — 1st
ed. — Boston : Little, Brown, c1981.

         xvi, 268 p. : ill. ; 24 cm.

         Bibliography: p. 253-259.
         Includes index.
         ISBN 0-316-56292-0 : $12.95

         1. Cetacea.   2. Whaling.   I. Title.

         QL737.C4M36   1981   333.95'9—dc19   81-5958
                                                AACR 2   MARC

     Library of Congress

Title Card

```
QL737      So remorseless a havoc
CLM36
           McNally, Robert, 1946-
              So remorseless a havoc : of dolphins, whales, and men / by
           Robert McNally ; illustrations by Pieter Arend Folkens. — 1st
           ed. — Boston : Little, Brown, c1981.

              xvi, 268 p. : ill. ; 24 cm.
              Bibliography: p. 253-259.
              Includes index.
              ISBN 0-316-56292-0 : $12.95




              1. Cetacea.   2. Whaling.    I. Title.
           QL737.C4M36   1981          333.95'9—dc19            81-5958
                                                              AACR 2   MARC
           Library of Congress
```

broad outline of information. For example, the article on dolphins
in the *Encyclopedia Americana* (1986) gives details about the physical makeup of the species, their eating habits, and their repro-
ductive cycle. It then concentrates on the most familiar variety,
the bottlenose dolphin. It provides historical data on the relationship between human beings and dolphins, and ends with a summary of recent findings about the species' intelligence, ability to
imitate human speech, and extensive use of a faculty like sonar.

Sometimes articles in encyclopedias conclude with suggestions for further reading (a **bibliography**), which can start you on
your way toward compiling a list of materials to read or consult.
Below is a listing of encyclopedias, dictionaries, bibliographies,
and other reference aids that you will find useful in the early
stages of your research. Ask your reference librarian about additional sources.

General reference aids

Articles on American Literature, 1900–1950; 1950–1967; 1968–1975.

Cambridge Bibliography of English Literature, 1941–1957. 5 vols.; *New Cambridge Bibliography of English Literature,* 1969–1977. 5 vols.

Cambridge Histories: Ancient, 12 vols., rev. ed. in progress; Medieval, 8 vols.; Modern, 13 vols.; *New Cambridge Modern History,* 14 vols.

Collier's Encyclopedia.

Columbia Lippincott Gazetteer of the World, 1962.

Contemporary Authors, 1962– .

Current Biography, 1940– . "Who's News and Why."

Dictionary of American Biography, 1928–1937. 20 vols. Supplements 1–7, 1944–1981.

Dictionary of American History, rev. ed., 1976–1978. 8 vols.

Dictionary of National Biography, 1885–1901. 22 vols. main work and 1st supplement; supplements 2–7, 1912–1971.

Encyclopedia Americana. Supplemented by the *Americana Annual.* 1923– .

Encyclopedia Judaica, 1972. 16 vols. Supplemented by its *Yearbook.*

Encyclopedia of Philosophy, 1967. 8 vols.

Encyclopedia of Religion, 1987. 15 vols.

Encyclopedia of Religion and Ethics, 1908–1927. 13 vols.

Encyclopedia of World Art, 1959–1968. 15 vols. Supplement, 1983.

Encyclopedia of World History, 5th ed., 1972.

Essay and General Literature Index, 1900– . "An Index to . . . Volumes of Collections of Essays and Miscellaneous Works."

Facts on File; a Weekly World News Digest . . . , 1940– .

Information Please Almanac, 1947– .

International Encyclopedia of the Social Sciences, 1968. 17 vols. *Biographical Supplement,* 1979.

Literary History of the United States, 1974. 2 vols.

MLA International Bibliography of Books and Articles on the Modern Languages and Literatures, 1919– .

McGraw-Hill Encyclopedia of Science and Technology. 6th ed., 1987. 20 vols. Supplemented by *McGraw-Hill Yearbook of Science and Technology.*

McGraw-Hill Encyclopedia of World Drama. 2nd ed., 1984. 5 vols.

Mythology of All Races, 1916–1932. 13 vols.

New Catholic Encyclopedia, 1967–1979. 17 vols.

New Century Cyclopedia of Names, 1954. 3 vols.

New Encyclopaedia Britannica. Supplemented by *Britannica Book of the Year,* 1938– .

New Grove Dictionary of Music and Musicians, 1980. 20 vols.

Oxford Classical Dictionary, 2d ed., 1970.

Oxford Companion to American Literature, 5th ed., 1983.

Oxford Companion to English Literature, 5th ed., 1985.

Oxford Companion to Film, 1976.

Oxford History of English Literature, 1945– .

Princeton Encyclopedia of Poetry and Poetics, 1974.

Statesman's Yearbook: Statistical and Historical Annual of the States of the World, 1864– .

Statistical Abstract of the United States, 1878– .

Webster's Biographical Dictionary, 1980.

World Almanac and Book of Facts, 1868– .

The basic tool for finding books in the library is the catalog. It may be in the form of a card catalog, a microform catalog, or a computerized catalog. Books are listed alphabetically by author, title, and subjects with helpful cross-references that will steer you to new aspects of your topics. Reproduced on pp. 333–335 are four typical catalog cards—actually four copies of the same Library of Congress card filed for four different uses. Notice the typed title and subject headings.

In some libraries the card catalog has been supplemented or replaced by catalogs on microform. These new catalogs require comparatively little space and can be made available in locations outside the library. A COM (Computer Output Microform) catalog is commonly on microfiche or microfilm, and has author, title, and subject entries arranged in the same way as the card catalog. Computerized, or on-line, catalogs are being used by an increasing number of libraries to take advantage of the computer's capabilities to store and retrieve the information formerly found on catalog cards. These systems allow the library user to sit at a terminal and search for material by author, title, subject, or any combination of these. Many on-line catalogs also allow the user to search for library holdings in a variety of new ways, such as by publisher, year of publication, library classification number, or international standard book number. Often persons using computers with modems at locations away from the library can gain access to these catalogs.

Articles in magazines and newspapers are a rich source of information on almost every subject. Some of the more important periodical indexes are listed below. Some of them are books, some are data bases, some are microform indexes (that is, on microfiche or microfilm), and some are published in more than one form. *The Readers' Guide to Periodical Literature*, for example, is found in many libraries in large green buckram volumes in the Reference Department. It is also available as a database to be used on-line or on compact disc. Your reference librarian can tell you which indexes are available, in what format, and how you can use them.

Periodical indexes

Readers' Guide to Periodical Literature, 1900– .
An index to the most widely circulated American periodicals.

Magazine Index, 1977/78– .
A microform index covering all the periodicals in *Readers' Guide* and many more. Especially useful for current topics.

Nineteenth Century Readers' Guide to Periodical Literature, 1890–1899.
Author and subject index to some fifty English-language general periodicals of the last decade of the nineteenth century.

Poole's Index to Periodical Literature, 1802–1906.
An index by subject to the leading British and American periodicals of the nineteenth century.

Humanities Index, 1974– .

Social Sciences Index, 1974– . Preceded by *Social Sciences and Humanities Index*.

Social Sciences and Humanities Index, 1965–1974. Formerly *International Index*, 1907–1965.
Author and subject index to a selection of scholarly journals.

British Humanities Index, 1962– .
Supersedes in part *Subject Index to Periodicals*, 1915–1922, 1926–1961.
Subject index to British periodicals.

Applied Science and Technology Index, 1958– .
Cumulative subject index to a selection of English and American periodicals in such fields as aeronautics, automation, chemistry, electricity, engineering, physics.

Art Index, 1929– .
"Cumulative Author and Subject Index to a Selected List of Fine Arts Periodicals."

Biography Index, 1946– .
"Cumulative Index to Biographical Material in Books and Magazines."

Biological and Agricultural Index, 1964– .
Continues *Agricultural Index*, 1919–1964. "Cumulative Subject Index to Periodicals in the Fields of Biology, Agriculture, and Related Sciences."

Book Review Digest, 1905– .
Index to book reviews. Includes excerpts from the reviews.

Book Review Index, 1965– .

Business Periodicals Index, 1958– .
Cumulative subject index to periodicals in all fields of business and industry.

Business Index, 1979– .
A microform index useful for current business topics.

Current Index to Journals in Education, 1969– .
Covers "the core periodical literature in the field of education" and "peripheral literature relating to the field of education."

Education Index, 1929– .
"Cumulative Subject Index to a Selected List of Educational Periodicals, Proceedings, and Yearbooks."

General Science Index, 1978– .
Science literature for the nonspecialist.

Industrial Arts Index, 1913–1957.
In 1958 divided into the *Applied Science and Technology Index* and *Business Periodicals Index*. "Subject Index to a Selected List of Engineering, Trade and Business Periodicals."

Music Index, 1949– .
Index by author and subject to a comprehensive list of music periodicals published throughout the world.

New York Times Index, 1851– .
"Master-Key to the News Since 1851."

National Newspaper Index, 1979– .
An on-line index to the *New York Times, Wall Street Journal, Christian Science Monitor, Los Angeles Times, Washington Post,* and other newspapers.

Newsbank Index, 1982– .
A microfiche index of selected articles in over a hundred city newspapers in the United States.

Public Affairs Information Service. Bulletin, 1915– .
Subject index to periodicals and government publications chiefly in the social sciences.

Suppose you are writing about the current controversy over dolphins. Looking under **Dolphins** in the *Readers' Guide to Periodical Literature*, November 1987, you find the following entry:

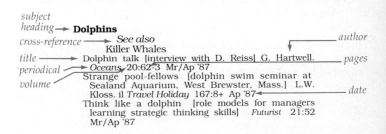

Consult indexes to periodicals in specific subject areas as well as the more general indexes such as the *Readers' Guide*. Under the heading **Dolphins and porpoises** in the *General Science Index* for November 1987, you find the following information:

Dolphins and porpoises
   Dolphin deaths raise pollution worries. M.
      Holderness. il *New Sci* 115:22 S 3 '87
   Habitats for cetaceans. *Oceans* 20:57 Jl/Ag '87
   Into the world of orcas. A. Morton. il *Int Wildl* 17:12-17
      S/O '87
   Keeping an ear on orcas. D. Hand. il *Oceans*
      20:10-19+ Jl/Ag '87
   Sonic punch: dolphins and whales generate "bangs"
      that may stun prey. T. M. Beardsley. *Sci Am* 257:36
      O '87

NOTE: If you do not know the abbreviation for a periodical, check
the front matter in the index.

With the information you have gathered from periodical indexes, you should be able to find articles on your subject. Check
the serials list or catalog to see whether the periodicals are in your
library. You probably will not have time to read carefully through
all the articles written generally on your topic; you can exclude
some merely by studying their titles in the periodical indexes.

Your **working bibliography** should grow as you proceed. Be
sure to include all the information that will help you find each
item listed: along with the author and title, you will need the library call number for books and the date, volume, and page
number for articles.

48c   Distinguish between primary and secondary sources and evaluate materials.

Primary sources are those about which other materials are written. *Moby-Dick* is a primary source; writings about *Moby-Dick* are
secondary sources. The terms distinguish between which material comes first (primary) and which follows (secondary). Some-

times what was once secondary—say, a book about Puritan New England—becomes primary material when it is the subject of later writings (in this instance, articles about the book). Primary sources for a study of tourists would consist of published and unpublished diaries, journals, and letters by tourists, interviews of tourists, and the like. The writings of journalists and historians about tourists would be secondary sources.

When considering which secondary sources to use in your research paper, you must know when a work was written, what information was available to its author, the reputation and reliability of the author, and, insofar as you can judge, the soundness of the author's argument and use of evidence. *The fact of publication is not a guarantee of truth, wisdom, objectivity, or perception.* Look with a critical eye at all the secondary material you discover in your search and rely only on those sources that are worthy (see p. 262).

48d Take accurate and effective notes from sources.

After you have compiled a working bibliography **(48b),** located some of the sources you wish to use, and done some preliminary reading, you are ready to begin collecting specific material for your paper. If you are writing a formally documented paper, make a **bibliography card** for each item as you examine it. This will be a full and exact record of bibliographical information, preferably on a 3 × 5 inch filing card. From these cards you will later compile your list of works cited. A sample card is shown on p. 344. The essential information includes the name of the author, the title of the work, the place and date of publication, and the name of the publisher. If the work has an editor or a translator, is in more than one volume, or is part of a series, these facts should be included. For later checking, record the library call number.

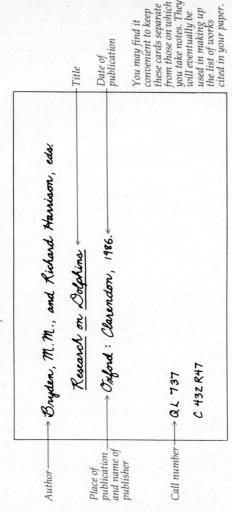

Bibliography Card

(reduced facsimile—actual size 3 X 5 inches)

Bryden, M. M., and Richard Harrison, eds.

Research on Dolphins

Oxford : Clarendon, 1986.

QL 737
C 432 R47

Author

Title

Date of publication

Place of publication and name of publisher

Call number

You may find it convenient to keep these cards separate from those on which you take notes. They will eventually be used in making up the list of works cited in your paper.

Paraphrased Notes

(reduced facsimile—actual size 3 X 5 inches)

Subject heading → *Dolphins in Captivity*

Cousteau and Diole' →

Page number → 158-59 *It is true that dolphins may discover much to like in a captive situation, and they appear to adjust well. Nevertheless, those who study them should remember that these animals have undergone a drastic change, and we cannot assume their behavior to be the same as that of dolphins in the open sea.*

Identification of source. Full bibliographical information has been taken down on the bibliography card.

Quotation

> ### Dolphins in Captivity
>
> Cousteau and Diolé
>
> 158-59 "But the behavior patterns which they develop in these conditions have very little to do with those which obtain when a dolphin lives at liberty in the sea./ We have succeeded in creating a personality common to *captive* dolphins" (italics mine).

Quotation and Paraphrase

> ### Dolphins in Captivity
>
> Cousteau and Diolé
>
> 158 Dolphins may discover much to like in a captive situation, and they appear to adjust well. "But the behavior patterns which they develop in these conditions have very little to do with those which obtain when a dolphin lives at liberty in the sea."

Quotation

Cooperation between Humans + Dolphins

McNally

58   "Dolphins do, of course, support
their own kind in distress, and in
rescuing a troubled human they are
simply extending that behavior to
another species."

Quotation

Legends about Dolphins

McNally

58   "Scientists also used to deride the
stories about dolphins carrying shipwrecked
and drowning people to safety ashore.
Some of these stories are the hallucina-
tions of people who have been pulled
back from the threshold of death, but
others have the ring of truth or the
corroboration of eyewitnesses."

Paraphrase

Mysteries of Dolphin Behavior

McNally

58-59 Strangely, dolphins do not act kindly toward humans just for the sake of reward. They help human beings in the water in the same manner as they would one of their own, but the question is how they understand that we need aid.

Quotation and Paraphrase

Mysteries of Dolphin Behavior

McNally

58-59 Dolphins will "cooperate or associate with humans" even when we do not reward them, and we are not sure why this is. Especially mysterious is how they "recognize that a human ... is in trouble" and "that taking this unknown creature ashore" is the correct action.

CAUTION: Carelessness in jotting down call numbers can lead to wasted time and confusion. Double-check to be sure you have recorded them correctly.

For **note-taking,** your next step, use cards or slips of paper uniform in size. Cards are easier to use than slips because they withstand more handling. Develop the knack of skimming a source so that you can move quickly over irrelevant material and concentrate on pertinent information. Use the table of contents, the section headings, and the index to find chapters or pages of particular use to you. As you read and take notes, consider what subtopics you will use. The two processes work together: Your reading will give you ideas for subtopics, and the subtopics will give direction to your note-taking.

At this point you are already in the process of organizing and outlining the paper. Suppose you wish to make a study of current attitudes toward dolphins. You might work up the following list of tentative subjects:

Aspects of dolphin intelligence

Captivity vs. freedom for dolphins

Cooperation between dolphins and humans

References to dolphins in ancient and modern times

Use of dolphins in military situations

Mysteries surrounding dolphins

These headings may not be final. Always be ready to delete, add, and change headings as you read and take notes. At this stage, it is neither possible nor necessary to determine the final order of headings.

To illustrate the methods of note-taking, suppose you have found the following passage about dolphins kept in captivity.

In our marinelands, dolphins find companions in captivity. They do tricks. They participate in shows. They have fans. But the behavior patterns which they develop in these conditions have very little to do with those which obtain when a dolphin lives at liberty in the sea. We have succeeded in creating a personality common to captive dolphins. And it is that personality that is being studied, without taking into sufficient account that we are dealing with animals that have been spoiled and perverted by man.

JACQUES-YVES COUSTEAU AND PHILIPPE DIOLÉ, Dolphins

You may make notes on this passage by paraphrasing, by quoting, or by combining short quotations with paraphrasing (see **48f**). The card on p. 345 identifies the source, gives a subject heading, indicates the page number, and then records relevant information in the student's own words. It *extracts* items of information instead of merely recasting the entire passage and line of thought in different words. Notice the careful selection of details and the fact that the paraphrase is considerably shorter than the original. The first card on p. 346 records a direct quotation, and the second combines quotation with paraphrase.

If you cannot determine just what information you wish to extract when you are taking notes, copy the entire passage. For later reference you must be careful to show by quotation marks that it is copied verbatim.

NOTE: The writer inserted a slash [/] in the quotation on the first card on p. 346 to indicate a break between pages.

A note card should contain information from only one source. If you keep your notes on cards with subject headings, you can later arrange all your cards by topics — a practical and an orderly procedure. Remember, the accuracy of your paper depends largely on the accuracy of your notes.

A photocopying machine can guarantee accuracy and save you time. At an early stage in your research it is not always possible to know exactly what information you need. Photocopy some of the longest passages, and then you can study them, digest them, and take notes later.

Read the following passage, which deals with the cooperation between dolphins and human beings.

> Sometimes cetaceans cooperate or associate with humans even when there appears to be nothing in it for them. Scientists . . . used to deride the stories about dolphins carrying shipwrecked and drowning people to safety ashore. Some of these stories are the hallucinations of people who have been pulled back from the threshold of death, but others have the ring of truth or the corroboration of eyewitnesses. Dolphins do, of course, support their own kind in distress, and in rescuing a troubled human they are simply extending that behavior to another species. Yet how does the dolphin recognize that a human, a species it rarely encounters, is in trouble, and how does it figure out that taking this unknown creature ashore is the right thing to do?
>
> ROBERT MCNALLY,
> *So Remorseless a Havoc: Of Dolphins, Whales and Men*

Now study the note cards on pp. 347–348 which are based on this passage. Observe the variety in subject headings and treatments.

48e   Produce an effective outline.

Since a research paper is usually longer and more complex than ordinary college papers, a good outline is likely to be of even greater help in your attempts to organize, expand, and delete materials. Consult **44d** about the various kinds of outlines.

After you have worked out a tentative outline, study it to be sure that you have included all the areas you wish to cover, that you have grouped subjects under the most appropriate headings, and that you have arranged the aspects of your discussion in the order that will produce the maximum effectiveness.

The thought that you put into a full and coherent outline is an excellent investment, which will pay off when you write the paper. You will find that you have worked out many of the problems of organization and made essential connections in preparing the outline that you would otherwise have to face during the composition of the paper. See the model outline on p. 371.

48f Acknowledge your sources; avoid plagiarism. Quote and paraphrase accurately.

Show your indebtedness to others by giving full details of sources. Using others' words and ideas as if they were your own is a form of stealing called **plagiarism.**

All direct quotations must be blocked or placed in quotation marks and acknowledged in your text.

Even when you take only a phrase or a single distinctive word from a source, you should enclose it in quotation marks and indicate where you got it. Compare the sources below with the passages that plagiarize them.

SOURCE

More than any previous explorer, Cook was well prepared to chart his discoveries and fix their locations accurately. He sailed at a time of rapid advances in methods of navigation; his ship was equipped with every available type of scientific instrument; he had the services of professional astronomers; and he himself had a far more sophisticated understanding of astronomy, mathematics, and surveying techniques than most ship captains.

LYNNE WITHEY,
Voyages of Discovery: Captain Cook and the Exploration of the Pacific

PASSAGE WITH PLAGIARISM

Although we often think of the famous Captain Cook as someone who was more of an adventurer than a systematic explorer, he actually was better prepared than any previous explorer to discover and fix new locations accurately. Many improvements were taking place in sailing. For example, his ship was furnished out with every available type of scientific instrument, and Cook himself had a far more sophisticated understanding of navigation than is often realized.

SOURCE

Although Poe's protagonists question their thoughts and feelings as well as their motivations and analyze the amount of harm they have done, they rarely grow in understanding. They lack the detachment necessary to rectify the situation and the will to carry out their decisions once these are made. Solipsistic in every way, they are caught in the stifling world of their own choice.

BETTINA L. KNAPP,
Edgar Allan Poe

PASSAGE WITH PLAGIARISM

Poe's main characters do examine themselves, but they rarely grow in understanding. They are not objective enough to change, and they lack the will to carry out their decisions once these are made. They are weird, or solipsistic in every way and therefore get stifled in their own choice.

These passages with plagiarism do contain some paraphrasing, but they also use some of the words of their sources without employing quotation marks, and neither indicates a source. If the source were acknowledged at the end but no quotation marks were used around words and phrases taken from the source, the writer would still be guilty of plagiarism. The writer of the passage about Poe was not only dishonest but also careless. He or she obviously did not know the meaning of the word *solipsistic* in the source, guessed that it meant something like "weird," and thus composed a sentence that does not make sense. The writer assumed that the reader would not know what *solipsistic* means either and would not have read the source. Thus plagiarism is also insulting to the reader and impractical since it often calls attention to itself.

Good and bad paraphrasing

A good paraphrase expresses the ideas found in the source (for which credit is always given) but not in the same words. It preserves the sense, but not the form, of the original. It does not retain the sentence patterns and merely substitute synonyms for the original words, nor does it retain the original words and merely alter the sentence patterns. It is a genuine restatement. It is briefer than its source.

SOURCE

> Although Poe's protagonists question their thoughts and feelings as well as their motivations and analyze the amount of harm they have done, they rarely grow in understanding. They lack the detachment necessary to rectify the situation and the will to carry out their decisions once these are made. Solipsistic in every way, they are caught in the stifling world of their own choice.

IMPROPER PARAPHRASE

> Even though Poe's heroes ask themselves about their ideas and emotions and also their reasons for acting and figure out how much damage they have left behind, they do not often gain more wisdom. They do not have the impartiality mandatory to alter the condition and the determination to follow through on their resolutions when they are formulated. Self-involved in all manner, they are snared in the smothering realm of their making (Knapp 155).

PROPER PARAPHRASE

> Poe's main characters do engage in self-examination, but they seldom benefit from it. They are too close to their own problems to solve them, too weak to change. Their whole world is within themselves, and they are destroyed by it (Knapp 155).

Frequently a combination of quotation and paraphrase is effective.

SOURCE

> More than any previous explorer, Cook was well prepared to chart his discoveries and fix their locations accurately. He sailed at a time

of rapid advances in methods of navigation; his ship was equipped with every available type of scientific instrument; he had the services of professional astronomers; and he himself had a far more sophisticated understanding of astronomy, mathematics, and surveying techniques than most sea captains.

QUOTATION AND PARAPHRASE

One of Captain Cook's distinctions was the care he took in readying himself for his voyages. He "was well prepared to chart his discoveries and fix their locations accurately." He did not sail without good equipment and competent navigators, and "he himself had a far more sophisticated understanding of astronomy, mathematics, and surveying techniques than most sea captains" (Withey 87–88).

PARAPHRASE

One of Captain Cook's distinctions was the care he took in readying himself for his voyages. He did not sail without good equipment and competent navigators. Indeed, he was well versed in the several sciences so important in long-distance sailing (Withey 87–88).

■ Exercise 1

Choose an article from a periodical; avoid those that are mainly factual or statistical. Then select two passages from one page of the article and make a photocopy (number the passages 1 and 2). In ten to fifteen words, paraphrase the first passage (which should be thirty to fifty words long). Do not state any ideas of your own. Do not use words from the article. In about twenty-five words, paraphrase the second passage (which should be sixty to seventy-five words). This time combine some of your own ideas with the paraphrase of the source. Turn the photocopy in with your paraphrases.

■ Exercise 2

Turn in to your teacher a photocopy of a single page from an article in a periodical. (Do not use the same page that you used for Exercise 1.)

*Draw circles around three quotations. Submit with the photocopy the
following: (a) a sentence that you quote with no writing of your own,
(b) a sentence of your own with short quotations in it from the source,
and (c) a sentence of your own that introduces a quoted sentence.
Write your part, followed by a comma or a colon, then the complete
quoted sentence.*

48g Follow an accepted system of documentation.

The forms of documentation vary with fields, periodicals, and
publishers. Instructors frequently have preferences that determine what specific system you will need to conform to in your research paper. The following style books and manuals are often
used in general studies.

Achtert, Walter S., and Joseph Gibaldi. *The MLA Style Manual.* New York: Modern Language Assn. of America, 1985.

Chicago Manual of Style. 13th ed. Chicago: U of Chicago P,
1982.

Gibaldi, Joseph, and Walter S. Achtert. *MLA Handbook for
Writers of Research Papers.* 3rd ed. New York: Modern Language Assn. of America, 1988.

Publication Manual of the American Psychological Association.
3rd ed. Washington: American Psychological Assn., 1983.

Skillin, Marjorie E., Robert M. Gay, et al. *Words into Type.* 3rd
ed. Englewood Cliffs: Prentice, 1974.

Turabian, Kate L. *A Manual for Writers of Term Papers, Theses,
and Dissertations.* 5th ed. Chicago: U of Chicago P, 1987.

Webster's Standard American Style Manual. Springfield, MA:
Merriam-Webster, 1985.

The model paper on pp. 369–415 follows the system of documentation in the *MLA Handbook for Writers of Research Papers,* 3rd ed., and *The MLA Style Manual.* This system is the most widely used in the humanities. The three sections that follow will give you the information you need to learn and utilize this system.

For the method presented in the *Publication Manual of the American Psychological Association* (APA), most frequently used in the social sciences, see pp. 416–421.

48h Prepare a list of works cited in the research paper.

At the end of a research paper, after the text and after the notes (or endnotes), comes a section called "Works Cited." Here you list alphabetically all the sources that you refer to in the text (see the list for the model paper, pp. 411–415). Study the examples below of forms used for various kinds of sources.

A BOOK BY A SINGLE AUTHOR

Bell, Bernard, W.   The Afro-American Novel and Its
    Tradition.   Amherst: U of Massachusetts P,
    1987.

Marcus, Millicent.   Italian Film in the Light of
    Neorealism.   Princeton: Princeton UP, 1986.

NOTE: A **pamphlet** is treated as a book.

AN EDITED BOOK

Murry, John Middleton, ed.   Journal of Katherine
    Mansfield.   New York: Knopf, 1952.

A BOOK WITH TWO EDITORS OR AUTHORS

```
Manley-Casimir, Michael, and Carmen Luke, eds.
    Children and Television: A Challenge for
    Education.  New York: Praeger, 1987.
```

NOTE: On the title page of this book the following cities are listed as places of publication: New York; Westport, Connecticut; and London. In your entry, use only the first city named.

A BOOK WITH MORE THAN THREE EDITORS OR AUTHORS

```
Kagan, Sharon L., et al., eds.  America's Family
    Support Programs.  New Haven: Yale UP, 1987.
```

NOTE: The title page of this book lists four editors: Sharon L. Kagan, Douglas R. Powell, Bernice Weissbourd, and Edward F. Zigler. Use only the first, followed by *et al.* ("and others").

A TRANSLATED BOOK

```
Palomino, Antonio.  Lives of the Eminent Spanish
    Painters and Sculptors.  Trans. Nina Ayala
    Mallory.  Cambridge: Cambridge UP, 1987.
```

A BOOK IN A SERIES

```
Jaffe, Jacqueline A.  Arthur Conan Doyle.  Twayne's
    English Authors Series 451.  Boston: Twayne,
    1987.
```

A MULTIVOLUME WORK

Hendrick, Burton J. The Life and Letters of Walter
     H. Page, 1855 to 1918. 2 vols. Garden City:
     Doubleday, 1927.

A REPUBLISHED BOOK

Langdon, William Chauncy. Everyday Things in
     American Life, 1776-1876. 1941. New York:
     Scribner's, 1969.

NOTE: The first date is that of original publication.

SECOND OR LATER EDITION OF A BOOK

Brooks, Cleanth, and Robert Penn Warren. Modern
     Rhetoric. 2nd ed. New York: Harcourt, 1958.

AN ESSAY IN A COLLECTION OF ESSAYS OR AN ANTHOLOGY

Powell, Douglas R. "Day Care as a Family Support
     System." America's Family Support Programs.
     Ed. Sharon L. Kagan, et al. New Haven: Yale
     UP, 1987. 115-32.

AN INTRODUCTION, FOREWORD, PREFACE, OR AFTERWORD IN A BOOK

Gibson, James. Introduction. The Complete Poems
     of Thomas Hardy. London: Macmillan, 1976.
     xxxv-xxvi.

Tobias, Andrew. Foreword. <u>Extraordinary Popular</u>
    <u>Delusions and the Madness of Crowds</u>. By
    Charles Mackay. 1841. New York: Harmony,
    1981. xii-xvi.

NOTE: The word is *foreword,* not *forward.* The second book is a
modern printing of an older work.

MORE THAN ONE WORK BY SAME AUTHOR

Phillips, Derek L. <u>Abandoning Method</u>. San
    Francisco: Jossey, 1973.

---. <u>Toward a Just Social Order</u>. Princeton:
    Princeton UP, 1986.

---. <u>Wittgenstein and Scientific Knowledge: A</u>
    <u>Sociological Perspective</u>. Totowa, NJ: Rowman,
    1977.

NOTE: Name the state when the city (Totowa) is not likely to be
known.

SIGNED ARTICLE IN A REFERENCE WORK

Emmet, Dorothy. "Ethics." <u>International Encyclo-</u>
    <u>pedia of Social Sciences</u>. 1968 ed.

UNSIGNED ARTICLE IN A REFERENCE WORK

"Domino." <u>Encyclopedia Americana</u>. 1986 ed.

GOVERNMENT PUBLICATION

United States. Dept. of Commerce. Internal Trade
    Administration. <u>United States Trade: Perform-
    ance in 1985 and Outlook</u>. Washington: GPO,
    1986.

ARTICLE IN A MONTHLY PERIODICAL

Clark, Earl. "Oregon's Covered Bridges." <u>Travel-
    Holiday</u> Jan. 1987: 71-72.

ARTICLE IN A WEEKLY PERIODICAL

Bernstein, Jeremy. "Our Far-Flung Correspondents."
    <u>New Yorker</u> 14 Dec. 1987: 47-105.

ARTICLE IN A QUARTERLY PERIODICAL (WITH CONTINUOUS
PAGINATION)

Handlin, Oscar. "Libraries and Learning." <u>American
    Scholar</u> 56 (1987): 205-18.

ARTICLE IN A JOURNAL (NOT WITH CONTINUOUS PAGINATION)

Ardoin, John. "A Pride of Prima Donnas." <u>Opera
    Quarterly</u> 5.1 (1987): 58-70.

NOTE: **The issue number (1) has been added.**

ARTICLE WITH TWO AUTHORS IN A JOURNAL

```
Gottfries, Nils, and Henrik Horn.  "Wage Formation
     and the Persistence of Unemployment."
     Economic Journal 97 (1987): 877-84.
```

BOOK REVIEW IN A PERIODICAL

```
Davin, Delia.  Rev. of Revolution Postponed: Women
     in Contemporary China, by Margery Wolf.
     Public Affairs 59 (1986-87): 684-85.
```

SIGNED ARTICLE IN A DAILY NEWSPAPER

```
Patton, Scott.  "Rules of the Ratings Game."
     Washington Post 19 Jan. 1988: D7.
```

NOTE: "D" refers to the section of the paper; "7," to the page within that section. Entry for an unsigned article would begin with the title.

UNSIGNED EDITORIAL IN A DAILY NEWSPAPER

```
"The Odds of Ignorance."  Editorial.  Miami Herald
     19 Jan. 1988: A10.
```

NOTE: Entry for a signed editorial would begin with the author's last name.

UNPUBLISHED DISSERTATION

```
Kenney, Catherine McGehee.  "The World of James
     Thurber: An Anatomy of Confusion."  Diss.
     Loyola of Chicago, 1974.
```

ABSTRACT IN *DISSERTATION ABSTRACTS INTERNATIONAL*

```
Kenney, Catherine McGehee.  "The World of James
     Thurber: An Anatomy of Confusion."  DAI 35
     (1974): 2276A.  Loyola of Chicago.
```

48i Document sources in parenthetical references in your text.

The list of Works Cited indicates clearly what sources you used, but precisely what you derived from each entry must also be revealed at particular places in the paper. Document each idea, paraphrase, or quotation by indicating the author (or the title if the work is anonymous) and the page reference at the appropriate place in your text.

> The extent of dissension that year in Parliament has been pointed out before (Levenson 127). *[Writer cites author and gives author's name and page number in parentheses.]*

> Accordingly, no "parliamentary session was without severe dissension" (Levenson 127). *[Writer quotes author and gives author's name and page number in parentheses.]*

> Levenson points out that "no parliamentary session was without severe dissension" (127). *[Writer names author, places quotation marks at beginning of quotation and before parenthesis, and gives only page number in parentheses.]*

These references indicate that the quotation is to be found in the work by Levenson listed in Works Cited at the end of the text of the paper.

If two authors in your sources have the same last name, give first names in your references.

> It has been suggested that the general's brother did not arrive until the following year (Frederick Johnson 235).
>
> The authenticity of the document, however, has been questioned (Edwin Johnson 15).

If two or more works by the same author are listed in Works Cited, indicate which one you are referring to by giving a short title: (Levenson, *Battles* 131). The full title listed in Works Cited is *Battles in British Parliament, 1720–1721.*

If a work cited consists of more than one volume, give the volume number as well as the page: (Hoagland 2:173–74).

Some sources—the Bible and well-known plays, for example—are cited in the text of the paper but not listed as sources in Works Cited. Use the following forms:

> . . . the soliloquy (*Hamlet* 2.2). [The numbers designate act and scene. Some instructors prefer roman numerals: *Hamlet* II.ii.]
>
> . . . the passage (1 Kings 4.3). [That is, chapter 4, verse 3.]

For further illustrations of parenthetical references to works cited, see the model research paper.

Forms of Parenthetical Reference: APA System

Compare the following examples of parenthetical documentation recommended by the *Publication Manual of the American Psycho-*

logical Association (APA) with the examples on pp. 363–364, which follow the system of the Modern Language Association of America.

> In 330 B.C. Aristotle wrote with relative accuracy of dolphins in his *History of Animals*, and Pliny the Elder, who died in A.D. 79, related in his *Natural History* the story of a dolphin that "would daily carry a boy on his back across the Bay of Baiae to Puteoli, which is near Naples" (Glueck, 1965, p. 359).
>
> According to Robert McNally, "there is little new in the New Age view of the cetaceans" (1981, p. 231).
>
> By gradually "untraining" them, their liberators proved that "civilized" dolphins can be turned back to the wild state successfully (Linden, 1987).
>
> Other researchers (Morris, 1986; Klinowska, 1986; Ridgway, 1986) approach the question of dolphins' intelligence from a different perspective.

48j Follow accepted practices in using notes for comments, explanations, and references to supplementary sources.

You will probably need few numbered notes (called "footnotes" when at the bottom of the page, "notes" at the end of the paper) because sources are referred to in the text itself and listed after the body of the paper. Notes are used to explain further or to comment on something you have written. To include incidental information in the text itself would be to interrupt the flow of the argument or to assign undue importance to matters that add to the substance only tangentially. Make your decision as to where to place such information—in the text or in a note—on the basis of its impact and direct relevance.

Notes are also useful in referring to sources other than those mentioned in the text or in commenting on sources. If you wish to list several books or articles in connection with a point you are making, it may prove awkward to include all of this information in parentheses. Therefore, a note is preferable.

The sign of a note is an Arabic numeral raised slightly above the line at the appropriate place in the text. The *MLA Handbook* recommends that notes be grouped at the end of the paper. Notes should be numbered consecutively throughout.

Examples

[1] See also Drummond, Stein, Van Patten, Southworth, and Langhorne.

[Lists further sources. Full bibliographic information given in Works Cited at end of paper.]

[2] After spending seventeen years in Europe, he returned to America with a new attitude toward slavery, which he had defended earlier.

[Remark parenthetical to main argument but important enough to include in a note.]

[3] This biography, once considered standard, is shown to be unreliable by recent discoveries.

[Evaluates a source.]

[4] Detailed census records are available only for the 1850–1880 period. Earlier censuses do not provide the exact names of inhabitants, nor any financial or social information. Later census schedules that do have detailed information on individuals are not available to the public; one may obtain only summaries of the data gathered.

[Provides background on a source.]

[5] Andrews uses the term "koan" to mean any riddle. To prevent confusion, however, "koan" will be used in this paper to designate only riddles in the form of paradoxes employed in Zen Buddhism as aids to meditation.

[Clarifies terminology.]

For further illustrations of notes, see model research paper, pp. 402–409.

▪ Exercise 3

In preparation for writing the final draft of your research paper, turn in the following:

1. Your title page.
2. A tentative list of Works Cited following the forms shown on pp. 357–363 (or the system preferred by your instructor).

Model research paper

A model research paper, with an outline and accompanying explanations, is given on the following pages.

GENERAL APPEARANCE AND MECHANICS

Allow ample and even margins.

Indent five spaces for paragraphs.

Leave two spaces after periods and other terminal punctuation.

Leave one space after other marks of punctuation.

Double-space between lines in the text, the notes, and entries in the Works Cited section.

Set off a quotation of five or more typed lines. Begin a new line, indent ten spaces from the margin, do not add quotation marks, and double-space unless your instructor specifies single spacing. If you quote only one paragraph, do not indent the first line.

Compose a title page for your research paper if your instructor requires it. (MLA does not require it.) Balance the material on the page. Center the title and place it about one-third of the way down from the top of the page. Include your name and the name and section number of the course as indicated on the opposite page, or follow the specific preferences of your instructor.

The Dolphin Controversy

By Curtis Washington

English 101

Section 3

If your instructor requests that you submit an outline with your paper, it should occupy a separate, unnumbered page following the title page and should follow the form for the outline illustrated on pp. 235–237, 371.

If your instructor requests that you include a thesis statement as part of your outline, place it between the title and the first line of the outline.

The Dolphin Controversy

I. Appeal of dolphins

    A. In modern times

    B. In ancient times

II. Dolphin as center of controversy

    A. Recentness of debate

    B. Nature of debate

III. Question of dolphin intelligence

    A. Dolphins as equals to humans

    B. Dolphins as inferior to humans

IV. Question of keeping dolphins in captivity

    A. U.S. Navy's training of dolphins

    B. Use of dolphins in Persian Gulf

    C. Arguments for and against such use

V. Emotional ingredients in controversy

    A. Dolphins as evokers of love, sympathy, mystery

    B. Dolphins as benevolent superbeings

    C. Attitudes of humans as reflections of their own deep needs

Center the title on the page. Allow four spaces between the title and the first line of the text.

The page number for the first page may be omitted or centered at the bottom.

The first and second paragraphs make up the introductory section of this paper. The writer first establishes the current popularity of dolphins, then illustrates that dolphins have long captured the human imagination. The reader's interest is thus stimulated by the writer's calling attention to this long tradition of human involvement with dolphins.

Flipper is underlined because it is the title of a television series. Titles of individual episodes within a series are placed in quotation marks rather than underlined.

The parenthetical reference to Glueck illustrates the most frequently used form of documentation: author's last name, no punctuation, page number.

The Dolphin Controversy

Perhaps no creature is currently more widely revered than the dolphin. Its exuberance, intelligence, and benevolence have captured the modern imagination. Its image is to be seen on restaurant advertisements and book covers and on motel logos. Its form has been imitated by the manufacturers of children's stuffed toys and by the makers of plastic floats for use in water. A professional football team is called the Dolphins, and for many years young people have thrilled to the adventures of a dolphin in the television series _Flipper_ (now in reruns).

The popularity of dolphins is not, however, strictly a modern phenomenon. In ancient times, "the dolphin alone or in association with male and female deities occurred frequently in sculptural or mosaic or painted form on the mainlands and islands of the entire Mediterranean" (Glueck 349). Classical Greek and Roman literatures abound with references to dolphins and their interaction with human beings. In his _Lives_ the first-century biographer

Place page numbers in the upper right-hand corner, two lines above the first line of text. Use Arabic numerals; do not put a period after the number. (According to MLA style, you may add your last name before the number on each page.)

The reference to an entry in the *Encyclopedia Americana* cites an unsigned article. No page number is needed for references to entries in encyclopedias.

The sentence beginning with "Delphi" illustrates the technique of combining one's own words with quoted words.

When a source has coauthors, cite the last names of both. Accent marks (as in Diolé) should be carefully reproduced.

Place note numbers slightly above the line of type and after marks of punctuation. Do not leave a space before the number; do not place a period after the number. Number notes consecutively throughout the paper.

Delphis is not documented; the translation or definition of words requires no documentation.

Plutarch tells how a dolphin saved Odysseus' son, Telemachus, from drowning. Long believed to be legends, such stories now appear to rest "in part at least, on factual grounds" (<u>Encyclopedia Americana</u>). Delphi, "the most famous sanctuary of Greece" and, according to ancient belief, "the center of the world," was given its name--if a long-standing explanation is to be believed--because it was thought that the god Apollo, who supposedly dwelt in that place, "first appeared there in the form of a dolphin" (Cousteau and Diolé 237).[1] The Greek word for dolphin is <u>delphis</u>. In 330 B.C. Aristotle wrote with relative accuracy of dolphins in his <u>History of Animals</u>, and Pliny the Elder, who died in A.D. 79, related in his <u>Natural History</u> the story of a dolphin that "would daily carry a boy on his back across the Bay of Baiae to Puteoli, which is near Naples" (Glueck 359).

Human beings have been fascinated with dolphins for so long that some scientists, anthropologists, and sociologists feel that the current (or "New Age") interest is merely a continuation of past attitudes. According to Robert McNally,

In the third paragraph the writer states the thesis: that despite a continuing fascination with dolphins, human beings have recently begun to quarrel in earnest about them—a new phenomenon.

Within the quotation brackets have been used to explain the term *cetaceans* since this definition is needed and is not a part of McNally's statement. The writer has added an interpolation, for which brackets rather than parentheses are used. Since the author of this quotation has already been identified ("According to Robert McNally"), only a page number is needed in parentheses after the quotation.

Underlining should be done sparingly. Here the writer underlines *has* because of the emphasis he wishes to place on that word within this centrally important sentence.

At the end of this paragraph, the writer clearly indicates that he will be discussing three specific questions that are basic to the modern controversy centering on dolphins. By stating these questions succinctly, he thus gives a strong direction to his essay. Readers know precisely where they will be going.

In the paragraph beginning with "Scientists know," the writer begins to address the problem of understanding dolphins' makeup, emphasizing that mystery still prevails in many areas.

"there is little new in the New Age view of the
cetaceans [the general term for the whale family,
of which the dolphin is a member]. It is only the
anthropocentrism of the centuries with a contemporary twist" (231). Despite this opinion, something new and highly significant _has_ become a part
of the modern concern with dolphins: heated controversy. Dolphins have been popular with humankind for centuries, but never before have they been
the center of intense debate. Ironically, opinions
about these kindly mammals long thought to be our
guardian angels of the deep are now pitting humans
against each other with startling intensity. Though
the dolphin controversy is many-sided, three aspects
of it, which can be expressed as questions, are
especially prominent: (1) What _is_ a dolphin?
(2) Should dolphins be kept in captivity? (3) Is
it immoral to use dolphins for military purposes?

Scientists know much more than ever before
about dolphins--about the large size of their
brains, their ability to use their splendid sonar-
like faculty for "echolocation," their recently
discovered weapon "in the form of a sound beam . . .

Single quotation marks are used to show quoted words within a quotation.

The parenthetical references to *Newsweek* and *U.S. News & World Report* cite unsigned articles in weekly magazines. No page numbers are needed in these instances because the articles are only one page long each.

The writer now turns to the most important aspect of this issue of dolphin nature: intelligence.

4

to debilitate or 'stun' their prey" (Morris 394).[2]
Some researchers now hypothesize that dolphins have
a "magnetic receptor system" (Klinowska 401), which
enables them to find their way over long distances.[3]
Yet each discovery appears to raise new questions
and to fuel debate. The more we learn about dolphins, the greater the mystery. For example, dead
dolphins have recently washed ashore along the
Atlantic Coast in large numbers. Investigators
have undertaken to explain why they are dying. Some
"scientists suspect a viral or bacterial agent"
(Newsweek). Others argue vehemently that pollution
is the culprit. Like so much else having to do
with this fascinating mammal, comments one reporter,
"the cause of the dolphin deaths may remain a mystery as deep as the sea itself" (U.S. News & World
Report).

Scientists and others avidly interested in
dolphins can disagree in friendly fashion over what
is causing the deplorable "die-off," as it is
called. But they are less coolly objective when
another and much larger issue is raised--the intelligence of dolphins. This subject is at the heart

In introducing the quotation from John C. Lilly, the writer gives the date of the author's book, 1961, not because such information in this position is always necessary or even advisable but because in this particular instance he wishes to show something of the chronology of the debate.

Prose quotations of five lines or more should be set off ten spaces as indicated here. Leave the right margin unchanged. Double-space unless instructed otherwise. Do not indent the first paragraph; indent for paragraphs thereafter. Do not use quotation marks around quotations that are set off.

When an ellipsis (. . .) is used to indicate omitted words at the end of a sentence, add a period (. . . .).

The name of the author of the quotation that is set off has been given before the quotation; therefore, it should not be mentioned again in parentheses after the quotation. The title of the work quoted is ordinarily not needed since that information is included in the list of Works Cited at the end of the paper. It is given here because two books by the same author are referred to in the paper, and thus it is needed for clarification.

of the question about what the dolphin is, what its place is in the hierarchy of nature. After extensive exploration of their intelligence, John C. Lilly boldly made the following statement in 1961:

> Eventually it may be possible for humans
> to speak with another species. I have
> come to this conclusion after careful
> consideration of evidence gained through
> my research experiments with dolphins.
> . . . We must strip ourselves, as far as
> possible, of our preconceptions about
> the relative place of homo sapiens in the
> scheme of nature. . . . If we are to seek
> communication with other species, we must
> first grant the possibility that some
> other species may have a potential (or
> even realized) intellectual development
> comparable to our own. (Man and Dolphin
> 17-18)

Lilly's determination to place dolphins on an equal footing with human beings and his attempts to break the language barrier between species brought forth a host of supporters and an army of

Both the title of the work cited and the names of its authors are given before the quotation beginning with "attacking," so only the page number is needed in parentheses. The small Roman numeral *x* indicates that the quotation is taken from the front matter, in this instance the preface.

In the quotation beginning with "the dolphin brain," the word *could* is underlined because it appears in italic type in the original. If it had been printed in regular type and the writer of this paper had wished to underline it, he could do so, but he would have had to add in parentheses after the quotation "italics mine" or "emphasis added."

Enough information about the motion picture *The Day of the Dolphin* is given here so that no parenthetical documentation is needed. Note that the title of a motion picture is underlined.

detractors. Karl-Erik Fichtelius and Sverre Sjölander aligned themselves with Lilly's point of view in their book, <u>Smarter Than Man?</u> They admit openly to "attacking the deeply rooted notion that man is the most remarkable thing God ever created" (x). Their "surprising conclusion" is that "the dolphin brain <u>could</u> be superior to ours" (40). These spokesmen for the dolphin's high intelligence attracted such attention that in 1973 Joseph E. Levine produced a motion picture based upon a French novel by Robert Merle called <u>The Day of the Dolphin</u>, starring George C. Scott as a Lilly-like scientist devoted to teaching dolphins the English language and marveling at their intelligence, capacity for love, and unswerving loyalty.

Controversy about Lilly and his followers continues to the present; name-calling on both sides is not rare. Robert McNally has concluded that Lilly is a "poor authority" (230), and Lilly has accused other scientists of retreating in arrogance and cowardice from what he terms "interlock research" with dolphins (<u>Programming</u> 95). Defenders of Lilly and his views claim that "his contributions

Whenever possible, consult directly the authorities that you quote or cite. In this instance, Curtis Washington did not have access to the writings of René-Guy Busnel but wished to cite his idea. He did so by giving the title of the book in which he found Busnel's views discussed. Since Busnel's actual words are not quoted, the parenthetical entry reads "cited in" rather than "quoted in."

Underlining for emphasis should be used sparingly, but since the writer has not made use of it often and since he is summarizing an important part of the argument, it is effective to underline *is*.

to our knowledge of cetaceans are legion, and his work has probably saved millions of animals by making the public aware of their intelligence and gentle sensitivity" (Gormley 177-78). That "gentle sensitivity," however, is more imagined than real, according to René-Guy Busnel, who insists that dolphins are no more sensitive and no more capable of feeling loyalty and affection than other animals-- perhaps less than some (cited in Cousteau and Diolé 88). Recently Dudok van Heel has written that although many scientists wish to place dolphins in an "elevated niche in the Animal Kingdom," others "maintain that there are not enough arguments to assume that man is not alone in attaining a level of reason, intelligence and emotions, which seem to have made this species unique so far" (163).[4] What, then, is a dolphin--a creature equal or even superior to human beings in intelligence or merely a large-brained mammal about which there has been much romanticizing? The question still is unanswered as the adversaries remain locked in an intellectual wrestling match, the dolphin looking on with that playful but enigmatic smile.[5]

In the paragraph beginning with "As the argument," the writer turns to the second phase of the dolphin controversy—the question of keeping dolphins in captivity. The organization of the paper is thus tightly controlled; the writer is on course; the reader in tow.

Again, the writer desires to use an important quotation to which he does not have direct access. He indicates where he found the quotation. Such a practice is acceptable only if rarely employed.

As the argument over the intelligence and sensitivity of dolphins has raged, a parallel debate has been increasing in intensity on the question of keeping them in captivity. At one point, John Lilly released all the dolphins that he had been working with because, he said, "I no longer wanted to run a concentration camp for my friends" (quoted in McNally 228).[6] Jacques Cousteau and Philippe Diolé expressed strong objections to keeping dolphins in aquariums and marinelands (158-59), and Gerard Gormley has referred to captive dolphins as having to serve "life sentences in oceanaria" (40). In 1983 a Global Conference on "Whales Alive" was held in Boston; it "clearly showed to what extent opinions are divided on the ethics of keeping cetaceans in captivity" (Dudok van Heel 163). Demands for the rights of dolphins were reminiscent of rallying cries in the civil-rights movement of some years ago. A popular weekly magazine commented that "dolphins have such high intelligence that several animal-rights groups campaign against their confinement in any conditions, likening it to jailing an innocent person" (U.S. News & World Report).

Personal interviews with important and knowledgeable people can be useful secondary sources. Such interviews should be set up in advance and should be conducted with due consideration to the interviewee's time. The interviewer should come well prepared with a list of specific questions. If any part of the interview is to be published, permission of the person being interviewed should be sought. Since all pertinent information documenting the interview is given before the quotation and in the list of Works Cited, no parenthetical entry is needed.

On the other hand, many researchers and trainers of dolphins make a strong case for such facilities as Marineland of Florida. Michael Bright has written that "dolphinaria provided the first and generally the best opportunity of observing dolphin behavior. Marineland of Florida, for instance, pioneered the early work on the sounds that dolphins make for communication and echolocation" (36). In an interview with Gregory Pyle, assistant director of shows at Marineland of Florida, I raised the question of locking up dolphins to serve "life sentences." Mr. Pyle strongly defended the usefulness of oceanaria, though he is critical of facilities where making money has overshadowed all other activities. To close such attractions as Marineland, he stated, would be to deprive thousands of people of the "aesthetic pleasure derived from seeing dolphins"; it would deprive children especially of the "sheer joy of watching dolphins from close up."

Many who feel that the objections of conservationists and some scientists to dolphins' being retained in cramped pools are misdirected point out that once dolphins are habituated to captivity,

The parenthetical reference to Linden is to a signed article in a weekly magazine. No page number is needed since the article covers only a single page.

Beginning with "No issue concerning dolphins," the writer now introduces the third and final phase of the dolphin controversy: the question of training dolphins for use in military situations.

they seem to like it so well that they often refuse
to leave even if given the opportunity. If forced
to leave, they frequently cannot survive in the
open sea. That view was generally accepted until
recently, when two dolphins that had been in captivity for seven years were freed off the coast of
Georgia. By gradually "untraining" them, their
liberators proved that "civilized" dolphins can be
turned back to the wild state successfully (Linden).
Still, whether marinelands and aquariums should all
be closed and all scientists be required to study
dolphins in the wild state continues to be hotly
debated, with emotions running high on both sides.

No issue concerning dolphins, however, is more
explosive than that of their use for military purposes. Most of the fireworks appear on one side,
for seldom do spokesmen for the military come forth
with any kind of justification for their training
of dolphins or with information about their experiments involving them. Nongovernment scientists
generally try to steer clear of the military. The
overall situation is fairly accurately presented in
a scene from the motion picture The Day of the

Set off dialogue in a motion picture or a play and use quotation marks as indicated here. If the writer were quoting part of a scene from a play, he would need to identify the act and scene (I.iii). Since motion pictures do not designate acts and scenes, no further documentation is required here.

The writer has added the word *dolphins* to the quotation for clarity. Such additions are always enclosed in brackets. Note also that, in order to make the sentence grammatical in the quotation set off on the next page, the word *training* has been added.

<u>Dolphin</u>, in which a scientist, Dr. Jacob Terrell,
responds to questions after presenting a brief talk
on dolphins. The dialogue is as follows:

>Woman in audience: "What about the
>experiments that the military--"

>Dr. Terrell (interrupts): "I don't
>know anything about the military."

>Woman: "But surely you have heard
>about the misuse of animals like dolphins
>that the government is rumored to--"

>Dr. Terrell: "Just a moment, please.
>I am not a political scientist. My de-
>grees are in biology and zoology and
>behavioral psychology. The government
>and I pay very little attention to each
>other."

Cousteau and Diolé have commented that "the
Navy is reluctant to have it known that these animals [dolphins] are being trained for military
service" (75-76). Although the United States government has denied that this training involves any
risk to dolphins, the notion persists that the animals may constitute a sort of modern-day kamikaze

After a quotation that is not set off, place the period *after* the parenthesis. When the quotation is set off, the period comes *before* the parenthesis.

After a quotation that has been set off, you do not necessarily have to begin a new paragraph. Here the same paragraph continues, and "Bright" is not indented.

squad to be sent on suicide missions to blow up enemy ships. Michael Bright's statement is representative of this widespread suspicion:

> It is generally known that naval authorities of several countries are currently [training], or have in the past trained, dolphins to fix explosives to the hulls of enemy vessels, to discover or destroy enemy mines, or to help detect the presence of enemy submarines. If they can be trained to do that, it is not a far stretch of the imagination to consider them in front-line attacks, perhaps exploding underwater mines--and killing themselves in the process. (53)

Bright goes on to comment on other possible uses of dolphins in war but remarks that little is actually known: "Since for each nation military research is a top-secret operation, there is little information available." He concludes that "public outcry has certainly deterred the use of such peaceful animals for naval warfare, but it may be that experiments

The parenthetical page reference reads (53, 55), not (53–55) because the passage quoted does not run consecutively but occurs on the two pages indicated, with illustrations occupying the intervening page.

The two words quoted, "Public outcry," do not need to be documented because the reader can clearly see that they are taken from the quotation above, the source of which has already been given.

The writer found this information about the military's killing of whales in several sources; therefore, it can be considered common knowledge for which no specific source is required.

The writer has indicated that these quotations are taken from a news story in the *New York Times*. Since the story carries no by-line and is all on a single page, no parenthetical reference is added.

In quotations that are run in with the text (that is, not set off), use single quotation marks to designate a quotation within the quotation.

continue, only now with still greater secrecy" (53, 55).

"Public outcry" indeed there has been, especially since it has come to light that American military airplanes used whales for target practice in the late 1940s and obliged Icelandic fishermen some years later by slaughtering killer whales. Charges of cruelty and insensitivity, however, have not prevented the Navy from continuing its work with dolphins. On October 24, 1987, the New York Times reported that "dolphins apparently trained to search for mines are the latest addition to American forces in the Persian Gulf. The Navy acknowledged Thursday that it had sent five dolphins at the request of the American commander in the Gulf, 'to provide an underwater surveillance and detection capacity.'" As usual, few details were available. The Pentagon refused to answer any questions about the operation but stated that the Navy "has never trained nor does it intend to train marine animals to perform a task which could result in intentional injury or death to the animal."

Note that the tone of the discussion remains essentially objective as the writer makes his way through the phases of the controversy. When dealing with highly volatile current issues, there may be a strong temptation to express one's own feelings with excessive zeal. In doing so, however, a writer runs the risk of alienating the audience, which Curtis Washington has deemed to be general readers rather than special interest groups. If he were composing for any of those groups, the tone might be substantially different. In any case, a careful consideration of audience is necessary for an effective essay.

The final paragraph brings the writer full circle. He begins with the phenomenal appeal dolphins have for humans, and he ends with the same idea. For his conclusion, however, he has added an important and thoughtful idea, that we reach out to dolphins and sometimes even think of them as benevolent aliens because of our loss of faith in our own kind. He ends the paper with a strong punch and at the same time offers a viable reason, in his view, for the intensity of the controversy.

Such pronouncements have failed to quiet the controversy, for even if dolphins were not trained for suicidal missions, there would still be widespread opposition to their being used to further military objectives of any kind. Yet if dolphins are indeed anxious to help preserve humankind from the sharks of the deep, as countless stories attest, then why not allow them to protect us from other forms of sharks--our nation's enemies?[7] So goes the argument in favor of enlisting our friends the dolphins for duty in the military. They may be our friends, but even so, they have unwittingly stirred up considerable trouble among us.

The reason for this trouble is not merely scientific disagreements. The controversy over dolphins is much more emotional than usual issues dealing with animals because these particular mammals have a special appeal. Indeed, it is difficult for some people to think of them as mere animals at all. They evoke not only sympathy, love, and admiration but also a deep sense of mystery. Michael Bright reports that "some claim dolphins have ESP and can telepathically understand a man's thoughts

Writers often summarize and draw together in their conclusions the material that has been discussed in the paper. Since the three aspects of the controversy have been so clearly put forth here, it would be redundant simply to describe them again at the end.

and moods" (6). Because they are clearly intelligent and, unlike human beings, essentially nonaggressive, qualities (like ESP) are often attributed to them without adequate proof. It is no wonder, then, that widespread outrage develops when news of their victimization in any form is reported.[8] As experiments increasingly reveal startling new details about their abilities, they take on the aura of benevolent extraterrestrial beings with whom we should communicate for the salvation of the human race. Gradually, Flipper seems to have merged with ET. Dolphins have become our latest heroes partly because we no longer seem to be able to find any heroes among our own kind.

The word *Notes* is centered on the page. Double-space throughout unless instructed otherwise.

Indent the first line of every note five spaces; do not indent succeeding lines. Note numbers are raised slightly above the line. Leave a space between the number and the first word of the note.

As note 1 illustrates, bibliographic references in notes are identical in form to parenthetical documentation in the body of the paper. This note gives further information about ancient associations with the dolphin. One of the primary functions of notes is to include details or arguments that are germane but that would somewhat clutter the text were they presented there. Notes assist in preserving a tight structure in the body of the paper while making it possible to include materials that add further interest or evidence.

Notes

[1] From early times the dolphin was associated with the supernatural. Glueck points out that for some ancient people "the dolphin symbol . . . became an attribute of their chief goddess, standing for succor in peril, safety in danger, security and promise of blessing in the unknown and hereafter" (353). Later, the dolphin became in some circles the symbol of Christ and of rebirth (Cousteau and Diolé 247).

[2] Although these sounds "cannot be heard by human beings, apparently they can be _felt_, at least under certain circumstances," in the form of a light tingle (Ellis 67).

[3] "My conclusion," states Klinowska, "is that these animals are certainly using geomagnetic topography as a base map and may also be using local geomagnetic time cues to provide information about their relative position on that map" (402). Thus an answer to why dolphins mysteriously strand themselves on beaches from time to time--an enigma that two thousand years ago Aristotle puzzled over--has

Note 5 contains general information ("common knowledge"), which requires no documentation.

The writer found the information given in note 6 not in Lilly's own writings but in a book by another author, which is cited in the parenthetical reference. Though what is reported here may be well known, the writer found it only in a single source and could not assume, therefore, that it is common knowledge, for which documentation would not be needed. The passage from Gormley is given below so that it may be compared with the *paraphrase* of it in note 6.

Within a few weeks after he stopped his research, five of the eight dolphins at his laboratory apparently took their own lives. Some starved themselves; others simply stopped breathing. Dr. Lilly freed the remaining three animals and closed his laboratory, saying he would never again experiment with dolphins unless the animals could come and go as they pleased, working with him when they wished and returning to the sea when they did not. Dr. Lilly devoted the next several years to continued isolation tank and LSD experiments, then in 1975 began another attempt to communicate with dolphins, using a computer language he called Janus. . . . Unless conditions have changed since this writing, his dolphins are captives. (178)

been offered in terms that satisfy some scientists: the dolphins "make mistakes" in the use of their magnetic sense, "which result in the accidents we know as live strandings" (427).

4 Despite all the postmortem examinations of dolphin brains and extensive experimentation with live dolphins, some prominent scientists feel that the reason for the large brain size is still to be determined. "An explanation as to why the dolphin brain is so large, and to whether its brain is functionally primitive must await more studies of dolphin anatomy, physiology, and behaviour" (Ridgway 68).

5 The dolphins seen in such attractions as Marineland and Sea World are almost always of the bottlenose variety, which has a fixed expression that resembles a kindly but mischievous smile.

6 After Lilly had let his last three dolphins go--five that he had ceased working with a short time earlier seemed to have willed their own deaths and died--he shut down his laboratory and declared that he would experiment with dolphins in the future only if they were allowed to be free to

The quotation in note 7 is from a personal letter, not a published work. If time allows, it is often practical and enlightening to carry your research outside the library. Mr. Gormley kindly responded in a full and interesting letter to a written inquiry, and he granted permission to be quoted. No parenthetical documentation is needed here since the writer and the source of the quotation have already been identified. The entry in the list of Works Cited gives the date of the letter.

visit him and return to the sea as they wished.
After an interval during which he conducted experiments with LSD and with isolation tanks, he resumed
his work with dolphins, now attempting to break
through the language barrier by utilizing computers,
but he was compelled to go against his earlier
statements and to keep his dolphins in captivity.

[7] Gerard Gormley, author of A Dolphin Summer,
indicated in a letter that he is opposed generally
to the exploitation of animals but took a position
on the use of dolphins in military situations that
is both sensible and appealing:

> Given the apparent inevitability of war,
> I can go along with the noncombatant use
> of dolphins to detect mines and save
> downed airmen or sailors cast adrift.
> This may risk dolphin lives, but we do
> that every time we buy "light meat" tuna
> or fish caught in drift nets. Besides,
> each trained dolphin represents such a
> major investment that military people
> aren't likely to take unnecessary risks
> with them. Still, if dolphins are to be

used for noble causes, let their deeds
and sacrifices be made public. This
would elevate them in everyone's eyes,
and might help with better treatment for
their kind in the wild.

[8] The very title of Farley Mowat's book <u>Sea of
Slaughter</u> suggests the extent of the author's emotional involvement with these victims of humankind.

Begin on a new page for the list of Works Cited. Center the title. Double-space throughout unless instructed otherwise.

Do not indent the first line of an entry; indent succeeding lines five spaces.

List only those sources actually used in your paper and referred to in parenthetical documentation.

Authors are listed with surnames first. If a book has more than one author, the names of authors after the first one are put in normal order (see the second and third entries).

List entries alphabetically by the authors' last name. If a name is not known, arrange the entry by the first word of the title, excluding *A, An,* and *The* (note that the entry for *The Day of the Dolphin* comes in between "Cousteau" and "Dolphin" rather than later on in the list under *T*).

Give the inclusive pages for articles.

Notice that the important divisions of entries are separated by periods.

The first entry illustrates the standard form for a book.

The entry for Cousteau and Diolé shows the proper method to list a book (a) that has more than one author, (b) that has been translated, and (c) that is part of a series (in this case an unnumbered series).

Entries for films should include the title, director, main actors, distributor, and date of release.

The entry for "Dolphin" illustrates the proper way to list an unsigned article in an encyclopedia.

Unsigned articles in weekly periodicals should be listed as indicated by the entries for "The Dolphin Die-off" and "What Is Killing the Atlantic's Dolphins?"

Be careful with foreign words and names. "Dudok van Heel" is the surname of the author, not "Heel" or "van Heel." This entry illustrates the proper way to list an essay in a collection.

For the proper form in listing an article in a monthly periodical, see the entry for Ellis. An entry for an article in a quarterly periodical is shown on p. 361.

Works Cited

Bright, Michael. Dolphins. New York: Gallery, 1985.

Bryden, M. M., and Richard Harrison, eds. Research on Dolphins. Oxford: Clarendon, 1986.

Cousteau, Jacques-Yves, and Philippe Diolé. Dolphins. Trans. J. F. Bernard. The Undersea Discoveries of Jacques-Yves Cousteau. Garden City: Doubleday, 1975.

The Day of the Dolphin. Dir. Mike Nichols. With George C. Scott. Twentieth Century-Fox, 1973.

"Dolphin." Encyclopedia Americana, 1986 ed.

"The Dolphin Die-off." U.S. News & World Report 24 Aug. 1987: 12.

"Dolphins Hunt Gulf Mines." New York Times 24 Oct. 1987: 3.

Dudok van Heel, W. H. "From the Ocean to the Pool." Research on Dolphins. Ed. M. M. Bryden and Richard Harrison. Oxford: Clarendon, 1986. 163-82.

Ellis, Richard. "Dolphins: The Mammal Behind the Myth." Science Digest Jan. 1982: 62-67.

Carefully reproduce all markings, especially in foreign words, as illustrated in the names of the authors in the entry for Fichtelius.

The second entry for Gormley shows how to list a personal letter.

When more than one work by the same author is listed, do not repeat the name but type three unspaced hyphens followed by a period in place of the author's name in entries after the first. (See the entry that follows that for Lilly's book *Man and Dolphin*.)

The entry for Linden shows the proper way to list a signed article in a weekly magazine.

Fichtelius, Karl-Erik, and Sverre Sjölander.
Smarter than Man? Intelligence in Whales, Dol-
phins, and Humans. Trans. Thomas Teal. New
York: Pantheon, 1972.

Glueck, Nelson. Deities and Dolphins. New York:
Farrar, 1965.

Gormley, Gerard. A Dolphin Summer. New York:
Taplinger, 1985.

---. Letter to the author. 30 Jan. 1988.

Klinowska, M. "The Cetacean Magnetic Sense--Evi-
dence from Strandings." Research on Dolphins.
Ed. M. M. Bryden and Richard Harrison. Oxford:
Clarendon, 1986. 401-32.

Lilly, John C. Man and Dolphin. Garden City:
Doubleday, 1961.

---. Programming and Metaprogramming in the Human
Biocomputer. 2nd ed. New York: Julian, 1972.

Linden, Eugene. "Joe and Rosie Go for It." Time
17 Aug. 1987: 72.

McNally, Robert. So Remorseless a Havoc: Of Dolphins, Whales and Men. Boston: Little, 1981.

Morris, Robert J. "The Acoustic Faculty of Dolphins." Research on Dolphins. Ed. M. M. Bryden

The entry for Pyle shows the method for listing a personal interview.

This list of Works Cited includes several essays from the volume *Research on Dolphins*. Generally a writer should not rely upon a single collection. To do so often suggests that the researcher has not ranged widely but has taken a shortcut by obtaining necessary data from one convenient source. It is clear, however, that Curtis Washington has not done that. His research paper refers to many other sources and uses *Research on Dolphins* in several instances only because it contains some of the latest information on pertinent topics.

and Richard Harrison.   Oxford: Clarendon, 1986.

369-99.

Mowat, Farley.   *Sea of Slaughter*.   Boston: Atlantic,

1984.

Pyle, Gregory.   Personal interview.   11 Dec. 1987.

Ridgway, S. H.   "Dolphin Brain Size."   *Research on*

Dolphins.   Ed. M. M. Bryden and Richard

Harrison.   Oxford: Clarendon, 1986.   59-70.

"What Is Killing the Atlantic's Dolphins?"   *News-*

week 24 Aug. 1987: 51.

The APA Style of Documentation

An alternate method of documentation—used widely in the sciences and the social sciences—is that explained in the *Publication Manual of the American Psychological Association* (APA), 1983. Opposite are examples of the forms that follow that manual.

Note that the list of works at the end of the paper is not called "Works Cited" but "References," that in the entries the date of publication comes immediately after the author's name, that initials are used instead of given names, that only the first word of a title is capitalized (except where there is a colon), that no quotation marks are used for titles, and that there are other differences from the method recommended by the Modern Language Association.

Follow the preferences of your instructor as to which method you use. Compare the entries opposite with those for the same works in the list of Works Cited, pp. 411–415.

References

Bright, M.   (1985).   Dolphins.   New York: Gallery
    Books.

Bryden, M. M., & Harrison, R.   (Eds.).   (1986).
    Research on dolphins.   Oxford: Clarendon
    Press.

Cousteau, J., & Diolé, P.   (1975).   Dolphins (J. F.
    Bernard, Trans.).   Garden City: Doubleday.

Dolphin.   (1986).   Encyclopedia Americana.

The dolphin die-off.   (1987, August 24).   U.S. News
    & World Report, p. 12.

Dolphins hunt Gulf mines.   (1987, October 24).   The
    New York Times, p. 3.

Dudok van Heel, W. H.   (1986).   From the ocean to
    the pool.   In M. M. Bryden & R. Harrison
    (Eds.), Research on dolphins (pp. 163-183).
    Oxford: Clarendon Press.

Ellis, R.   (1982, January).   Dolphins: The mammal
    behind the myth.   Science Digest, pp. 62-67.

Fichtelius, K., & Sjölander, S.   (1972).   Smarter
    than man? Intelligence in whales, dolphins,
    and humans (T. Teal, Trans.).   New York:
    Pantheon.

The second entry for Gormley in the list of Works Cited is not included here because in the APA system, personal letters are not listed in References. The letter would be documented parenthetically in the text as follows:

(personal communication, January 30, 1988).

If more than one work by a single author appears in the list of References, they should be arranged *chronologically*, the work published earliest coming first.

Glueck, N. (1965). Deities and dolphins. New York: Farrar, Straus and Giroux.

Gormley, G. (1985). A dolphin summer. New York: Taplinger.

Klinowska, M. (1986). The cetacean magnetic sense--evidence from strandings. In M. M. Bryden & R. Harrison (Eds.), Research on dolphins (pp. 401-432). Oxford: Clarendon Press.

Levine, J. E. (Producer), & Nichols, M. (Director). (1973). The day of the dolphin [Film]. Twentieth Century-Fox.

Lilly, J. C. (1961). Man and dolphin. Garden City: Doubleday.

Lilly, J. C. (1972). Programming and metaprogramming in the human biocomputer (2nd ed.). New York: Julian.

Linden, E. (1987, August 17). Joe and Rosie go for it. Time, p. 72.

McNally, R. (1981). So remorseless a havoc: Of dolphins, whales and men. Boston: Little, Brown.

Morris, R. J. (1986). The acoustic faculty of dolphins. In M. M. Bryden & R. Harrison

(Eds.), <u>Research on dolphins</u> (pp. 369-399).

Oxford: Clarendon Press.

Mowat, F. (1984). <u>Sea of slaughter</u>. Boston:

Atlantic Monthly Press.

Ridgway, S. H. (1986). Dolphin brain size. In

M. M. Bryden & R. Harrison (Eds.), <u>Research on</u>

<u>dolphins</u> (pp. 59-70). Oxford: Clarendon

Press.

What is killing the Atlantic's dolphins? (1987,

August 24). <u>Newsweek</u>, p. 51.

GLOSSARY OF USAGE

49 Glossary of Usage   *gl / us*

Many items not listed here are covered in other sections of this book and may be located through the index. For words found neither in this glossary nor in the index, consult a good dictionary. The usage labels (*informal, dialectal,* and so on) affixed to words in this glossary reflect the opinions of two or more of the dictionaries listed on p. 195.

A, an Use *a* as an article before consonant sounds; use *an* before vowel sounds.

a nickname	*an* office
a house	*an* hour
(the *h* is sounded)	(the *h* is not sounded)
a historical novel	*an* honor
(though the British say *an*)	*an* uncle
a union	
(long *u* has the consonant sound of *y*)	

Accept, except As a verb, *accept* means "to receive"; *except* means "to exclude." *Except* as a preposition also means "but."
   Every legislator *except* Mr. Whelling refused to *accept* the bribe.
   We will *except* (exclude) this novel from the list of those to be read.

Accidently A misspelling usually caused by mispronunciation. Use *accidentally.*

Advice, advise Use *advice* as a noun, *advise* as a verb.

Affect, effect *Affect* is a verb meaning "to act upon" or "to influence." *Effect* may be a verb or a noun. *Effect* as a verb means "to cause" or "to bring about"; *effect* as a noun means "a result," "a consequence."
   The patent medicine did not *affect* (influence) the disease.
   The operation did not *effect* (bring about) an improvement in the patient's health.
   The drug had a drastic *effect* (consequence) on the speed of the patient's reactions.

Aggravate Informal in the sense of "annoy," "irritate," or "pester." Formally, it means to "make worse or more severe."

Agree to, agree with   *Agree to* a thing (plan, proposal); *agree with* a person.

>He *agreed to* the insertion of the plank in the platform of the party.
>He *agreed with* the senator that the plank would not gain many votes.

Ain't   Nonstandard or illiterate.

All ready, already   *All ready* means "prepared, in a state of readiness"; *already* means "before some specified time" or "previously" and describes an action that is completed.

>The riders were *all ready* to mount. (fully prepared)
>Mr. Bowman had *already* bagged his limit of quail. (action completed at time of statement)

All together, altogether   *All together* describes a group as acting or existing collectively; *altogether* means "wholly, entirely."

>The sprinters managed to start *all together.*
>I do not *altogether* approve of the decision.

Allusion, illusion   An *allusion* is a casual reference. An *illusion* is a false or misleading sight or impression.

Alot   Nonstandard for *a lot.*

Alright   Nonstandard for *all right.*

Among, between   *Among* is used with three or more persons or things; *between* is used with only two.

>It will be hard to choose *among* so many candidates.
>It will be hard to choose *between* the two candidates.

Amount, number   *Amount* refers to mass or quantity; *number* refers to things which may be counted.

>That is a large *number* of turtles for a pond which has such a small *amount* of water.

An   See **A.**

And etc.   See **Etc.**

Anxious, eager   *Anxious* is not a synonym for *eager. Anxious* means "worried or distressed"; *eager* means "intensely desirous."

>The defendant was *anxious* about the outcome of the trial.
>Most people are *eager* to hear good news.

Anyways   Prefer *anyway.*

Anywheres   Prefer *anywhere.*

As Weak or confusing in the sense of *because*.

> The client collected the full amount of insurance *as* her car ran off the cliff and was totally demolished.

At this (*or* that) point in time Avoid. Wordy and trite.

Awful A trite and feeble substitute for such words as *bad, shocking, ludicrous, ugly*.

Awhile, a while *Awhile* is an adverb; *a while* is an article and a noun.

> Stay *awhile*.
> Wait here for *a while*. (object of preposition)

Bad, badly See pp. 80–81.

Because See **Reason is because.**

Being as, being that Use *because* or *since*.

Beside, besides *Beside* means "by the side of," "next to"; *besides* means "in addition to."

> Mr. Potts was sitting *beside* the stove.
> No one was in the room *besides* Mr. Potts.

Between See **Among.**

Between you and I Wrong case. Use *between you and me*.

Bring, take Use *bring* to indicate movement toward the place of speaking or regarding. Use *take* for movement away from such a place.

> *Take* this coupon to the store and *bring* back a free coffee mug.

Bug Informal or slang in almost every sense except when used to name an insect.

Bunch Informal for a group of people.

Bust, busted Slang as forms of *burst*. *Bursted* is also unacceptable.

Can, may In formal English, *can* is still used to denote ability; *may*, to denote permission. Informally the two are interchangeable.

> FORMAL
> *May* (not *can*) I go?

Capital, capitol *Capitol* designates "a building that is a seat of government"; *capital* is used for all other meanings.

Center around Illogical: use *center in* (or *on*) or *cluster around*.

Climactic, climatic *Climactic* pertains to a climax; *climatic* pertains to climate.

Compare, contrast   Do not use interchangeably. *Compare* means to look for or reveal likenesses; *contrast* treats differences.

Compare to, compare with   In formal writing use *compare to* when referring to similarities and *compare with* when referring to both similarities and differences.

> The poet *compared* a woman's beauty *to* a summer's day.
> The sociologist's report *compares* the career aspirations of male undergraduates *with* those of females.

Complement, compliment   As a verb, *complement* means to "complete" or "go well with"; as a noun, it means "something that completes." *Compliment* as a verb means "to praise"; as a noun it means "an expression of praise."

> Her delicate jewelry was an ideal *complement* to her simple but tasteful gown.
> Departing guests should *compliment* a gracious hostess.

Conscience, conscious   *Conscience,* a noun, refers to the faculty that distinguishes right from wrong. *Conscious,* an adjective, means "being physically or psychologically aware of conditions or situations."

> His *conscience* dictated that he return the money.
> *Conscious* of their hostility toward him, the senator left the meeting early.

Continual, continuous   Use *continual* to refer to actions that recur at intervals, *continuous* to mean "without interruption."

> The return of the bats to the lake every evening is *continual.*
> Breathing is a *continuous* function of the body.

Contractions   Avoid contractions (*don't, he's, they're*) in formal writing.

Contrast   See **Compare.**

Cool   Slang when used to mean "excellent" or "first-rate."

Could care less   Illogical and nonstandard for "could not care less."

Could of, would of   See **Of.**

Criteria, phenomena, data   Plurals. Use *criterion, phenomenon* for the singular. *Data,* however, can be considered singular or plural.

Cute, great, lovely, wonderful   Often poor substitutes for words of approval.

Different from, different than   Prefer *different from* in your writing.

> Children's taste in music is often much *different from* that of their parents.

Differ from, differ with   *Differ from* means "to be unlike"; *differ with* means "to disagree."

The economic system of Poland *differs from* that of New Zealand.

Poland *differs with* some neighboring countries on economic policy.

Disinterested, uninterested   Use *disinterested* to mean someone is "unbiased, objective"; use *uninterested* to mean someone is "not interested, indifferent."

A *disinterested* person is helpful in solving disputes.

Uninterested members of an audience seldom remember what a speaker says.

Don't   Contraction of *do not;* not to be used for *doesn't,* the contraction of *does not.*

Double negative   Avoid such uneducated phrases as *can't help but, didn't have scarcely,* and so on.

Due to   Objectionable to some when used as a prepositional phrase modifying a verb.

OBJECTIONABLE

Due to the laughter, the speaker could not continue.

BETTER

Because of the laughter, the speaker could not continue.

Each and every   Redundant. Use one or the other, not both.

Each other, one another   When two persons are involved, use the expression *each other;* when three or more persons are involved, use the expression *one another.*

The poet and her editor wrote *each other* frequently.

Arguing heatedly with *one another,* the jury deliberated the case.

Eager   See **Anxious.**

Early on   Redundant. Use *early.* Omit *on.*

Effect   See **Affect.**

Elicit, illicit   *Elicit,* a verb, means "to evoke or bring forth." *Illicit,* an adjective, means "not permitted" or "unlawful."

A pianist's innovative style will sometimes *elicit* a negative response from the critics.

Authorities discovered his participation in an *illicit* trade involving weapons.

Emigrate, immigrate   *To emigrate* means "to leave one's country and settle in another." *To immigrate* means "to enter another country and reside there."

Luis *emigrated from* Spain to the United States when he was only five years old.

My grandmother *immigrated to* this country from the city of Messina, Sicily, in 1919.

Enthused   Use *enthusiastic* in formal writing.

Etc.   Do not use *and etc. Etc.* means "and so forth," or "and others."

Ever, every   Use *every* in *every day, every other, everybody, every now and then;* use *ever* in *ever and anon, ever so humble.*

Exam   Considered informal by some authorities. *Examination* is always correct.

Except   See **Accept.**

Expect   Informal for *believe, suspect, think, suppose,* and so forth.

Explicit, implicit   *Explicit* means "directly expressed or clearly defined." *Implicit* means "implied or understood."

Hitler confronted Neville Chamberlain with *explicit* demands.

The Prime Minister did not have to answer; his disappointment was *implicit.*

Fabulous   Informal for *extremely pleasing.*

Fantastic   Informal for *extraordinarily good.*

Farther, further   Generally interchangeable, though many persons prefer *farther* in expressions of physical distance and *further* in expressions of time, quantity, and degree.

My car used less gasoline and went *farther* than his.

The second speaker went *further* into the issues than the first.

Feel like   Nonstandard for "feel that."

NOT
I feel like I could have been elected.

CORRECT
I feel that I could have been elected.
See **Like.**

Fewer, less   Use *fewer* to denote number; *less,* to denote amount or degree.

With *fewer* advertisers, there will also be *less* income from advertising.

Finalize Bureaucratic. Avoid.

Fine Often a poor substitute for a more exact word of approval or commendation.

Fix Informal for the noun *predicament*.

Flunk Informal: prefer *fail* or *failure* in formal usage.

Funny Informal for *strange, remarkable,* or *peculiar*.

Further See **Farther.**

Good Incorrect as an adverb. See **10.**

Got to In formal writing prefer *have to, has to,* or *must*.
  People must (not *got to*) understand that voting is a great privilege.

Great Informal for "first-rate."

Hanged, hung Both *hanged* and *hung* are the past tense and past participle forms of *hang*, but they are not interchangeable. *Hanged* means "executed by hanging"; *hung* means "suspended."
  In modern times criminals are seldom *hanged*.
  The decorator *hung* a reproduction of Picasso's *Portrait of a Woman* in the living room.

Hardly See **Not hardly.**

He, she Traditionally, *he* has been used to mean *he* or *she*. Today this usage is unacceptable. For additional discussion, alternatives, and examples, see p. 64.

Himself See **Myself.**

Hopefully When *hopefully* is used as a sentence modifier in the sense "it is hoped," it is often unclear who is doing the hoping—the writer or the subject.

VAGUE
Hopefully, the amendment will be approved.

CLEAR
Most local voters hope that the amendment will be approved.

CLEAR (but with a different meaning)
I hope the amendment will be approved.

If, whether Use *if* to indicate a condition; use *whether* to specify alternatives.
  The reception will be held outdoors *if* it does not rain.
  The reception will be held indoors *whether* it rains or not.

Illusion   See **Allusion.**

Impact on   Sociological and bureaucratic jargon. Avoid *impact* as a verb.

Imply, infer   *Imply* means "to hint" or "suggest"; *infer* means "to draw a conclusion."

>The speaker *implied* that Mr. Dixon was guilty.
>The audience *inferred* that Mr. Dixon was guilty.

In, into   *Into* denotes motion from the outside to the inside; *in* denotes position (enclosure).

>The lion was *in* the cage when the trainer walked *into* the tent.

Infer   See **Imply.**

Individual   Avoid using for *person.*

In regards to   Unidiomatic: use *in regard to* or *with regard to.*

Into   See **In.**

Irregardless   Nonstandard for *regardless.*

Is when, is where   Ungrammatical use of adverbial clause after a linking verb. Often misused in definitions and explanations.

NONSTANDARD
>Combustion *is when* (or *is where*) oxygen unites with other elements.

STANDARD
>Combustion occurs when oxygen unites with other elements.
>Combustion is a union of oxygen with other elements.

Its, it's   *Its* is the possessive case of the pronoun *it; it's* is a contraction of *it is* or *it has.*

>*It's* exciting to parents when their baby cuts *its* first tooth.

Kind of, sort of   Informal as adverbs: use *rather, somewhat,* and so forth.

INFORMAL
>Mr. Josephson was *sort of* disgusted.

FORMAL
>Mr. Josephson was *rather* disgusted.

FORMAL (not an adverb)
>What *sort of* book is that?

Kind of a, sort of a   Delete the *a;* use *kind of* and *sort of.*
>What *kind of* (not *kind of a*) pipe do you smoke?

Lay, lie   See p. 40.

Lead, led *Lead* is an incorrect form for the past tense *led*.

Learn, teach *Learn* means "to acquire knowledge." *Teach* means "to impart knowledge."
> She could not *learn* how to work the problem until Mrs. Smithers *taught* her the formula.

Less See **Fewer.**

Liable See **Likely.**

Lie See p. 40.

Like A preposition. Instead of *like* as a conjunction, prefer *as, as if,* or *as though.*

PREPOSITION
> She acted *like* a novice.

CONJUNCTION
> She acted *as if* she had never been on the stage before. (correct)
> She acted *like* she had never had a date before. (informal)

Such popular expressions as "tell it like it is" derive part of their appeal from their lighthearted defiance of convention.
Do not use *like* (the verb) for *lack.*
Do not use *like* for *that* as in *feel like.*
See **Feel like.**

Likely, liable Use *likely* to express probability; use *liable,* which may have legal connotations, to express responsibility or obligation.
> You are *likely* to have an accident if you drive recklessly.
> Since your father owns the car, he will be *liable* for damages.

Literally Do not use for *figuratively.*
> She was literally walking on clouds. (Means that she was *actually* stepping from cloud to cloud.)

Loose, lose Frequently confused. *Loose* is an adjective; *lose* is a verb.
> She wore a *loose* and trailing gown.
> Speculators often *lose* their money.

Lot of, lots of Informal in the sense of *much, many, a great deal.*

Lovely See **Cute.**

Mad Informal when used to mean "angry."

Man (mankind) Objectionable to many. Prefer *humankind* or *human beings.*

May   See **Can.**

Most   Informal for *almost* in such expressions as the following:
He is late for class *almost* (not *most*) every day.

Myself, yourself, himself, herself, itself   These words are reflexives or intensives, not strict equivalents of *I, me, you, he, she, him, her, it.*

INTENSIVE
I *myself* helped Father cut the wheat.
I helped Father cut the wheat *myself.*

REFLEXIVE
I cut *myself.*

NOT
The elopement was known only to Sherry and *myself.*

BUT
The elopement was known only to Sherry and *me.*

NOT
Only Kay and *myself* had access to the safe.

BUT
Only Kay and *I* had access to the safe.

Nice   A weak substitute for more exact words like *attractive, modest, pleasant, kind,* and so forth.

Not hardly   Double negative. Avoid.

Nowheres   Dialectal. Use *nowhere.*

Nucular   A misspelling and mispronunciation of *nuclear.*

Number   See **Amount.**

Of   Not to be used for "have."
Had he lived, the emperor could *have* (not *of*) prevented the war.
The physician would *have* (not *of*) come had he known of the illness.

Off of   *Off* is sufficient.
He fell *off* (not *off of*) the water tower.

O.K., OK, okay   Informal.

Per   Do not use for "a" or "an" in formal writing.
Guests paid fifty dollars *a* (not *per*) plate at the political dinner.

Percent, percentage   *Percent* refers to a specific number: 8 percent. *Percentage* is used when no number is specified: a percentage of the stock.

The % sign after a percentage (8%) is acceptable in business and technical writing. Write out the word *percent* in formal writing. The number before percent is given in figures except at the start of a sentence.

Employees own *8 percent* of the stock.

Eight percent of the stock is owned by employees.

Percent can be singular or plural. See **7g.**

A *percentage* takes a singular or a plural verb. See **7g.**

Phenomena   See **Criteria.**

Photo   Informal.

Plus   Avoid using for the conjunction *and.*

Precede, proceed   *Precede* means "to come before." *Proceed* means "to move onward."

Freshmen often *precede* seniors on the waiting list for campus housing.

The instructor answered a few questions and then *proceeded* with the lecture.

Principal, principle   Use *principal* to mean "the chief" or "most important." Use *principle* to mean "a rule" or "a truth."

The *principal* reason for her delinquency was never discussed.

The *principal* of Brookwood High School applauded.

To act without *principle* leads to delinquency.

Provided, providing   *Provided,* the past participle of the verb *provide,* is used as a conjunction to mean "on condition that." *Providing,* the present participle of the verb *provide,* is often mistakenly used for *provided.*

The cellist will compete in the Canadian Music Festival *provided* (not *providing*) she wins the regional competition.

Quote   A verb: prefer *quotation* as a noun.

Raise, rise   See p. 40.

Real   Informal or dialectal as an adverb meaning *really* or *very.*

Reason is (was) because   Use *the reason is (was) that.* Formally, *because* should introduce an adverbial clause, not a noun clause used as a predicate nominative.

NOT

The *reason* Abernathy enlisted *was because* he failed in college.

BUT

The *reason* Abernathy enlisted *was that* he failed in college.

OR
> Abernathy enlisted *because* he failed in college.

Respectfully, respectively   *Respectfully* means "with respect"; *respectively* means "each in the order given."
> He *respectfully* thanked the president for his diploma.
> Crossing the platform, he passed *respectively* by the speaker, the dean, and the registrar.

Revelant   A misspelling and mispronunciation of *relevant*.

Sensual, sensuous   *Sensual* connotes the gratification of bodily pleasures; *sensuous* refers favorably to what is experienced through the senses.

Set, sit   See p. 40.

Shall, will   In strictly formal English, to indicate simple futurity, *shall* is conventional in the first person (I *shall*, we *shall*); *will*, in the second and third persons (you *will*, he *will*, they *will*). To indicate determination, duty, or necessity, *will* is formal in the first person (I *will*, we *will*); *shall*, in the second and third persons (you *shall*, he *shall*, they *shall*). These distinctions are weaker than they used to be, and *will* is increasingly used in all persons.

Should of   See **Of.**

So, so that   Use *so that* instead of *so* to express intent or purpose.
> Most people use credit cards *so that* (not *so*) they can pay their bills at the end of the month.

Sometime, some time   *Sometime* is used adverbially to designate an indefinite point of time. *Some time* refers to a period or duration of time.
> I will see you *sometime* next week.
> I have not seen him for *some time*.

Sort of   See **Kind of.**

Sort of a   See **Kind of a.**

Stationary, stationery   An adjective, *stationary* means "not moving." A noun, *stationery* refers to writing materials or office supplies.

Super   Informal for *excellent*.

Sure   Informal as an adverb for *surely, certainly*.

INFORMAL
> The speaker *sure* criticized his opponent.

FORMAL
> The speaker *certainly* criticized his opponent.

Sure and, try and   Use *sure to, try to.*
Be *sure to* (not *sure and*) notice the costumes of the Hungarian folk dancers.

Suspicion   Avoid as a verb; use *suspect.*

Teach   See **Learn.**

Than, then   Do not use one of these words for the other. *Than,* a conjunction, is used in comparisons. *Then,* an adverb, relates to time.
Calculus is more complicated *than* algebra.
Drizzle the pizza with oil; *then* bake it at 350°.

That, which   When introducing a relative clause essential to the meaning of the sentence (a restrictive clause), use *that.* Use *which* in a relative clause that provides the sentence with additional, but not necessary, information (a nonrestrictive clause). Note that the nonrestrictive clause is set off with commas.
The driver of the car *that* ran the red light has been fined.
This jacket, *which* is several years old, has large pockets and a detachable hood.

Their, there   Not interchangeable: *their* is the possessive of *they; there* is either an adverb meaning "in that place" or an expletive.
Their dachshund is sick.
There it is on the corner. (adverb of place)
There is a veterinarian's office in this block. (expletive)

These (those) kind, these (those) sort   *These (those)* is plural; *kind (sort)* is singular. Therefore use *this (that) kind, this (that) sort; these (those) kinds, these (those) sorts.*

Thusly   Prefer *thus.*

Toward, towards   Although both are acceptable, prefer *toward.*

Try and   See **Sure and.**

Uninterested   See **Disinterested.**

Unique   Means "one of a kind"; hence it may not logically be compared. *Unique* should not be loosely used for *unusual* or *strange.*

Use   Sometimes carelessly written for the past tense, *used.*
Thomas Jefferson *used* (not *use*) to bathe in cold water almost every morning.

Wait on   Unidiomatic for *wait for. Wait on* correctly means "to serve."

Ways   Prefer *way* when designating a distance.
a long *way.*

NOT
a long *ways*

When, where   See **Is when.**

Where   Do not misuse for *that*.
I read in the newspaper *that* (not *where*) you saved a child's life.

While   Do not use *while* in a sentence when it can be taken to mean "although."

AMBIGUOUS
While I prepared dinner, Ann did nothing.

Who, which   *Who* refers to people; *which* refers to things.
Some listeners are amused at a newscaster *who* cannot pronounce names correctly.
Copies of the author's last novel, *which* was published in 1917, are now rare.

Whose, who's   *Whose* is the possessive of *who; who's* is a contraction of *who is.*

Wicked   Slang when used for *excellent* or *masterly.*

-wise   A suffix overused in combinations with nouns, such as *budgetwise, progresswise,* and *businesswise.*

Wonderful   See **Cute.**

Would of   See **Of.**

You know   annoying, repetitious, and meaningless when used as a question inserted in a sentence.
Avoid: He was just scared, you know?

GLOSSARY OF
GRAMMATICAL
TERMS

50   Glossary of Grammatical Terms   *gl / gr*

This is by no means a complete list of terms used in discussing grammar. See "Grammar" (pp. 2–27), the index, other sections of this book, and dictionaries.

Absolute phrase   See **20L.**

Active voice   See **Voice.**

Adjectival   A term describing a word or word group that modifies a noun.

Adjective   A word that modifies a noun or a pronoun. (See pp. 8–9.)
Her young horse jumped over *that high* barrier for *the first* time.

Adjective clause   See **Dependent clause.**

Adverb   A word that modifies a verb, an adjective, or another adverb. (See pp. 9–10.)

Adverbial clause   See **Dependent clause.**

Agreement   The correspondence between words in number, gender, person, or case. A verb agrees in number and person with its subject. A pronoun must agree in number, person, and gender with its antecedent.
Flannery O'Connor is best known for well-crafted short stories.

Antecedent   A word to which a pronoun refers.

           antecedent   *pronoun*
              ↓   ↓
When the ballet *dancers* appeared, *they* were dressed in pink.

Appositive   A word, phrase, or clause used as a noun and placed beside another word to explain it.

        appositive
            ↓
The poet *John Milton* wrote *Paradise Lost* while he was blind.

Article   *A* and *an* are indefinite articles; *the* is the definite article.

Auxiliary verb   A verb used to help another verb indicate tense, m or voice. Principal auxiliaries are forms of the verbs *to be* and *to do*. (See p. 7.)

> I *am* studying.
> I *do* study.
> I *shall* go there next week.
> He *may* lose his job.

Case   English has remnants of three cases: subjective, possessive, and objective. Nouns are inflected for case only in the possessive *(father, father's)*. An alternative way to show possession is with the "of phrase" *(of the house)*. Some pronouns, notably the personal pronouns and the relative pronoun *who*, are still fully inflected for three cases:

SUBJECTIVE (acting)
> I, he, she, we, they, who

POSSESSIVE (possessing)
> my (mine), your (yours), his, her (hers), its, our (ours), their (theirs), whose

OBJECTIVE (acted upon)
> me, him, her, us, them, whom

Clause   A group of words containing a subject and a predicate. See **Independent clause; Dependent clause.** See pp. 25–26.

Collective noun   A word identifying a class or a group of persons or things. See p. 3.

Comma splice (or comma fault)   An error that occurs when two independent clauses are incorrectly linked by a comma with no coordinating conjunction.

Comparative and superlative degrees   See **10a** and **10b.**

Complement   A word or group of words used to complete a predicate. Predicate adjectives, predicate nominatives, direct objects, and indirect objects are complements. See pp. 19–21.

Complex, compound, compound-complex sentences   A *complex sentence* has one independent clause and at least one dependent clause. A *compound sentence* has at least two independent clauses. A *compound-complex sentence* has two or more independent clauses and one dependent clause or more. See pp. 26–27.

Compound structures   See p. 17.

Conjugation The inflection of the forms of a verb according to person, number, tense, voice, and mood. See the abbreviated form of the conjugation of the verb *walk* in **4.**

Conjunction A word used to connect sentences or sentence parts. See also **Coordinating conjunctions, Correlative conjunctions, Subordinating conjunctions,** and pp. 11–12.

Conjunctive adverb An adverb used to relate two independent clauses that are separated by a semicolon: *however, therefore, moreover, then, consequently, besides,* and so on (see **22a**).

Contraction The shortening of two words combined by replacing omitted letters with an apostrophe.
   I've for *I have. Isn't* for *is not.*

Coordinate clause See **Independent clause.** When there are two independent clauses in a compound or a compound-complex sentence, they may be called coordinate clauses.

Coordinating conjunction A simple conjunction that joins sentences or parts of sentences of equal rank *(and, but, or, nor, for, yet, so)*. See p. 11.

Correlative conjunctions Conjunctions used in pairs to join coordinate sentence elements. The most common are *either—or, neither—nor, not only—but also, both—and.*

Dangling modifier A modifier that is not clearly attached to a word or element in the sentence.

   DANGLING MODIFIER
   Following a regimen of proper diet and exercise, Alan's weight can be controlled.

   REVISED
   Following a regimen of proper diet and exercise, Alan can control his weight.

Declension The inflection of nouns, pronouns, and adjectives in case, number, and gender. See especially **9.**

Degrees (of modifiers) See **10a** and **10b.**

Demonstrative adjective or pronoun A word used to point out *(this, that, these, those).*

Dependent (subordinate) clause A group of words that contains both a subject and a predicate but that does not stand alone as a sentence. A dependent clause is frequently signaled by a subordinator *(who, which,* *what, that, since, because,* and so on) and always functions as an adjective, adverb, or noun.

ADJECTIVE
The tenor *who sang the aria* had just arrived from Italy.

NOUN
The critics agreed *that the young tenor had a magnificent voice.*

ADVERB
When he sang, even the sophisticated audience was enraptured.

Diagramming   Diagramming uses systems of lines and positioning of words to show the parts of a sentence and the relationships between them. Its purpose is to make understandable the way writing is put together. (See the example below.)

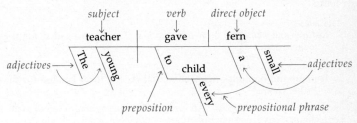

Direct object   A noun, pronoun, or other substantive receiving the action of the verb. (See p. 20.)
The angler finally caught the old *trout.*

Double negative   Nonstandard use of two negative words within the same sentence.

DOUBLE NEGATIVE
I do not have hardly any problems with my car.

REVISED
I hardly have any problems with my car.

Elliptical clause   A clause in which one or more words are omitted but understood.

understood
The director admired no one else as much as *(he admired* or *he did)* Faith DeFelce.

Expletive   See **7h.**

Faulty predication   Errors occur in predication when a subject and its complement are put together in such a fashion that the sentence is illogical or unmeaningful.

FAULTY
> A reporter taking pictures meant that there would be publicity.

BETTER
> Since a reporter was taking pictures, we knew that there would be publicity.

It is illogical to say that *taking pictures meant.*

Fragment   Part of a sentence written and punctuated as a complete sentence.

FRAGMENT
> *Jostling and bantering with one another.* The team headed for the locker room.

REVISED
> Jostling and bantering with one another, the team headed for the locker room.

Fused (or run-on) sentence   An error that occurs when two independent clauses have neither punctuation nor coordinating conjunctions between them.

FUSED
> The average adult has about twelve pints of blood this amount is roughly 9 percent of total body weight.

REVISED
> The average adult has about twelve pints of blood; this is roughly 9 percent of total body weight.

Gender   The classification of nouns and pronouns into masculine, feminine, or neuter categories.

Gerund   See **Verbal.**

Indefinite pronoun   A pronoun not pointing out a particular person or thing. Some of the most common are *some, any, each, everyone, everybody, anyone, anybody, one,* and *neither.*

Independent (main) clause   A group of words which contains a subject and a predicate and which grammatically can stand alone as a sentence.

Indirect object A word which indirectly receives the action of the verb. (See p. 20.)

> The actress wrote the *soldier* a letter.

Infinitive See **Verbal.**

Inflection A change in the form of a word to indicate its grammatical function. Nouns, adjectives, and pronouns are declined; verbs are conjugated. Some inflections occur when *-s* or *-es* is added to nouns or verbs or when *'s* is added to nouns.

Intensifier A modifier (such as *very*) used to lend emphasis. *Use sparingly.*

Intensive pronoun A pronoun ending in *-self* and used for emphasis.

> The director *himself* will act the part of Hamlet.

Interjection A word used to exclaim or to express an (usually strong) emotion. It has no grammatical connections within its sentence. Some common interjections are *oh, ah,* and *ouch.* See pp. 14–15.

Interrogative pronoun See **9i.**

Intransitive verb See **Voice.**

Inversion A change in normal word order, such as placing an adjective after the noun it modifies or placing the object of a verb at the beginning of a sentence.

Irregular verb A verb that does not form its past tense and past participle by adding *-d* or *-ed* to its infinitive form. For example, *give, gave, given.*

Linking verb A verb that does not express action but links the subject to another word that names or describes it. See pp. 7, 19 and **10c.** Common linking verbs are *be, become,* and *seem.*

Main clause See **Independent clause.**

Misplaced modifier A modifier that causes confusion because it is mistakenly placed away from the word(s) it is intended to modify and appears to modify the word(s) it is near.

MISPLACED MODIFIER

> Most trout fishermen catch fish wearing rubber boots.

REVISED

> Most trout fishermen wear rubber boots while catching fish.

Mixed construction A sentence with two or more parts that are not grammatically compatible.

MIXED CONSTRUCTION
    By cutting welfare benefits will penalize many poor families.

REVISED
    Cutting welfare benefits will penalize many poor families.

Modifier   A word (or word group) that limits or describes another word.
See pp. 103–106.

Mood   The mood (or mode) of a verb indicates whether an action is to
be thought of as fact, command, wish, or condition contrary to fact.
Modern English has three moods: the indicative, for ordinary statements and questions; the imperative, for commands and entreaty; and
the subjunctive, for certain idiomatic expressions of wish, command, or
condition contrary to fact.

INDICATIVE
    Does she *play* the guitar?
    She *does.*

IMPERATIVE
    Stay with me.
    Let him stay.
    The imperative is formed like plural present indicative, without *-s.*

SUBJUNCTIVE
    If I *were* you, I would go.
    I wish he *were* going with you.
    I move that the meeting *be* adjourned.
    It is necessary that he *stay* absolutely quiet.
    If this *be* true, no man ever loved.

The most common subjunctive forms are *were* and *be.* All others are
formed like the present-tense plural form without *-s.*

Nominal   A term for a word or a word group that is used as a noun. For
example, the *good,* the *bad,* the *ugly.*

Nominative case   See **Case.**

Nonrestrictive modifier   A modifier that is not essential to understanding. See **20e.**

Noun   A word that names and that has gender, number, and case.
There are proper nouns, which name particular people, places or
things *(Thomas Jefferson, Paris,* the *Colosseum);* common nouns, which
name one or more of a group *(alligator, high school, politician);* collective
nouns (see **7d** and **8c**); abstract nouns, which name ideas, feelings, beliefs, and so on *(religion, justice, dislike, enthusiasm);* concrete nouns,

which name things perceived through the senses *(lemon, hatchet, worm)*.

Noun clause   See **Dependent clause.**

Number   A term to describe forms that indicate whether a word is singular or plural.

Object of preposition   See **Preposition, 9b,** and p. 21.

Objective case   See **Case.**

Parallelism   Parallelism occurs when corresponding parts of a sentence are similar in structure, length, and thought.

FAULTY
The staff was required to wear black shoes, red ties, and *shirts that were white.*

PARALLEL
The staff was required to wear black shoes, red ties, and white shirts.

Participle   See **Verbal.**

Parts of speech   See pp. 2–15

Passive voice   See **Voice.**

Person   Three groups of forms of pronouns (with corresponding verb inflections) used to distinguish between the speaker (first person), the person spoken to (second person), and the person spoken about (third person).

Personal pronoun   A pronoun like *I, you, he, she, it, we, they, mine, yours, his, hers, its, ours, theirs.*

Phrase   A group of closely related words without both a subject and a predicate. There are subject phrases *(the new drill sergeant),* verb phrases *(should have been),* verbal phrases *(climbing high mountains),* prepositional phrases *(of the novel),* appositive phrases (my brother, *the black sheep of the family),* and so forth. See pp. 22–24.

Predicate   The verb in a clause (simple predicate) or the verb and its modifiers, complements, and objects (complete predicate). See pp. 18–21.

Predicate adjective   An adjective following a linking verb and describing the subject (see p. 19 and **10c**).
The rose is *artificial.*

Predicate nominative   A noun following a linking verb and naming the subject.

Predication   See **Faulty predication.**

Preposition   A connective that joins a noun or a pronoun to the rest of a sentence. See pp. 13, 22.

Pronominal adjective   An adjective that has the same form as a possessive pronoun (*my* book, *their* enthusiasm).

Pronoun   A word which stands for a noun. See **Personal pronoun; Demonstrative pronoun; Reflexive pronoun; Intensive pronoun; Interrogative pronoun; Indefinite pronoun; Relative pronoun.**

Reflexive pronoun   A pronoun ending in *-self* and indicating that the subject acts upon itself. See **Myself** (Glossary of Usage).

Relative pronoun   See **9i.**

Restrictive modifier   A modifier essential for a clear understanding of the element modified (see **Nonrestrictive modifier**).

Run-on sentence   See **Fused sentence.**

Simple sentence   A sentence consisting of only one independent clause and no dependent clauses. See p. 26.

Subject   A word or group of words about which the sentence or clause makes a statement. (See pp. 15–17.)

Subjective case   See **Case.**

Subordinate clause   See **Dependent clause.**

Subordinating conjunction   A conjunction that connects a subordinating clause to the rest of the sentence. Some common subordinating conjunctions are *because, since, though, although, if, when, while, before, after, as, until, so that, as long as, as if, where, unless, as soon as, whereas, in order that.* See pp. 11–12.

Substantive   A noun or a sentence element that serves the function of a noun.

Superlative degree   See **10a** and **10b.**

Syntax   The grammatical ways in which words are put together to form phrases, clauses, and sentences.

Transitive verb   See **Voice.**

Verb   A word or group of words expressing action, being, or state of being. (See p. 7.)
     Automobiles *burn* gas.
     What *is* life?

Verb phrase   See **Phrase.**

Verbal   A word derived from a verb and used as a noun, an adjective, or an adverb. A verbal may be a gerund, a participle, or an infinitive. See pp. 22–24.

Voice   Transitive verbs have two forms to show whether their subjects act on an object (active voice) or are acted upon (passive voice). See pp. 47–48.

INDEX

ABBREVIATIONS Used in Marking Papers

ab abbreviation, 157, 188
abst abstract word, 219
adj adjective, 8, 78
adv adverb, 9, 78
agr agreement:
    pronoun, antecedent, 62
    subject, verb, 52
' apostrophe, 183
archaic archaic word, 199
[ ] brackets, 152, 392
cap capital letters, 185
c case, 70
chop choppy sentences, 86
coh coherence, 281
: colon, 149
, comma, 122
cs / fus comma splice, 32
no, unnecessary comma, 140
comp comparisons, 94
compl completeness, 93
conc conclusion, 248, 285
con connotation, 221
cons consistency, 98
coord coordination, excessive, 86
— dash, 151
dial dialect, 198
d diction, 194
dg dangling modifier, 103
exact exactness, 205
! exclamation point, 159
fig figurative language, 223
fl flowery language, 225
frag fragment, 30
fus fused sentence, 32
gl / gr glossary, grammatical, 423
gl / us glossary, usage, 439
- hyphen, 180
id idiom, 200
intro introduction, 248, 285
ital italics, 171
log logic, 260

mod modifier, position of, 103
mo mood, subjunctive, 50
ms manuscript form, 166
num numbers, 189
paral parallelism, 109
( ) parentheses, 151
. period, 156
? question mark, 158
" " quotation marks, 152
ref reference, vague
    pronoun, 65
rep repetition, 215
; semicolon, 145
sep separation of
    elements, 108
sl slang, 198
sp spelling, 174
sub subordination,
    excessive, 89
tech technical diction, 203
t tense, 42
ts topic sentence, 272
tr transition, 248, 291
trite triteness, 204
vag w vague words, 219
var variety, 113
vf verb form, 38
vocab vocabulary, 207
vo voice, 47
w wordiness, 212

GENERAL EDITING MARKS:
awk awkward
⌒ close up
δ delete
× obvious error
∧ insert
insert space
o omission
¶ paragraphing
⌐⌐ transposed